BEER HIKING SOUTHERN ROCKIES

54 hikes and microbreweries in Colorado, New Mexico, Arizona and Utah

Beer Hiking Southern Rockies
54 Hikes and Microbreweries in Colorado, New Mexico, Arizona and Utah

By: Yitka Winn and Kevin Holsapple

ISBN: 978-3-03964-081-2
Published by Helvetiq, Lausanne/Basel, Switzerland
Graphic design and illustration: Daniel Malak, Jędrzej Malak (maps)

Printed in China
First Edition 2025

info@helvetiq.ch
www.helvetiq.com/us
www.facebook.com/helvetiq_usa
instagram: @helvetiq_usa

helvetiq.com

MIX
Paper from responsible sources
FSC® C167893

BEER HIKING SOUTHERN ROCKIES

54 hikes and microbreweries in
Colorado, New Mexico, Arizona and Utah

TABLE OF CONTENTS

1. INTRODUCTION 7

About the Authors 8
About the Southern Rockies 10
Choose the Beer or the Hike 12
Trail and Beer Ratings 13
Hiking Safety in the Southern Rockies 14
Trail Etiquette 16
A Note on the Beers 17
Before Setting Off 18
Map 20
Hikes 22
Breweries & Beers 23

2. TRAILS 25

Utah 27
Arizona 77
New Mexico 111
Colorado 183

1

INTRODUCTION

ABOUT THE AUTHORS

Yitka Winn grew up some 650 miles away from Colorado's mountains, all the way across the neighboring state of Kansas. Every summer, her family road-tripped out west, braving the drive across the high plains and wheat fields to spend a couple weeks in a cabin in the Rocky Mountains. Many of her childhood's finest memories are from these trips—craggy, snow-capped peaks, the fragrant scent of sagebrush, the shrieks of yellow-bellied marmots sunning themselves on talus slopes. Hiking was always her family's first mode of choice for exploration, lacing up their boots in pursuit of soaring ridgelines and sparkling alpine lakes.

In later years, when a job opportunity arose in a mountain town in western Colorado, Yitka moved there without hesitation. By then, she'd also developed a healthy appetite for good beer—stouts and porters, especially, though in the process of working on this book, she wound up falling in love with IPAs, too. (Since you asked, her favorite dark beer featured in this book is the Broken Compass Coconut Porter in Breckenridge. Her favorite IPA is Rock Cut Brewing's Galactic Portal IPA in Estes Park.) She also can't resist a good sour.

She has a degree in Creative Writing from Oberlin College and now works professionally as a writer and editor in the outdoor industry. Her writing has appeared in *Trail Runner, Outdoors NW, Outside Online, REI Co-op Journal, RootsRated, Red Bull Adventure, iRunFar, Gear Institute,* and more. If she's not writing or at work, she's probably playing in the mountains.

Yitka is the author of the Colorado chapters.

Kevin Holsapple has lived in the mountains of northern New Mexico for more than 35 years, moving there from Arizona. He is retired from a career as a community developer, but he has not chosen a sedentary retirement. Kevin has published the blog Prime Passages to inspire lovers of beer, hiking, and travel for more than a decade. Prime Passages features hundreds of photo essays from beery travels in North America, Europe, and Asia.

Kevin's love of beer hiking traces to his experience in the Army stationed in the Franconian region of Bavaria, where sampling beers along weekend hikes became a regular pursuit. Part of his duties involved managing beer halls in military camps, which required negotiating with the local German breweries. He also organized recreational tours throughout Europe. Kevin is a certified FORA Travel Advisor specializing in designing and planning trips that combine beer culture, outdoor adventure, and travel throughout the world.

Kevin is the author of the New Mexico, Arizona, and Utah chapters.

ABOUT THE SOUTHERN ROCKIES

The focus of *Beer Hiking Southern Rockies* are the Four Corners States of Colorado, Utah, New Mexico, and Arizona. These are the only four states in the US that meet at a common border, and the only place where it is possible to stand in four states at once. It is also a land of dramatic contrasts, offering an array of landscapes and hiking experiences that cater to every taste and ability.

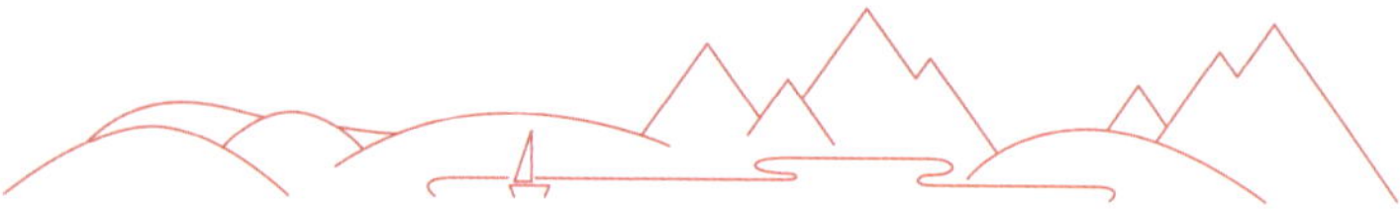

Majestic mountains with towering peaks offer challenging climbs and breathtaking panoramas throughout the region. Rugged canyons showcase stunning rock formations sculpted by wind and water. Trails wind among towering buttes and mesas and through narrow gorges and alongside towering cliffs. Ancient deserts and colorful badlands offer stark beauty, with vast open spaces, unique and colorful geological formations, surreal landscapes, and a sense of solitude. Lush forests of spruces, firs, and ponderosa pines are everywhere in the high country. Mountain meadows and aspen groves blaze with color in the fall. Snow-capped peaks rise above most of the region.

The hiking experiences range from strenuous climbs to challenging traverses to canyon exploration. Our hikes lead to stunning panoramas on mountain peaks, remote valleys or more intimate exploration along canyon walls. And of course, fascinating archaeological sites, including ancient cliff dwellings, abound.

Beyond the landscapes, the Southwest is home to a rich tapestry of cultures with a strong Native American presence. Hiking in certain areas may require permits or guides, offering a chance to learn about the traditions and history of the region's indigenous people. Dark Sky areas with minimal light pollution make the night sky come alive with countless stars, constellations, planet viewing, and the Milky Way. Quaint towns and villages dot the region, offering places to rest and refuel after a day of hiking. Many have vibrant arts and culture scenes, and great craft beer venues and restaurants are all over.

If there's anywhere that offers a front seat to the craft beer experience in America combined with the majesty of outdoor experience, it's the Southern Rockies. With more than 400 breweries, Colorado ranks near the top of the craft beer pecking order. New Mexico has more than 100 breweries and brewery taprooms, and some have given it the nickname "The Frontier of Beer." Arizona is home to more than 130 breweries and brewery taprooms, and Utah to more than 40. The beer cultures in the four states each possess distinctive features and local traditions.

Many craft beer venues are situated near (or even at!) trailheads that serve as gateways to the mountains. And, perhaps unsurprisingly, many are owned by outdoor enthusiasts and conservationists. Breweries and beers are named for peaks, canyons, trails, and river rapids; taproom walls are decorated with trail maps, landscape imagery, skis, bicycles, kayak paddles, and lots of trophies for outstanding beer achievements. And, let's be honest—at the end of a long hike in the Mountain West sun, there's nothing quite as wonderful as sipping a cold, fine beer.

This guidebook is your ticket to that simple pleasure, to the sublime undertaking of earning one's ales with miles on the trails. Hikes range from short and sweet strolls in the woods to rugged high-altitude sojourns among peaks and canyons. The beers span a broad range—juicy IPAs, decadent porters, malty lagers, nutty brown ales, and plenty of experimental flavor combinations.

Like the Southern Rockies topography itself, there truly is something for everyone.

CHOOSE THE BEER OR THE HIKE

HIKE LOCATION

NAME OF THE BEER

MAP

DIMPLE DELL

GET YOUR HIKE ON, THEN GET HOPPY

STARTING POINT	OBJECTIVE
WRANGLER TRAILHEAD	DIMPLE DELL
BEER	HIKE TYPE
FEELIN' HAZY DOUBLE IPA	MODERATE
FEES	SEASON
NONE	YEAR ROUND
MAP REFERENCE	DOG FRIENDLY
USGS 825927	DOGS MUST BE LEASHED
DURATION	LENGTH
3 HOURS	5.8 MILES
LOW POINT / HIGH POINT	ELEVATION GAIN
4,673 FEET / 5,106 FEET	627 FEET

34

ALCOHOL 8.5% CONTENT

DOUBLE IPA

HAZY GOLDEN

CITRUS NOSE

HOPPY, MALTY

BITTERNESS IBU: 45

SWEETNESS

35

INFORMATION ABOUT THE BEER

INFORMATION ABOUT THE HIKE

TRAIL AND BEER RATINGS

All ratings in this book—both beer notes and hike difficulties—are subjective. Some hikers might find what we have called a "Moderate" hike to be difficult or even easy. Just like some craft beer drinkers may think that the bitterness or sweetness of a specific beer differs from the tasting notes we have described. Please do not consider the ratings as definitive but as a reference to help you choose the right hike or beer for your taste.

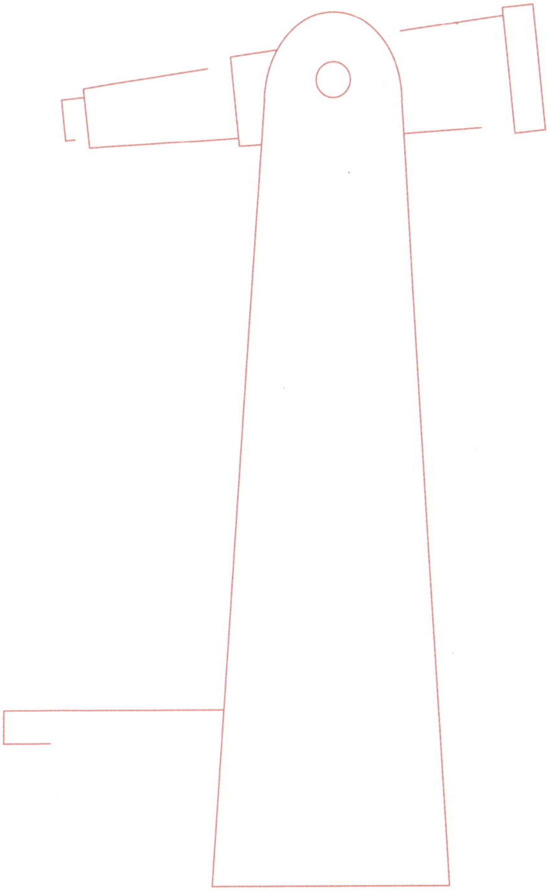

HIKING SAFETY IN THE SOUTHERN ROCKIES

Hiking in many parts of the Southern Rockies poses some unique risks. In addition to the usual precautions one should take when hiking—notifying someone of your itinerary, carrying the ten essentials, knowing how to navigate by map and compass, etc.—there are some special factors to be aware of as well, especially if you're visiting from lower-elevation locales.

Many of the hikes in this book venture above tree line, areas that are especially beautiful but also high-risk should thunder clouds roll in. If you can hear thunder, lightning is close enough to strike you; do not venture above tree line in these conditions, or if you're already above it, do everything you can to get below tree line immediately.

Start your hikes early in the day. Afternoons in July and August are often the most dangerous windows of time in the Southern Rockies; however, do bear in mind that thunderstorms can strike at any time. Check the weather forecast ahead of time, plan accordingly, and, most of all, be willing to modify your plans on the fly for safety reasons.

Additionally, most of the hikes in this book occur at higher altitudes than a vast majority of hikes elsewhere in the continental U.S. Be sure to bring a hat, sunscreen, sunglasses, and plenty of water, especially on hikes that are more exposed. It is easier to get sunburned at altitude than at sea level.

For high-elevation hikes, pay attention to any signs of altitude sickness, such as shortness of breath, nausea, fatigue, or headaches. Especially if you're coming from sea level, exerting yourself above 8,000 feet can trigger symptoms—and even more intensely so once you get above 12,000 feet. For mild symptoms, drink plenty of water, slow your pace, and take plenty of breaks. For more severe symptoms (such as an unsteady gait, intensifying nausea, vomiting, or shortness of breath even when resting), get yourself down to a lower elevation as soon as possible and, if symptoms persist, seek medical attention.

In the winter and spring, avalanches are also a risk factor in higher elevation areas—most notably for backcountry skiers or snowboarders, mountaineers, and snowshoers. Of the hikes in this book, the ones in the backcountry are written primarily with summer and/or occasionally autumn use in mind. Do not attempt any routes when large swaths of snow are still present unless you've done your homework ahead of time on avalanche safety awareness and preparation.

The mountains and deserts of the Southern Rockies are home to many kinds of interesting wildlife, the vast majority of which pose no risk whatsoever to humans. However, it's wise to read up on wildlife encounters, safety precautions, and how to react should you come face to face with any critters that can, in rare situations, pose a danger to humans—namely, rattlesnakes, black bears, javelina, Gila monsters, tarantulas, moose, and mountain lions. Arm yourself with knowledge.

Be sure to check your skin for ticks after hiking.

Lastly, a word on beer-imbibing safety as well: be aware that, particularly after a hard hike at altitude, your body is likely to already be dehydrated, which can make alcohol feel as though it hits you much harder and faster. Drink plenty of water and consume ample food during and after your hikes. Don't expect your alcohol tolerance to feel equivalent to what it may be at lower elevations.

The majority of the trailheads and breweries in this book require a vehicle to access. Drink responsibly, and never drink and drive. Have a designated driver, or wait at least 45 minutes per beer you enjoy for the alcohol to clear your system before getting behind the wheel of a vehicle. Otherwise, plan to get a growler, six-pack, or cowboy can to go and enjoy your beer responsibly back at your home, campsite, cabin, RV, or hotel.

TRAIL ETIQUETTE

Though this is a book on hiking and beer drinking, not on how to be a decent human when you venture into the wild, we'd be remiss if we didn't provide a few tips on trail etiquette.

The Southern Rockies are a popular place for outdoor enthusiasts. This book includes a mix of lesser-known trails and more popular (i.e., crowded) hikes. Especially if you're hiking on weekends, you're unlikely to have many of the trails in this book to yourself. Be respectful of other trail users and the environment by following some simple rules:

- Stay on trail—don't cut switchbacks as you risk trampling delicate flora and encouraging erosion.
- Limit your group size—especially in designated wilderness areas, where groups of 12 or larger are prohibited.
- Keep your noise level to a respectful volume—leave your Bluetooth speakers at home, please.
- Observe Leave No Trace (LNT) principles—respect wildlife, pack out your trash, and educate yourself on how to handle bathroom needs in the backcountry. Learn more at LNT.org.
- Yield to uphill hikers, who have the right of way.
- On equestrian trails, yield to horses, giving them plenty of space to get by you.
- Stay aware of your surroundings (e.g., do not hike with noise-canceling headphones).

Finally, many of the hikes in this book (though not all) are dog-friendly. If you like to hike with a four-legged companion, please do so with the utmost respect for other trail users as well as the land manager's rules, including leash regulations, which are often in place to help protect wildlife and fragile ecosystems. Pick up your dog's waste—and please don't leave plastic baggies of poop on the side of the trail to pick up on your way back.

A NOTE ON THE BEERS

While we've tried to primarily recommend beers that can be enjoyed at the brewery year-round, there are many exceptions. Some breweries are more experimental and put out new beers on constant rotation, meaning there isn't a set of core beers always on tap. The craft beer scene in the area is a dynamic one, and new beers sometimes take the place of old favorites to keep up with the changing landscape.

We chose beers based on brewery recommendations, community reviews, and the authors' personal enjoyment. The highlighted beers are certainly not the only ones worth trying at any given brewery. We fully encourage you to sample any beer that catches your fancy; many breweries offer sampler "flights" to encourage just this.

Consider this book your sampler flight of hikes and brews in the Southern Rockies. There are many more incredible trails, breweries, and beers to discover on your own. Let this book be your springboard for a lifetime of beer-hiking explorations in the Four Corners States and beyond.

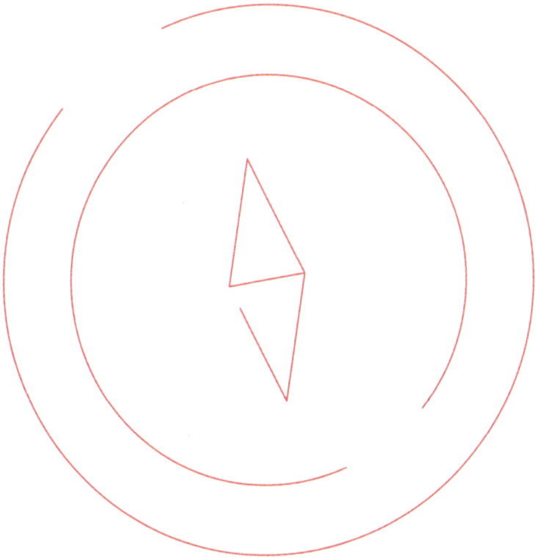

BEFORE SETTING OFF

TEN ESSENTIALS 

Even if you're just heading out on a day hike, you should always be prepared. Here's a list of the ten essentials you should take with you on the trail.

- Navigation: Maps in this book are for reference only. The most reliable form of navigation is a topographic paper map and compass. Batteries die—don't rely solely on your phone!
- Hydration: Water is essential when you're hiking. Make sure you bring plenty along to keep yourself hydrated and ward off the potential for dehydration and heat stroke. Don't worry—no matter how much water you drink, you'll still be thirsty enough for a beer!
- Nutrition: Bring extra food along just in case you're on the trail for longer than you expect. Foods that are high in protein and can be stored for a while can be kept in your pack for emergencies.
- Rain Gear and Insulation: The weather can change quickly! Rain gear is especially important; afternoon thunderstorms are common in the summer in the Southern Rockies. Bring an extra layer of clothing as temperatures fluctuate in the backcountry.
- Fire Starter: In case of emergency, a water-tight container of waterproof matches is invaluable to a lost hiker for warmth and cooking.
- First Aid: From minor cuts and scrapes to more major injuries, you need to be prepared.

- Tools: From a pocket knife to a multi-tool, these small tools take on big jobs in the backcountry. And never underestimate the power of duct tape!
- Illumination: Whether the hike took longer than you anticipated or you really wanted to catch that sunset from the top, you could get caught in the dark. Bring a flashlight or headlamp so you'll be able to see the trail.
- Sun Protection: Sunglasses, hats, and sunscreen keep you from getting sunburned and protect your eyes from the bright glare.
- Shelter: As simple as a space blanket or tarp—it could keep you dry and warmer in inclement weather or anunexpected overnight on the trail.

HIKING SEASON

Seasons are always a factor when hiking in the Southern Rockies. High-country trails may not be accessible between late fall and spring due to snow levels. Desert hikes may be brutal during the middle of the day in the summer. Always check with the land manager (listed for each hike) for current trail conditions before setting out. Local tourism offices can be a good resource as well.

WEATHER

Because conditions can change in an instant—especially in the mountains—it's best to always be prepared for wind, rain, snow, and anything else Mother Nature might throw your way. For accurate forecasts, check the following site:

- weather.gov

ADDITIONAL RESOURCES

For additional hiking and brewery information, we suggest the following sites:

HIKING

- arizonahiking.org
- gohikecolorado.com
- hikingproject.com
- alltrails.com

BREWERIES

- coloradocraftbrews.com
- coloradobrewerylist.com
- nmbeer.org
- chooseazbrews.com
- utahbrewersguild.org

BEER HIKING

- www.primepassages.com

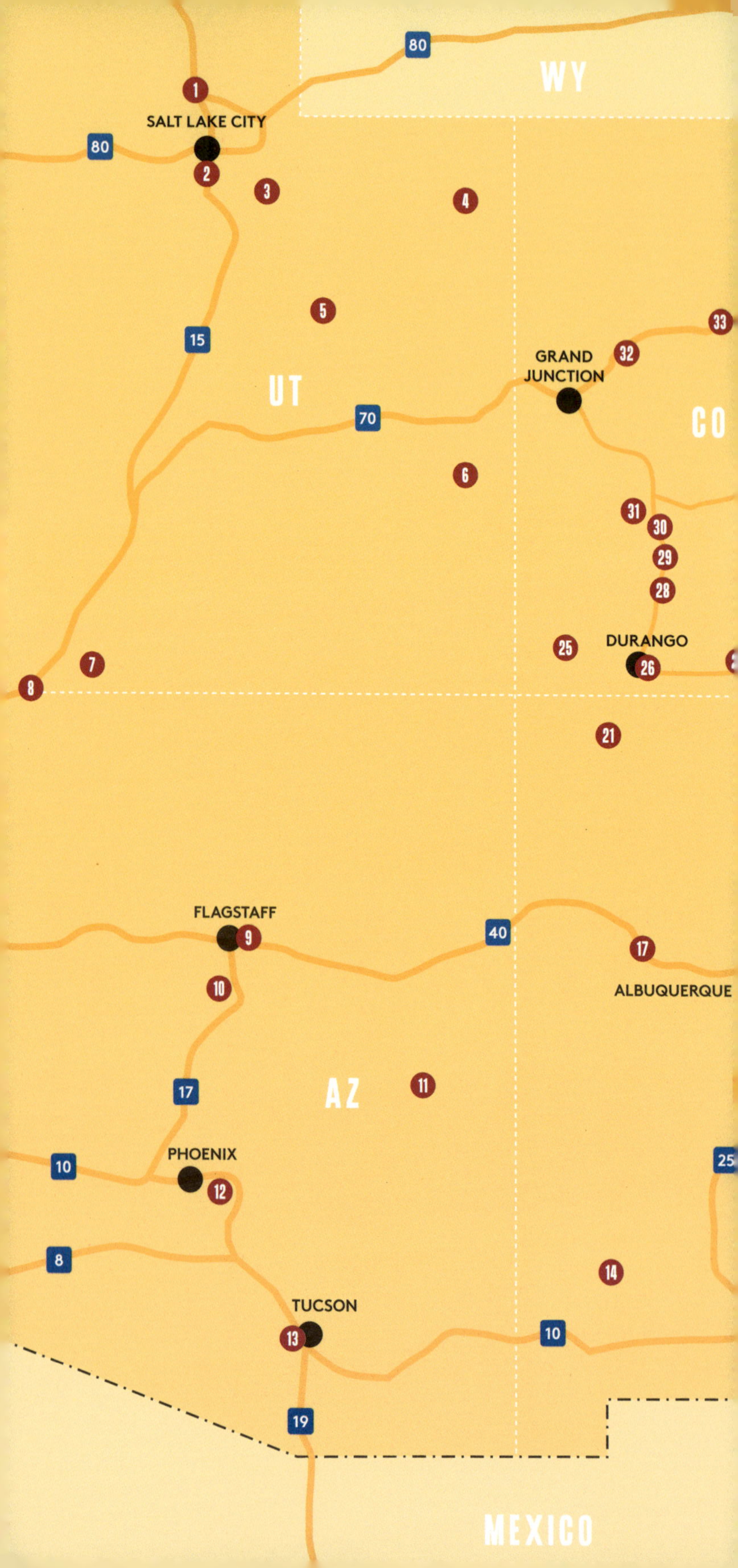

WY
SALT LAKE CITY
UT
GRAND JUNCTION
CO
DURANGO
FLAGSTAFF
ALBUQUERQUE
AZ
PHOENIX
TUCSON
MEXICO
80
15
70
40
17
10
8
19
25
1
2
3
4
5
6
7
8
9
10
11
12
13
14
17
21
25
26
28
29
30
31
32
33

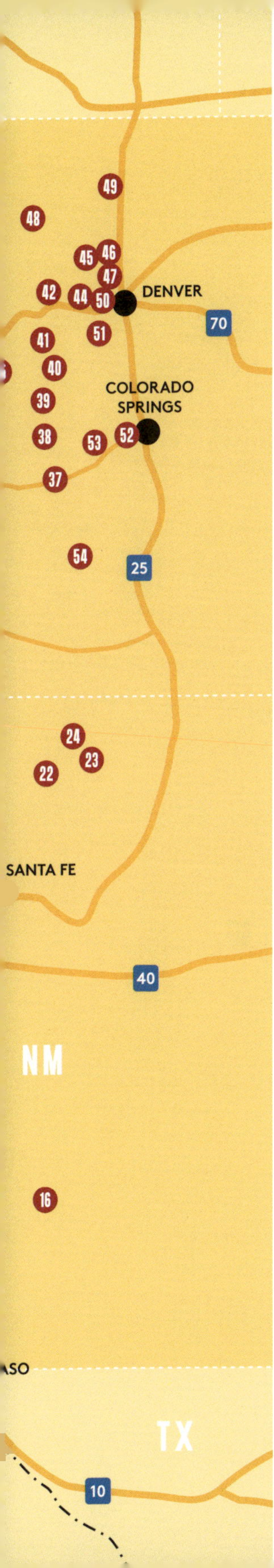

MAP

UTAH

1. Ogden Bay 28
2. Dimple Dell 34
3. Dutchman's Hollow 40
4. Sound of Silence 46
5. Gordon Creek Falls 52
6. Delicate Arch 58
7. Watchman Lookout 64
8. Turtle Wall 70

ARIZONA

9. Sandys Canyon 78
10. Thunder Mountain 84
11. Woodland Lake 90
12. Fat Man Pass 96
13. Bren Mountain 104

NEW MEXICO

14. Dragonfly Loop 112
15. Soledad Canyon 118
16. Grindstone Canyon 124
17. Lobo Canyon 130
18. Paseo del Bosque 136
19. Santa Fe River 144
20. Los Alamos Mesa 152
21. Animas River 158
22. El Salto del Agua Cañoncito 164
23. Tolby Canyon 170
24. Double Draw 176

COLORADO

25. Cortez 184
26. Durango 188
27. Pagosa Springs 192
28. Silverton 196
29. Ouray 200
30. Ridgway 204
31. Telluride 208
32. Palisade 212
33. Glenwood Springs 216
34. Carbondale 220
35. Aspen 224
36. Crested Butte 228
37. Poncha Springs 232
38. Buena Vista 236
39. Leadville 240
40. Fairplay 244
41. Breckenridge 248
42. Silverthorne 252
43. Steamboat Springs 256
44. Idaho Springs 260
45. Nederland 264
46. North Boulder 268
47. Boulder 272
48. Estes Park 276
49. Fort Collins 280
50. Golden 284
51. Evergreen 288
52. Colorado Springs 292
53. Manitou Springs 296
54. Alamosa 300

HIKES

HIKE	STATE	LENGTH	PAGE
Alamosa	Colorado	2.6 miles	300
Animas River	New Mexico	7.5 miles	158
Aspen	Colorado	4.1 miles	224
Boulder	Colorado	7.5 miles	272
Breckenridge	Colorado	7 miles	248
Bren Mountain	Arizona	3.8 miles	104
Buena Vista	Colorado	4 miles	236
Carbondale	Colorado	2 miles	220
Colorado Springs	Colorado	6 miles	292
Cortez	Colorado	5.5 miles	184
Crested Butte	Colorado	10.5-12.4 miles	228
Delicate Arch	Utah	3.3 miles	58
Dimple Dell	Utah	5.8 miles	34
Double Draw	New Mexico	3.6 miles	176
Dragonfly loop	New Mexico	3.5 miles	112
Durango	Colorado	2.5 miles	188
Dutchman's Hollow	Utah	5.36 miles	40
El Salto del Agua Cañoncito	New Mexico	5.2 miles	164
Estes Park	Colorado	8.4 miles	276
Evergreen	Colorado	6 miles	288
Fairplay	Colorado	3 miles	244
Fat Man Pass	Arizona	6 miles	96
Fort Collins	Colorado	6.1 miles	280
Glenwood Springs	Colorado	7.5 miles	216
Golden	Colorado	4.2 miles	284
Gordon Creek	Utah	6.3 miles	52
Grindstone Canyon	New Mexico	6.5 miles	124
Idaho Springs	Colorado	2 miles	260
Leadville	Colorado	5-6 miles	240
Lobo Canyon	New Mexico	4.3 miles	130
Los Alamos Mesa	New Mexico	6 miles	152
Manitou Springs	Colorado	3.4 miles	296
Nederland	Colorado	10.6 miles	264
North Boulder	Colorado	2.4 miles	268
Ogden Bay	Utah	6.3 miles	28
Ouray	Colorado	5.5 miles	200
Pagosa Springs	Colorado	6.2 miles	192
Palisade	Colorado	5.2 miles	212
Paseo del Bosque	New Mexico	3.9 miles	136
Poncha Springs	Colorado	8.6 miles	232
Ridgway	Colorado	3.75 miles	204
Sandys Canyon	Arizona	6.25 miles	78
Santa Fe River	New Mexico	7 miles	144
Silverthorne	Colorado	5.3 miles	252
Silverton	Colorado	7.7 miles	196
Soledad Canyon	New Mexico	3.8 miles	118
Sound of Silence	Utah	3.2 miles	46
Steamboat Springs	Colorado	4.9 miles	256
Telluride	Colorado	2.5 miles	208
Thunder Mountain	Arizona	4.25 miles	84
Tolby Canyon	New Mexico	8 miles	170
Turtle Wall	Utah	3.94 miles	70
Watchman Lookout	Utah	3.6 miles	64
Woodland Lake	Arizona	5 miles	90

BREWERIES & BEERS

BREWERY	BEER	PAGE
2 Row Brewing Company	Feelin' Hazy Double IPA	34
Angry James Brewery	Alpen Weisse	252
Arizona Wilderness Brewing Company	Don't F#%k It Up Blonde Ale	96
Avalanche Brewing Company	Pride of the West Porter	196
Bathtub Row Brewing Co-Op	Hoppenheimer IPA	152
Bristol Brewing Company	Laughing Lab Scottish Ale	292
Broken Compass Brewing	Coconut Porter	248
Carbondale Beer Works	Valley Girl Blonde	220
Colorado Boy Pub and Brewery	Irish Red Ale	204
Comanche Creek Brewing Company	Homestead Amber	170
Downshift Brewing Company	Hikin' Beer	124
Dragoon Brewing Company	Fall For You (Black IPA)	104
Eddyline Brewery	Jolly Roger Black Lager	236
Elevation Beer Company	Apis IV Belgian Quadrupel	232
Glenwood Canyon Brewpub	Burning Lotus Hazy IPA	216
Heber Valley Brewing Company	Bavarian Munich Helles	40
Helper Beer	Alt Bier	52
Highside Brewing	Rookie Guide Pale Ale	244
Ice Box Brewing Company	Black Ice Lager	118
Irwin Brewing Company	Oatmeal Stout	228
Junkyard on Route 66 Brewery	Junkyard Lager	130
La Cumbre Brewing	Elevated IPA	136
Lariat Lodge Brewing	Angry Elk Amber Ale	288
Main Street Brewery	Schnorzenboomer Amber Doppelbock	184
Manitou Brewing Company	High Ground IPA	296
Moab Brewery	Dead Horse Amber Ale	58
Mother Road Brewing Company	Tower Station IPA	78
Mountain Tap Brewery	HOPPY HIKER IPA	256
New Terrain Brewing Company	Cruise Ride American Cream Ale	284
Ogden Beer Company	Tmavé Dark Czech Lager	28
Open Space Brewing	NM-15 Hazy IPA	112
Ouray Brewery	Box Canyon Brown Ale	200
Palisade Brewing Company	Dirty Hippie Dark American Wheat	212
Pinetop Brewing Company	Blonde	90
Red River Brewing Company and Distillery	Catskinner IPA	176
Riff Raff Brewing Company	El Duende Verde Chile Ale	192
Rock Cut Brewing Company	Galactic Portal Hazy IPA	276
San Luis Valley Brewing Company	Valle Especial Mexican Lager	300
Sedona Beer Company	Red Rock Amber Lager	84
Silver Reef Brewing Company	Mas Fuego Rauchbier	70
Southern Sun Pub & Brewery	Annapurna Amber	272
Steamworks Brewing Company	Colorado Kölsch	188
Taos Mesa Brewing Mothership	Kolsch 45	164
Telluride Brewing Company	Face Down Brown Ale	208
Three Rivers Brewery	Piñon Hills Pils	158
Tommyknocker Brewery	Blood Orange IPA	260
Tumbleroot Brewery and Distillery	Patio Pale Ale	144
Two Mile Brewing Company	Camp Hale Pale Ale	240
Upslope Brewing Company - Lee Hill	Japanese Style Rice Lager	268
Vernal Brewing Company	Allosaurus Amber Ale	46
Very Nice Brewing Company	Very Nice Pale Ale	264
Westbound & Down Brewing Company	Italian Pils	224
Zion Brewing Company	Springdale Amber	64
Zwei Brewing	Zwei Pils Bavarian-style Pilsner	280

2

TRAILS

UTAH

OGDEN BAY

FROM WETLAND TRAILS TO WETTING YOUR WHISTLE

STARTING POINT	OBJECTIVE
OGDEN BAY SOUTH PARKING	**OGDEN BAY WATERFOWL MANAGEMENT AREA**
BEER	HIKE TYPE
TMAVÉ DARK CZECH LAGER	**EASY**
FEES	SEASON
NONE	**YEAR-ROUND**
MAP REFERENCE	DOG FRIENDLY
MAP AT TRAILHEAD, USGS 826477	**NOT ALLOWED**
DURATION	LENGTH
2.5 HOURS	**6.3 MILES**
LOW POINT / HIGH POINT	ELEVATION GAIN
4,209 FEET / 4,216 FEET	**36 FEET**

ALCOHOL **5.0%** CONTENT

CZECH LAGER TMAVÉ (CZECH DARK)

DARK BROWN WITH RUBY GLOW

ROASTY, HINT OF COCOA

MALT FORWARD, COFFEE NOTES

BITTERNESS
IBU: 20

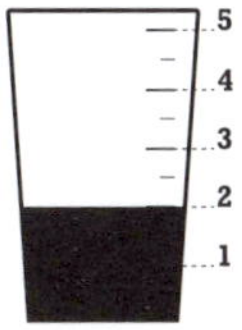

SWEETNESS

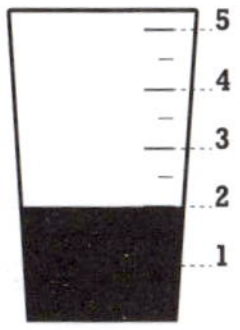

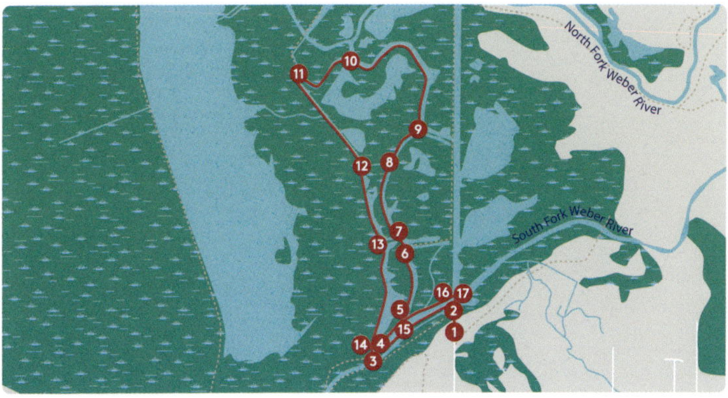

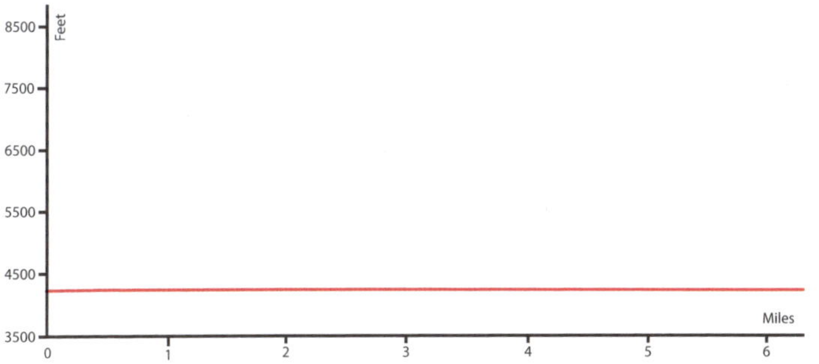

HIKE DESCRIPTION

Hiking in Bird Paradise and Savoring Local Brews

Just a short drive west of Ogden, Utah, is the Ogden Bay Waterfowl Management Area, a sprawling wetland sanctuary that is a haven for waterfowl, birdwatchers—and beer hikers. This enormous wetland encompasses an area larger than the states of Delaware and Rhode Island combined. It was created in 1938 as an early project funded by the Pittman-Robertson Act, landmark federal legislation that has revolutionized wildlife conservation in the United States.

Ogden is located about 40 miles north of Salt Lake City and is part of the Wasatch Front metro area encompassing a chain of cities from Ogen in the north down to Salt Lake City and Provo farther south. It was once a major passenger railroad junction and is still a railroad hub today. Ogden nestles right up against the Wasatch Mountains, providing quick access to hiking, skiing, and other outdoor mountain activities. Three downhill ski areas are nearby: Snowbasin, Powder Mountain, and Nordic Valley. Considered laid back by Salt Lake City standards, Ogden is home to Weber State University.

The land flattens out west of town approaching Great Salt Lake. The Ogden Bay Waterfowl Management Area is between the city and the huge lake. Trails and rough roads travel along the tops of many dikes that separate lagoons scattered throughout the reserve. The area features a combination of freshwater and salty wetlands, making it a unique habitat. While there is no shade to speak of, the open terrain allows for open views of the many birds, as well as the engaging scenery. To protect the nesting birds and other wildlife, dogs are not permitted in the Waterfowl Management Area. And it's a good idea to pack bug repellant!

The Ogden Bay Loop Hike route, accessible year-round, meanders along dikes that crisscross the marshes, providing panoramic views of the wetlands and the majestic Wasatch Mountains rising in the east. As we started the hike, we were greeted by a symphony of bird calls. The marshes are alive with chirps, whistles, and honks. You can spot a wide variety of bird species, including grebes, herons, sandpipers, cranes, egrets, ducks (cinnamon teal, gadwall, mallard, pintail, and northern shoveler), and geese. Some will be in the air, and others will be plodding through the waters of the lagoons. Keep a close lookout, and you may even see rarer species like the snowy plover, Wilson's phalarope, white-faced ibis, or a peregrine falcon.

If you're a birder, the best time to visit is September through May. In the fall, migratory birds pass through the area. Beginning in spring, nesting birds take over. About 15,000 ducks are born at Ogden Bay each year.

Check ahead to find out about duck hunting season closures. You'll see groupings of spent shotgun shells scattered here and there along the route, reminding you that the birds may be safe from dogs, but not necessarily from duck hunters.

We enjoyed the marshland hike after many days of hiking in mountain terrain, but if the marsh isn't your thing, there are plenty of nearby hike possibilities in the Wasatch as well as an inviting urban river hike starting at Ogden Beer Company. The Ogden River Trail is a 9.5-mile river trail connected to a larger system that extends into the foothills of the Wasatch Range.

TURN-BY-TURN DIRECTIONS

1. From the Ogden Bay Wildlife Management Area South Parking Area kiosk, follow the dirt road walking north and cross the bridge over the South Fork of the Weber River.
2. At 0.1 miles, turn left at the junction to walk on a dirt road on top of a dike between the river and a lagoon.
3. At 0.7 miles, turn right through the gate at the end of the lagoon.
4. At 0.8 miles, turn right and follow the path on a dike between two lagoons. The route will return to this point after a long loop.
5. At 1.0 miles, veer left at the junction onto the path with a lagoon to your right.
6. At 1.5 miles, continue straight at the junction with a trail to the right.
7. After 100 yards, continue straight at the junction with a trail to the left.
8. At 2.0 miles, continue straight at the junction with a trail to the left.
9. At 2.3 miles, continue straight at the junction with a trail to the right.
10. At 3.2 miles, continue straight where the lagoon to your right ends.
11. At 3.7 miles, turn left at the junction to walk southbound with a lagoon to your left.
12. At 4.3 miles, continue straight at the junction with a trail to the left.
13. At 4.8 miles, continue straight at the junction with a trail to the left.
14. At 5.5 miles, turn left at the junction and follow the path on a dike between two lagoons.
15. At 5.7 miles, continue straight at the junction with a trail to the left.
16. At 6.1 miles, turn right and cross the bridge.
17. After crossing the bridge, turn right on the dirt road and return to the parking area.

FIND THE TRAILHEAD

From the Hill Aerospace Museum exit on Interstate 15, take Utah Highway 97 (W 5600 S) 7.3 miles to S 7500 W Street. Turn right and travel 1.5 miles to the trailhead at the Ogden Bay Wildlife Management Area South Parking Area.

OGDEN BEER COMPANY

Ogden Beer Company (OBC) is located in downtown Ogden on the shady banks of the Ogden River. OBC replaced a previous brewery called Ogden River Brewing. A pair of local restauranteurs took over the old brewery, brought in a new head brewer, and re-opened as OBC in 2023. The head brewer, Jacquie King, is arguably the dean of women brewers in Utah. As I traveled the state talking to other brewers, her name and OBC were mentioned repeatedly.

OBC is a modern, attractive place with lots of outdoor seating on multiple levels overlooking the river. The food menu is a short but interesting list of pub food. A more extensive brunch is offered on weekends. Eleven draft beers were on offer, along with a big list of "high-point" beers in cans. High-point beer is a Utah thing to designate beers with an ABV greater than 5%. Two high-point beers were OBC-brewed, and the rest came from other breweries in Utah and beyond.

I chose a draft OBC Tmavé, a dark Czech-style lager that I encountered at several craft breweries in Utah. I hope they are starting a trend. Other OBC beers have names like Hopsteiner Experimental (a hazy pale ale), Hola Aloha (wheat ale), Cultura Cerveza (Mexican lager), 1851 (gateway lager), Cougar Juice (tangerine wheat ale), Pam-Ango Sour (mango sour on nitro), Prost Malone (Marzen), Cerveza Roja (red ale), Cerveza Obscura (a dark 6% ABV Mexican lager), and New Skool (a 7% IPA). Two of the beers offered were collaborations with other breweries and beer venues in the area. Kickstart Kolsch is a collaboration with local "beervenience" shop Salt & Hops, and the Tmavé is a collab with Kiitos, a Salt Lake City brewery. Collab beers are a regular part of Jacquie's brewing approach.

Other artisanal breweries in Ogden include Talisman Brewing Company, Cerveza Zólupez Beer Company, UTOG Brewing Company, and Roosters Brewing. Salt & Hops is a craft beer–themed convenience store offering a big range of artisanal choices. Regional pizza chain Saltfire features an impressive selection of craft beers from throughout the state and country and has several locations in the Wasatch Front Metro Area, including in Ogden.

CONTACT INFORMATION

Utah Division of Wildlife Resources
515 E. 5300 South
Ogden, UT 84405
+ 1 (801)-476-2740

BREWERY/RESTAURANT

Ogden Beer Company
358 Park Blvd,
Ogden, UT 84401
Distance from trailhead: 14 miles

DIMPLE DELL

GET YOUR HIKE ON, THEN GET HOPPY

STARTING POINT	OBJECTIVE
WRANGLER TRAILHEAD	DIMPLE DELL
BEER	HIKE TYPE
FEELIN' HAZY DOUBLE IPA	MODERATE
FEES	SEASON
NONE	YEAR ROUND
MAP REFERENCE	DOG FRIENDLY
USGS 825927	DOGS MUST BE LEASHED
DURATION	LENGTH
3 HOURS	5.8 MILES
LOW POINT / HIGH POINT	ELEVATION GAIN
4,673 FEET / 5,106 FEET	627 FEET

ALCOHOL
8.5%
CONTENT

DOUBLE IPA

HAZY GOLDEN

CITRUS NOSE

HOPPY, MALTY

BITTERNESS
IBU: 45

SWEETNESS

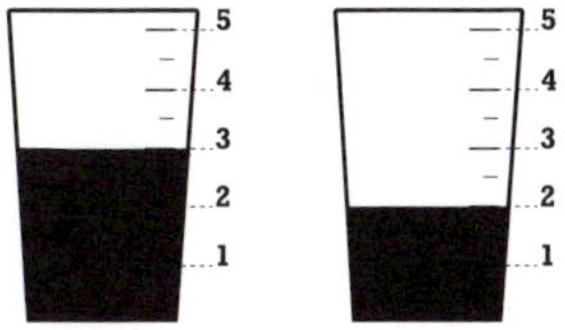

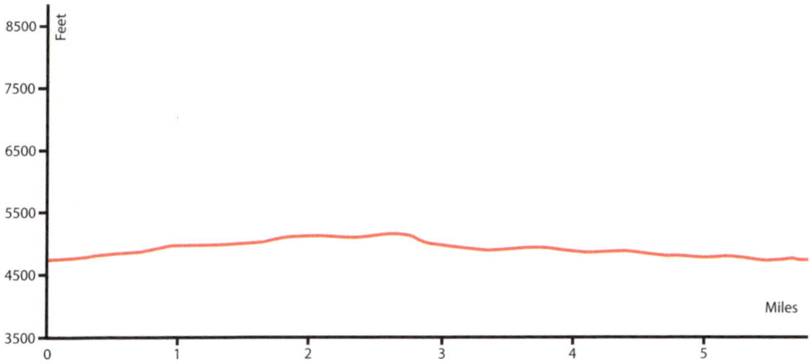

HIKE DESCRIPTION

Dimple Dell Loop, a hidden gem in the heart of Salt Lake City

The Dimple Dell Loop runs through an island of nature embedded in a busy urban area. Dimple Dell Regional Park is a sprawling 630-acre natural oasis following a ravine called Dry Creek, cutting through the urban landscape of Sandy, Utah. Like Midvale to the north, Sandy is one of a number of former small farming towns that have been absorbed into the urban milieu of the Salt Lake City Metro Area. The park features over 15 miles of multi-use trails, catering to hikers, bikers, and equestrians. I saw a horse or two along the way, but no bikes when I visited.

There was a farmer in the Dell back in the day. Dimple Dell was once a dairy farm, and there are still some visible remnants of those days. Over the years, the area has transformed into an important recreational space in Salt Lake City. There is also a prehistory here with an archaeological site in the park dating back 1,600 years. The hike begins at the Wrangler Trailhead, located on the northern ridge of the ravine adjacent to a shopping center. The trailhead offers plenty of parking, restrooms, picnic tables, and drinking water. The hike begins with a stiff uphill on a dirt path. Eventually, the hill is crested, and the path follows the ridge as it curves above the big ravine.

As expected in an urban area, there are many side trails offering route variations. Our route traverses the entire ridge on the east side of the park before dropping down into the Dell and looping all the way back through thick growth just above Dry Creek. On top of the ridge, the grassland is punctuated by a number of large shady trees. The nearby Wasatch range rises majestically to the east, with Gobblers Knob, O'Sullivan Peak, and Lone Peak providing a dramatic backdrop for the hike. Once you drop into the hollow, there are many scrub oak and other small trees along the way, so it feels more like hiking in a thicket. When you are in the Dell, it can be easy to forget you are in the middle of a bustling urban area. The creek lives up to its name—no running water in sight.

Most of the loop uses two trails. Up on the ridge is Dimple Dell Trail, and down in the hollow, the route uses Sego Lily Trail. The Sego Lily is Utah's state flower. A Sego Lily, a pretty white lily with an edible bulb, is a revered plant in Utah. It is a sacred plant to Native Americans, and it is credited with saving early Mormon settlers from starvation. If you are interested in this kind of thing, a short detour from the Dimple Dell trail can take you to visit Sego Lily Gardens, a small park featuring plantings of a broad range of drought-resistant plants that are important to a dry state like Utah.

Fortunately, Utah isn't totally dry, and a visit to 2 Row Brewing Company isn't far away.

TURN-BY-TURN DIRECTIONS

1. From the trailhead kiosk, follow the Dimple Dell Trail east up the hill.
2. At 0.1 miles, continue straight at the junction with Sego Lily Trail (Sego Lily Trail to the right is the return route).
3. At 0.3 miles, continue straight at a junction with Flanders Point Loop Trail.
4. At 0.6 miles, continue straight at a second junction with Flanders Point Loop Trail.
5. After 100 yards, continue straight at a junction with Primrose Loop Trail.
6. At 1.1 miles, continue straight at a second junction with Primrose Loop Trail.
7. At 1.6 miles, continue straight at a junction with Fox Point Loop Trail.
8. At 1.9 miles, continue straight at the junction with an unnamed connector trail.
9. At 2.0 miles, continue straight at a second junction with Fox Point Loop Trail.
10. At 2.1 miles, continue straight at a junction with Fox Hollow Trail.
11. At 2.2 miles, continue straight at a second junction with Fox Hollow Trail.
12. At 2.3 miles, continue straight at a junction with a neighborhood connector trail to the left.
13. At 2.6 miles, continue straight at a junction with another connector trail to the left.
14. At 2.7 miles, turn right to begin descending into the hollow on Sego Lily Trail.
15. At 3.1 miles, continue straight at the junction with Dry Creek Trail.
16. At 3.5 miles, continue straight at a junction with a connector trail to the left.
17. After 100 yards, continue straight at a junction with Mountain View Trail.
18. At 3.6 miles, continue straight at a junction with a connector trail to the right.
19. At 4.9 miles, continue straight at a second junction with Mountain View Trail.
20. At 5.0 miles, continue straight at a junction with Primrose Loop Trail.
21. After 50 yards, continue straight at another junction with Primrose Loop Trail to the right (Sego Lily Trail and Primrose Loop Trail share the same pathway for 50 yards).
22. At 5.6 miles, turn left at the junction with Dimple Dell Trail to return to the trailhead.

FIND THE TRAILHEAD

From exit 293 on I-15, exit onto W11400S heading east toward South State Street. Travel 2 miles and turn left onto S1300E. Travel north 1.25 miles and turn into the access road from Dimple Dell Regional Park. The parking lot entry and Wrangler Trailhead are 400 feet ahead on the right.

2 ROW BREWING COMPANY

After the hike, we headed to 2 Row Brewing in Midvale, Utah. 2 Row is literally a big box (16,000 square feet), occupying what must have formerly been a Staples or something like that in a strip shopping center. Founded in 2015 by award-winning homebrewer Brian Coleman, 2 Row is an example of turning a hobby into a thriving business. Brian took the time to sit with us and tell us about his journey. The big bump was in 2023 when 2 Row made the jump from being a brewery without a taproom to occupying its current space.

The sharp-looking brewhouse is in a roped-off section of the expansive space, and a good bit of floorspace is taken by indoor cornhole courts (are they called courts?) and space for other games. The feel is that of a big, friendly hangout space, and Brian told me that is what it is—a real community room. Sandwiches, salads, and a couple of entrees are on the menu, and there are plans to expand to a full kitchen.

I had heard that 2 Row is known for high-quality, full-flavored IPAs, so I dove right into one of their flagship beers, Feelin' Hazy. It is a New England–style double IPA, so in Utah that means it is a "high-point" beer served in a can. It weighs in at 8.5% ABV. There are thirteen taps, and the range includes names like Hipacrit IPA (unfiltered), Piney Peaks IPA (West Coast–style), Separation IPA, Lollygaggin' (Saison), Black Currant Sour, Inevitable Amber, Dos Filas, and Golden Sol (light mexi-lagers). I also tried out a totally pleasant Elderberry Blonde, which is made with real Elderberry fruit. Including the Feelin' Hazy, there were about a dozen high-point offerings in cans, with the strongest called "Barrel-aged Dark Alley" coming in at a hefty 14.6% ABV.

Brian was a great guy to chat with. The conversation ran the gamut from his brewing journey of discovery to his recommendations for other breweries and venues in the Salt Lake City Metro to Utah alcohol history. Believe it or not, Brigham Young once owned a distillery near here. I didn't believe it until I looked it up.

I counted more than 15 craft breweries in the Salt Lake City Metroplex, so there are plenty of hikes and beers to be paired up in the area. A block away from 2 Row, Bohemian Brewery makes various Czech and German-style lagers (my sweet spot) and even makes a Czechulator Doppelbock during strong beer season. Another favorite of mine was Templin Family Brewing (TF for short), located downtown. Great quality beers, a lively atmosphere, and what I'll call a "foam fetish" that you don't see every day made this a fun stop. I'll leave it at that.

CONTACT INFORMATION

Salt Lake County Parks & Recreation
2001 South State Street , Ste S4-700
Salt Lake City, Utah 84190
+ 1 (385) 468-1800

BREWERY/RESTAURANT

2 Row Brewing Company
73 W 7200 S
Midvale, UT 84047
Distance from trailhead: 6 miles

DUTCHMAN'S HOLLOW

EUROPEAN CHARM AND PANORAMIC VIEWS

STARTING POINT	OBJECTIVE
DUTCHMAN CANYON TRAILHEAD	DUTCHMAN OVERLOOK
BEER	HIKE TYPE
BAVARIAN MUNICH HELLES	MODERATE
FEES	SEASON
DAY USE VEHICLE PERMIT	SPRING-FALL
MAP REFERENCE	DOG FRIENDLY
POSTED AT TRAILHEAD-USGS 826139	YES
DURATION	LENGTH
3 HOURS	5.36 MILES
LOW POINT / HIGH POINT	ELEVATION GAIN
5,738 FEET / 6,339 FEET	696 FEET

ALCOHOL 5.0% CONTENT

HELLES

GOLDEN

GRAINY MALT, SLIGHT HOPPINESS

CLEAN, SLIGHTLY HOPPY

BITTERNESS
IBU: 22

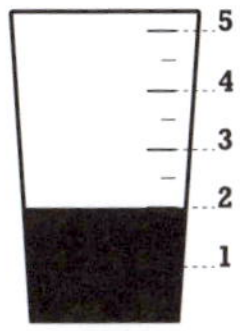

SWEETNESS

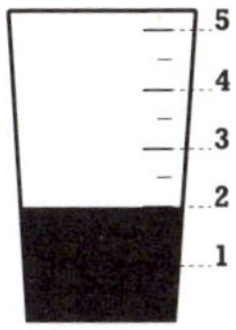

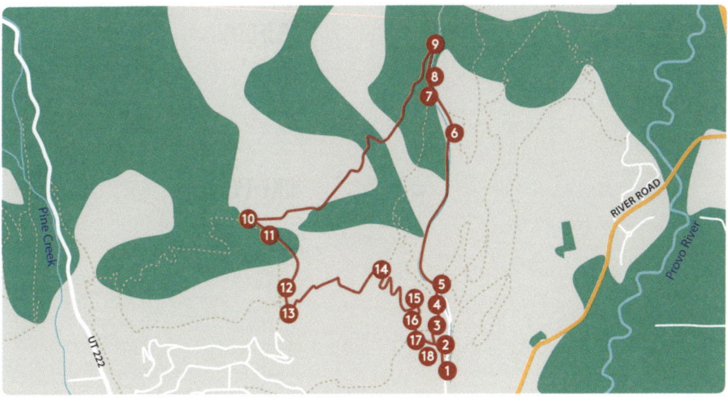

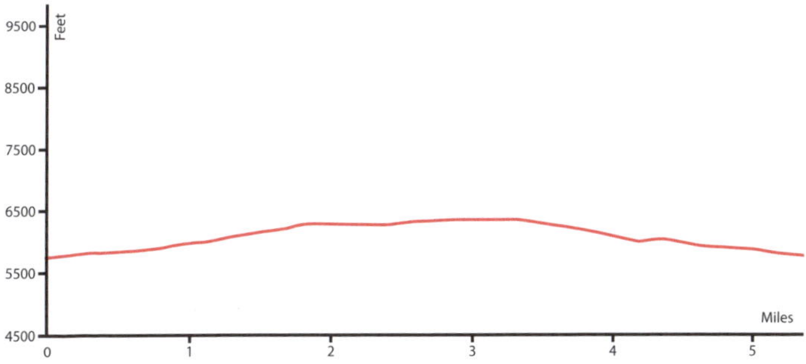

HIKE DESCRIPTION

Dutchman Hollow features hidden trails and stunning valley views—with a beer at the end.

Dutchman Hollow, near Midway in the Heber Valley of central Utah, offers miles of trails to explore. The area is riddled with pathways—a sure sign of mountain biker use. The trail system in the area is made up of mostly smooth single tracks and one old forest road leading up the canyon. There are some rocky sections, and shade is sporadic. The area is part of Wasatch Mountain State Park, a sprawling area encompassing 21,592 acres and sitting at an elevation of nominally 5,900 feet. Miles of trails and backcountry can be explored on foot, by mountain bike, or on horseback. In winter, there is cross-country skiing and snowshoeing. The park provided Nordic skiing venues for the 2002 Winter Olympics.

The Heber Valley is a broad valley on the eastern flank of the Wasatch Mountains. Due west over the Wasatch range—20 miles as the crow flies—is the Salt Lake City metro area. The area features towering peaks, lush valleys, and sparkling reservoirs. The closest town to Dutchman Hollow is Midway, a place settled by Swiss immigrants in the mid-19th century. As the story goes, the settlers were seeking a new life reminiscent of their homeland, and the valley's terrain harkened back to the Swiss Alps. Architecture and cuisine in the town build on Swiss tradition, and if you go at the right time in the summer, you can experience Midway Swiss Days, a celebration of Swiss culture and tradition. Midway provides an unexpected taste of European charm in the Mountain West.

The Dutch Canyon trailhead is marked by a small parking area and a big signboard that is covered with an array of smaller signs. Follow instructions on one of the signs to pay the state park day-use fee online. Dogs are welcome but must be leashed and under the owner's control at all times. Notices warn users that black bears and cougars may be present in the area.

The Dutchman Hollow Loop Hike route gradually ascends the canyon, passing a number of trail intersections. The hillsides are thick with scrub oak and other bushy plants. Stop for a few minutes anywhere, and you'll have an expansive view to the south overlooking Heber Valley. The proliferation of trails provides many options for adjusting your route to make for a longer, shorter, or steeper hike, depending on preference. We turned back when we reached the Prospect Trail, but we could have kept going up the canyon to get an even better view.

By the time we started descending back to the trailhead, I had worked up a noticeable thirst for something more than the water I had packed. Fortunately, a friendly neighborhood brewery is a short drive from Dutchman's Hollow.

TURN-BY-TURN DIRECTIONS

1. From the trailhead kiosk, follow the single-track trail called Dutchman Way.
2. At 0.1 miles, bear right at the junction and continue on Dutchman Way (to the left is a trail called Luge which will be the return route).
3. At 0.2 miles, bear right at the junction with Interlakken Trail and continue on Dutchman Way.
4. At 0.5 miles, turn right onto Donkey Ridge Trail.
5. At 0.6 miles, turn left onto Dutchman Hollow Trail.
6. At 1.3 miles, bear left to stay on Dutchman Hollow Trail.
7. At 1.5 miles, bear right onto Dutchman Way.
8. In about 150 feet, bear right and continue on Dutchman Way.
9. At 1.8 miles, switchback to the left onto Prospect Trail.
10. At 3.1 miles, switchback to the left and continue on Prospect Trail.
11. At 3.3 miles, bear left at the intersection with Phosphate Hill Trail and continue on Prospect Trail.
12. At 3.6 miles, bear left at the intersection with The Face Trail and continue on Prospect Trail.
13. At 3.7 miles, at the T intersection, turn left onto Donkey Ridge Trail.
14. At 4.4 miles, bear right at the intersection with Fenceline Trail and continue on Donkey Ridge Trail.
15. At 5.0 miles, turn right on Luge Trail.
16. At 5.1 miles, continue straight on Luge Trail.
17. At 5.2 miles, continue straight on Luge Trail.
18. At 5.25 miles, bear right onto Dutchman Way and return to the trailhead.

FIND THE TRAILHEAD

From the intersection of US 189 and US 40 in Heber City, travel north 0.3 miles and turn left on UT-113 W. Travel 2.8 miles and turn right on River Road N. Travel 0.4 miles and take the 3rd exit at the traffic circle onto River Road. Travel 0.3 miles and continue straight at the traffic circle to stay on River Road. Travel 0.5 miles and take the 2nd exit at the traffic circle onto E 440 N/River Road. Continue on River Road 0.8 miles. Turn left onto Dutch Canyon Road and travel 0.3 miles to Dutch Canyon trailhead

HEBER VALLEY BREWING COMPANY

Heber Valley Brewing Company in nearby Heber City is a neighborhood brewery and taproom operation. Heber City is the largest town in the valley and the Wasatch County seat. Named after Heber Kimball, a prominent Mormon leader, it was founded about the same time that those Swiss settlers were taking root in Midway. Heber City is a short drive from the ski town of Park City, and it struck me that a lot of the workforce for Park City lives in Heber City.

Heber Valley Brewing was started in 2019 by a former Olympic coach and an Olympic ski athlete, Greg Poirier and Clint Jones. Greg coached the Nordic ski team in multiple Olympics and Clint competed in multiple Olympics. Traveling all over, particularly in Europe, exposed the pair to lots of great beer. Their lineup features lots of traditional European brewing styles. Greg is the business guy and Clint is the head brewer. Greg told me that their vision is to create a friendly space focused on locals, but which welcomes visitors from all over the world.

The small taproom had a *Cheers* vibe, with small groups of obvious friends laughing over beers. While enjoying the HVBC rendition of a traditional Munich Helles-style brew, we enjoyed a giant soft pretzel with a killer cheese spread. This isn't just any pretzel! It is an authentic Bavarian pretzel that Greg told me is made fresh by a local German immigrant using her Oma's (grandma's) recipe. The cheese spread that came with it, reminiscent of obadza, is made from locally made cheeses. This is one of just a few food offerings, but the pretzel was memorable.

The draft beer list featured beers with names like Cold Fusion Kölsch, a Dunkelweiss (traditional dark wheat beer), Märzen (traditional amber lager), Dark Helmet Schwarzbier (black lager), Dark Sky Stout, Heber's Hazy IPA, Stellar Stream IPA (West Coast), White Wine Tart Ale (a sour), and Three C's American Pale Ale. For the strong-beer lovers who find themselves in Utah, several "high-point" (above 5% ABV) beers are often offered in cans or bottles with names like Snake Creek Imperial Stout, Bomegranate Sour, The Grunge IPA, and Citrocumulus Hazy IPA.

A brewery founded by Olympians, a taste of European brewing traditions, locally sourced soft pretzels, and a friendly neighborhood atmosphere after a scenic hike—what could be better?

CONTACT INFORMATION

Wasatch Mountain State Park
1281 Warm Springs Rd
Midway, UT 84049
+ 1 (435)-654-1791

BREWERY/RESTAURANT

Heber Valley Brewing Company
501 N Main Street
Heber City, UT 84032
Distance from trailhead: 6 miles

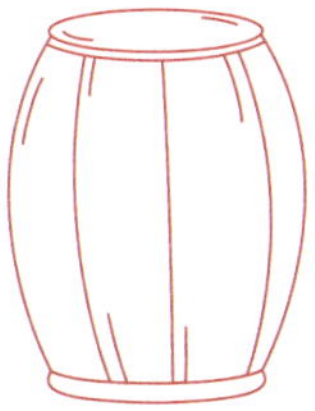

SOUND OF SILENCE

ANCIENT CANYONS, DINOSAUR FOSSILS, AND A THIRST-QUENCHING ALLOSAURUS

STARTING POINT	OBJECTIVE
SOUND OF SILENCE TRAILHEAD	SPLIT MOUNTAIN OVERLOOK
BEER	HIKE TYPE
ALLOSAURUS AMBER ALE	EASY
FEES	SEASON
NATIONAL PARK ENTRY FEE	SPRING-FALL
MAP REFERENCE	DOG FRIENDLY
POSTED AT TRAILHEAD - USGS 488111	NO
DURATION	LENGTH
1.5 HOURS	3.2 MILES
LOW POINT / HIGH POINT	ELEVATION GAIN
4,865 FEET / 5,131 FEET	328 FEET

ALCOHOL 5.0% CONTENT

AMBER ALE
RED ALE

REDDISH BROWN

FLORAL NOTES

MEDIUM BODY, BREADY

BITTERNESS
IBU: 28

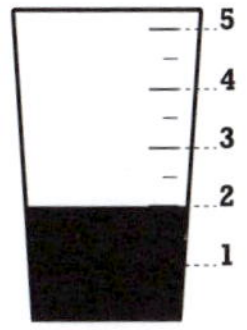

SWEETNESS

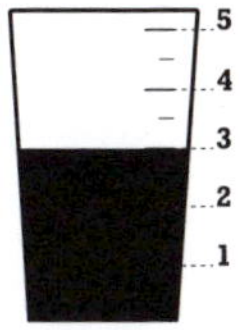

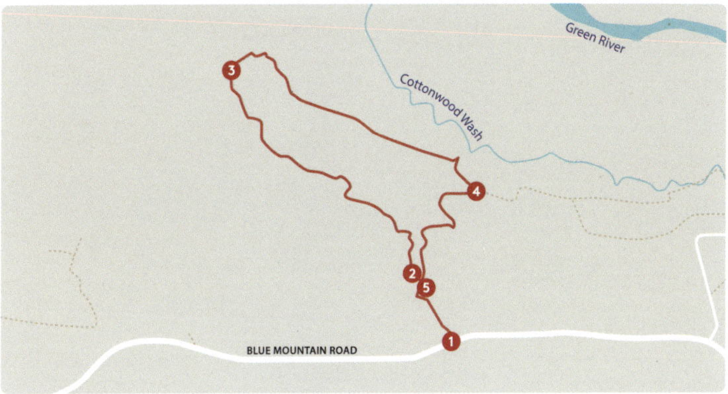

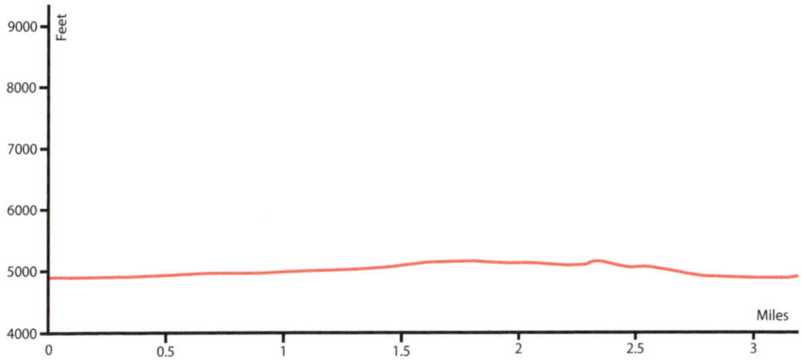

HIKE DESCRIPTION

Hike through colorful canyons and discover ancient secrets on the Sound of Silence Trail.

Dinosaur National Monument straddles a northern section of the border where Utah and Colorado meet. It is best known for its dinosaur fossils, which can be seen in the visitor centers and at the Quarry Exhibit Hall. "Dinosaur," as many people call it, also features a variety of landscapes, including mountains, deserts, rivers, and canyons. The Sound of Silence Trail is a sampler of this terrain.

The start of the trail is in a dry ravine that winds its way into wilderness. Upturned rock layers are exposed as you hike up the wash under the shade of occasional cottonwood trees. The route is easy to follow, as is expected in most national parks, and there are confidence markers at appropriate spots along the way. Eventually, the route leaves the main ravine and starts climbing through a series of narrow, red-earth gullies before topping out on a long ridge.

The route follows the ridge on a nearly straight path with ups and downs across several small gullies. All along this way are splendid views to the north of Split Mountain, a prominent landmark in the area. Split Mountain is a massive example of an anticline—a fold in the Earth's crust that pushed rock layers upward. The Green River cut right through the center of the anticline, creating the split, a spectacular canyon that divided the mountain into two distinct peaks.

Eventually, you reach the intersection with a trail called Desert Voices that loops down to the Green River. A longer hike is available by adding this loop to the route (adds about two miles), but it was too damn hot the day we were there to do that. Summertime temperatures can exceed 100 degrees, and there is little shade. Slather on the sunscreen, bring plenty of water, and hike early in the morning to avoid the heat.

The terrain gets a bit trickier on the descent down a big slab of slickrock, followed by a scramble through a mini-gorge back into the ravine. After that, turn back to the trailhead. It is all pretty easy if you take your time and watch your footing.

I love the name of this hike: Sound of Silence. It evoked memories of the Simon & Garfunkel song of that name. It planted a vision in my brain of a hike through an ancient, silent landscape, and that isn't a bad description for this hike.

Dinosaur National Monument is famous as a collecting point for dinosaur fossils. The fossils date back 150 million years to the Jurassic period, and large deposits are spotted around the 210,000-acre park. We didn't spot any dinosaur fossils along the route. No worries, though. A short drive from the trailhead is the Quarry Exhibit Hall, a huge shed protecting a natural cliff face exhibiting more than 1,500 dinosaur fossils embedded in the rock. Pretty cool!

TURN-BY-TURN DIRECTIONS

1. From the trailhead kiosk, proceed on the Sound of Silence trail.
2. At 0.2 miles, bear left at the trail junction to follow the ravine (to the right is your return route).
3. At 1.3 miles, the trail turns to the right and proceeds up a narrow arroyo.
4. At 2.4 miles, turn right at the junction with the Desert Voices trail.
5. At 2.9 miles, bear left at the junction and follow the trail back to the trailhead.

FIND THE TRAILHEAD

From Vernal, take U.S. Highway 40 E 12.2 miles to Jenson, UT. Turn left onto Utah Highway 149 for 7.8 miles and travel into Dinosaur National Monument. The Sound of Silence trailhead parking is along the highway about 2 miles past the park entry station.

VERNAL BREWING COMPANY

The combination of hiking the Sound of Silence Loop and enjoying a beer at Vernal Brewing Company made for a great day in Vernal. Vernal Brewing Company is a modern, stand-alone building with a garden on the grounds. Some would call the taproom a gastropub featuring garden-to-table and farm-to-table fare. The beers also incorporate local ingredients whenever possible, including honey.

I quenched my thirst with a flagship Allosaurus Amber Ale. The Allosaurus seems to be an iconic symbol of the area, and it shows up frequently in the names of places and products. Other beers on tap also pay homage to the locale with names like Little Hole Lager, Pilgrimage Extra Pale Ale, She's a Peach Wheat Ale, Ms. Bee Hiven (a honey blonde ale brewed with local honey), and several seasonals. Another unusual and well-crafted draft beer I tried is the She's a Fire Wheat Ale, a citrusy beer with a tinge of jalapeño heat. "High-point" can offerings included .50 Caliber India Pale Ale (103 IBU, 8.5% ABV) and Mama's Milk Imperial Milk Stout. Remember that in Utah, only beers of 5% ABV or lower are permitted to be served on tap. ABVs above that are called high-point beer and can only be served in packaged form.

Owner Ginger Bowden was stationed at the bar, overseeing the operation. Her family has lived in the area for at least five generations, and she is deeply committed to the community. She has welcomed community participation through a process called "Battle of the Beers," which gathers customer feedback to develop new beer recipes and tweak existing ones. This involves brewing small batches and having customers test each variation.

CONTACT INFORMATION

Dinosaur National Monument
4545 Hwy 40
Dinosaur, CO 81610
+ 1 (435) 781-7700

BREWERY/RESTAURANT

Vernal Brewing Company
55 S 500 E
Vernal, UT 84078
Distance from trailhead: 20 miles

GORDON CREEK

EXPLORE A HIDDEN VALLEY FOLLOWED BY A HELPER BEER

STARTING POINT	OBJECTIVE
GORDON CREEK TRAILHEAD	SUMMER HOUSE CABIN
BEER	HIKE TYPE
ALT BIER	MODERATE
FEES	SEASON
NONE	SPRING TO FALL
MAP REFERENCE	DOG FRIENDLY
USGS 826534	YES
DURATION	LENGTH
2.5 HOURS	6.3 MILES
LOW POINT / HIGH POINT	ELEVATION GAIN
6,211 FEET / 6,536 FEET	500 FEET

ALCOHOL
4.7%
CONTENT

ALT BIER
ALTBIER

BRONZE-ORANGE

GRAINY, SPICY HOP

WELL-BALANCED, CRISP, NUTTY HINTS

BITTERNESS
IBU: 35

SWEETNESS

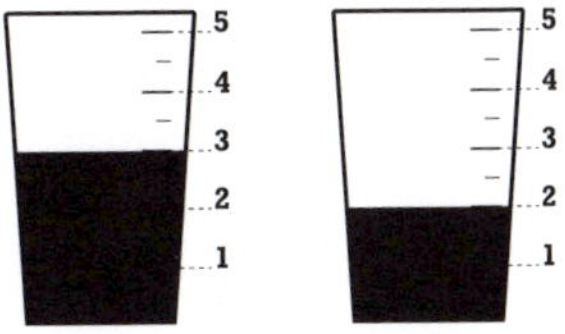

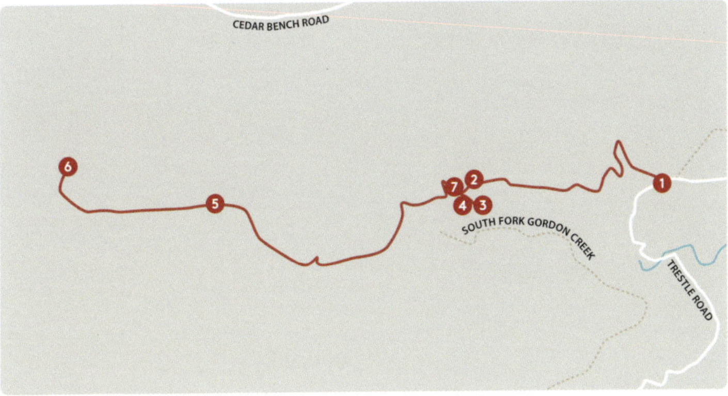

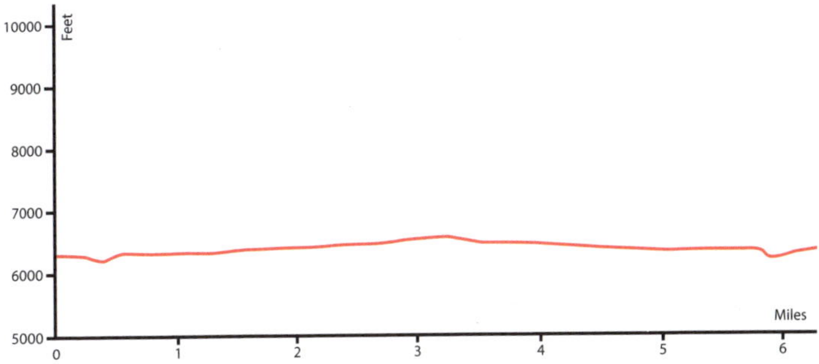

HIKE DESCRIPTION

Discover the rugged beauty of the Gordon Creek Trail, featuring stunning waterfalls, a historic trestle, and a glimpse into the lives of early settlers.

The Gordon Creek Trail descends rapidly into a narrow side canyon that feeds the Gordon Creek Valley before ascending a ridgeline above Gordon Creek. The route follows an old, closed road leading past impressive waterfalls to the turnaround point at an abandoned cabin. This 6.3-mile in-and-back hike offers a chance for immersion in the nature and history of the area.

This is rugged, well-adapted piñon-juniper woodland, typical of the mesas, canyons, and mountain slopes in the area. Typical native plants along the route are subtle but vibrantly colored Indian paintbrush and green rabbitbrush. For the Navajo, Indian paintbrush was seen as a protective talisman for hunters, while for the Paiute people, it was a harbinger of stormy weather. Rabbitbrush roots were used as chewing gum by the Paiute, and the Navajo used the red and yellow leaves as dyes. We encountered no storms, nor for that matter, any people at all, as we hiked in this remote area.

Typical wildlife in the area includes diverse birdlife, such as the blue-ish piñon jay and turkey vultures, and mammals like the white-tailed prairie dog. We didn't see any cattle or sheep, but as I understand it, the BLM issues grazing permits in this area. Hunt's bumblebees, identifiable by an orange stripe, collect pollen from the rabbitbrush.

The view east offers glimpses of the Gordon Creek Trestle, a historic steel girder rail bridge located a short distance away. The trestle spans 634 feet and stands 135 feet above the creek. It is one of the longest steel girder bridges in Utah, though it is no longer in use. Built in 1914, the bridge connected the towns of Hiawatha and Mohrland to the community of Martin, Utah.

The ridgeline follows the broad valley, eventually descending to a lookout over the creek and the Gordon Creek waterfalls. Gordon Creek is a year-round stream, and the 100-foot drop is a refreshing cascade over a series of sandstone ledges. The falls are arguably the highlight of this hike. Be careful if you decide to scramble down to the water, which I recommend, because it's a tranquil spot to hang out and gaze up at the impressive (by Mountain West standards) falls.

This valley has a ranching history rooted in summer grazing by sheepherders in the early 1900s. A family named Oman grazed sheep in the area and built a structure known as Summer House Cabin for shelter. The remains of the cabin still stand at the turnaround point of our hike.

Close your eyes and imagine what life must have been like for the Oman family summering in a remote spot like this. The Gordon Creek Falls Hike is an off-the-beaten-path journey through time, nature, and history.

In addition to the Gordon Creek Falls Hike, the "Carbon Corridor," as the tourism authorities in the area call it, offers a variety of hiking options. One that caught my eye that I'll check out next time I visit is called Buried Forest Concretions Trail. "Buried Forest" refers to an area of what was once thought to be a buried petrified forest that can be seen on an eroded cliffside. Some of the circular concretions that can be found exceed four feet in diameter.

TURN-BY-TURN DIRECTIONS

1. From the trailhead kiosk, follow the Gordon Creek Trail.
2. At 1.0 miles, bear left at the junction to walk downhill to the Gordon Falls overlook (to the right is your return route).
3. At 1.1 miles, reach the Gordon Falls overlook.
4. At 1.2 miles, bear left at the junction and head west further up the valley.
5. At 2.5 miles, continue straight on the trail heading west up the valley.
6. At 3.2 miles, reach the remains of Summer House Cabin. This is the turnaround point for the hike. Retrace your route back to the trailhead.
7. At 5.2 miles, reach the Y junction near the Falls and bear left on the trail back to the trailhead.

FIND THE TRAILHEAD

From Helper, head out of town South on US Highway 6, 2.2 miles to Consumers Road. Turn right on Consumers Road and travel 2.8 miles to Trestle Road. Turn left on Trestle Road and travel 3.4 miles to the trailhead on the right. There is a sign and small parking area for Gordon Creek Trail.

HELPER BEER

Helper Beer is a modern small brewery and pub located in historic Helper, Utah. Helper is a town with a rich history as a bustling coal mining and railroad hub in the early 20th century. The town took its name from the "helper" engines that assisted trains in climbing the steep railroad grades found in the area. Tough times came in the 1970s, when the coal industry (and reportedly the brothels) in the area declined. By appearances, Helper is having a bit of a comeback. There is a cool old main drag with vintage brick buildings, a nice community cafe/restaurant or two, an interesting private museum (more about that in a minute), and signs of artists and artisans sprinkled here and there. There is still an active Amtrak stop. And oh yes ... did I say there is a brewery?

Helper Beer is a short, enjoyable walk from the historic center. Helper Beer's head brewer, Jaron Anderson, learned his trade as a brewer with Templin Family (TF) Brewing in Salt Lake City. He is one of several brewers I encountered in Utah who trace their brewing journey to TF. In Jaron's case, he brought strong experience with brewing classic European-style beers with him, and that is evidenced in the Helper line-up. Sixteen taps pour beers with names like Schloss Tor (German-style pilsener), Lime Gose, Weisse Bier, Lifestyle Choices (hazy pale ale), Mindset Extra Pale Ale, and Feijoa Tart (made with Guavasteen). There are three pilseners on tap—a German-style, a Czech-style, and a Danish-style. My choice for a thirst quencher was the Helper Alt Bier, a gorgeous German-style ale that is the beer style of choice in Dusseldorf.

As is the case with most Utah breweries, Helper offers "high-point" beers in cans. High-point beers exceed the 5% ABV limit that Utah places on draft beers. These offerings included Circle Back (West Coast IPA), Total Rise (imperial IPA), Slow Fade (imperial tart), Power Coupling (West Coast pils), Idea Shower (cold IPA), an Italian pilsener, and Night Indoors (imperial stout at 12% ABV).

Brewery co-owner (and Jaron's wife) Amy told me they opened the brewery and pub in 2023. It is a family-friendly space with a small patio. The decor is minimalist Art Deco. The brewhouse is open to the seating area. Oven-fired pizzas, sandwiches, and salads make up the menu. Amy told me that their clientele splits about 50/50 between locals and visitors passing through on Utah's National Park Circuit. She figures there are more mountain bikers and ATVers than hikers. It feels remote, and there are only about 20,000 locals in the big, rural county, so this is definitely a small market brewery.

A nearby private museum called Vintage Motor Company (VMC) in Helper shows off a cool collection of vintage Harley Davidson and Indian motorcycles, classic cars, and memorabilia. Housed in a restored vintage building, it oozes character. The owners, who also own a number of AirBnBs in Helper, have made the community a personal project, meticulously restoring not only the museum but also many other buildings and homes in Helper. It's truly a unique place.

A visit to Helper Beer is not just about enjoying craft brews; it's an opportunity to experience the town's unique charm and history. The brewery is one of several symbols of Helper's revitalization progress.

CONTACT INFORMATION

U.S. Bureau of Land Management (BLM)
125 South 600 West
Price, UT 84501
+ 1 (435)-636-3600

BREWERY/RESTAURANT

Helper Beer
159 N Main Street
Helper, UT 84526
Distance from trailhead: 8 miles

DELICATE ARCH

HIKE TO AN ICONIC UTAH LANDMARK FOLLOWED BY A BREW AT ONE OF UTAH'S OLDEST CRAFT BREWERIES

STARTING POINT	OBJECTIVE
DELICATE ARCH TRAILHEAD	DELICATE ARCH

BEER	HIKE TYPE
DEAD HORSE AMBER ALE	MODERATE

FEES	SEASON
ARCHES NATIONAL PARK (RESERVATIONS AT PEAK TIMES)	YEAR-ROUND (CAUTION: HEAT AND ICE)

MAP REFERENCE	DOG FRIENDLY
HELLO.HELVETIQ.COM/BHNM	DOGS NOT ALLOWED

DURATION	LENGTH
1.5 HOURS	3.3 MILES

LOW POINT / HIGH POINT	ELEVATION GAIN
4,302 FEET / 4,884 FEET	617 FEET

ALCOHOL
5.0%
CONTENT

AMBER ALE

AMBER

SLIGHT HOPPINESS

CLEAN AND ROASTY

BITTERNESS
IBU: 24

SWEETNESS

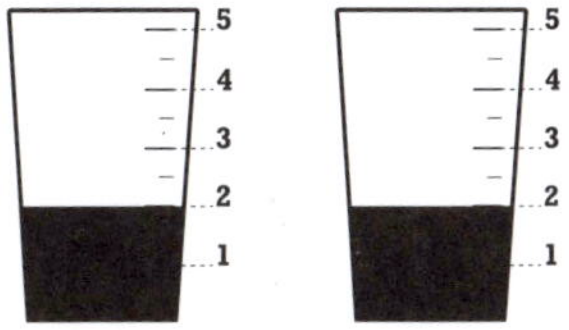

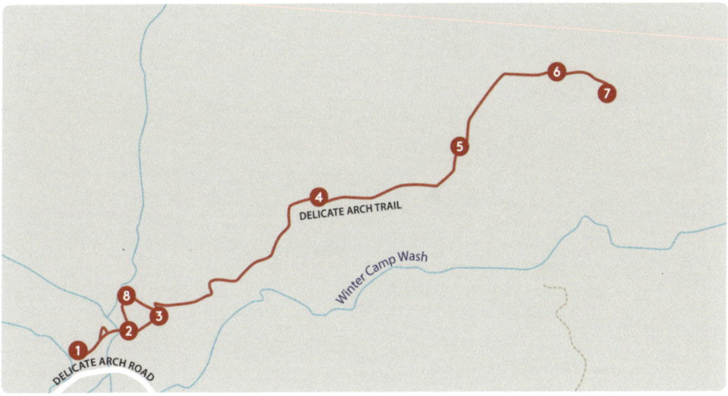

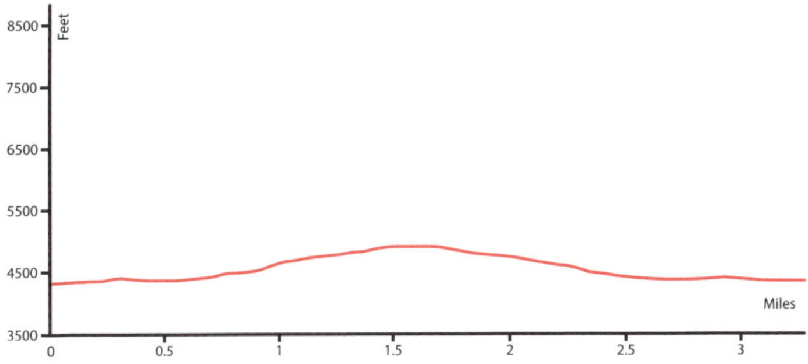

HIKE DESCRIPTION

Delicate Arch Hike is a scenic out-and-back climb to the iconic Delicate Arch, a massive freestanding arch that is frequently used as a symbol of Utah. Work up a thirst for a post-hike visit to the nearby Moab Brewery.

The Utah sun was starting to beat down over the eastern horizon on the road leading to the trailhead. Arches National Park is a dramatic place, and big views of the La Sal mountain range and rock formations with names like Courthouse Towers, Tower of Babel, Petrified Dunes, and Balanced Rock mark the drive to the Delicate Arch trailhead. A 6 AM start from Moab beat the worst heat of the day and some of the crowds. Delicate Arch Hike is one of the most popular hikes within Arches. It is an out-and-back hike with a spectacular pay-off hidden at the turnaround. Delicate Arch Trail is one of dozens of hikes in the park and one of hundreds of possibilities in the area.

The well-marked trailhead at Wolfe Ranch has a large parking lot, civilized restroom facilities, and plenty of informational signs. But proceed down the trail through a wash and up the slope, and civilization quickly fades away. The trail unfolds like a Martian landscape—red rock formations jut skyward, sculpted by eons of wind and water. A vast desert expanse stretches to the south of the route.

The trail climbs steadily to the base of a steep slickrock slope. The wear of foot traffic is faint on the hard, red rock but easy to follow. There is scarce shade along this trail, so sunscreen, a hat, and plenty of water are essential. Footgear with good traction is especially important on the sloping slickrock.

Cresting the slickrock, the route enters a series of up-and-down washes. Confidence markers are dotted through this part of the route to provide visual cues for staying on course. Occasionally, a giant boulder or outcropping offers a place to catch your breath out of the sun.

Emerging from this labyrinth, the route reaches what feels like a slickrock pass before ascending a ramp-like rock shelf with a steep drop on one side. This natural feature could be a feature in a skateboard park. After several hundred feet of climbing up this natural walkway, the route reaches another pass that affords the first view of Delicate Arch. The arch had been hidden between two ridgetops so far and is only seen on this hike when you reach it.

Delicate Arch is an impressive sight and an iconic symbol of Utah. The arch sits at the edge of a massive, sculpted bowl, which is an impressive feature in its own right. Framed by a vibrant blue sky, the massive arch is even more magnificent than in the many photos and license plate images you will see while traveling in Utah. The opening beneath the arch is 46 feet high and 32 feet wide. There are more than 2,000 arches in the National Park, and Delicate Arch is the largest freestanding one. Once called "Cowboy's Chaps," it was described as "delicate" in a 1934 article about the Arches National Monument Scientific Expedition, which described it as "the most delicately chiseled arch in the entire area." The name has stuck.

The descent back to the trailhead retraces your steps, except for a slight detour near the end to inspect a panel of petroglyphs and the remnants of Wolfe Ranch. Wolfe Ranch was a former cattle ranch where visitors can view a log cabin, dugout shed, and corral. Like the ascent, there was no wildlife save for the occasional lizard skittering across the trail or soaring bird. Enjoy the views from a different perspective on your way back.

TURN-BY-TURN DIRECTIONS

1. Park at the Wolfe Ranch/Delicate Arch Trail parking area. The trailhead is clearly marked.
2. Follow the trail .1 mile to the first junction with the petroglyph loop and stay right on the Delicate Arch Trail.
3. Travel another .1 mile to the conjunction with the petroglyph loop and stay right on the Delicate Arch Trail.
4. Travel another .6 miles to the base of the slickrock slope and proceed up the slope.
5. The trail continues at the top of the slick rock section and is occasionally marked with small posts to indicate the route.
6. Travel another 4 miles through a pass between ridges and a shelf leading up the mountainside to get the first look at the arch.
7. The descent to the base of Delicate Arch is a scramble across slickrock.
8. After enjoying the arch, retrace the route back to the start point, taking the petroglyph loop and checking out Wolfe Ranch near the parking area.

FIND THE TRAILHEAD

After entering Arches National Park, drive 11.7 miles north on the main road until you see the well-marked right-hand turn to Delicate Arch and Wolfe Ranch. Turn right on Delicate Arch Road and drive another 1.2 miles to the parking area on your left. Arches National Park may require an advance reservation for entry at peak times—check ahead on their website.

MOAB BREWERY

Moab Brewery dates back to 1998 when outdoor adventure tourism started booming here. While Moab may be best known as a mountain biking destination, recent data collection by a local tourism organization indicates that about 70% of visitors to the area hike, 40% play with off-road vehicles, and a mere 20% say they are bikers. Every one of these activities can work up a thirst—the Delicate Arch hike is no exception.

The brewery is on the main drag just south of the center. The aroma of a brew was a pleasant greeting before even entering. The interior celebrates Moab's place as a desert outdoor mecca. Kayak, mountain bike, and climber kitsch adorn nearly every available space.

The flagship Dead Horse Amber Ale is a roasty, traditional English mild ale that has been a constant through changing styles and trends over the years. It is part of a line-up that features a broad selection of styles from IPAs to Belgians to wheat beers to lagers. The "MOAB the Grand" imperial pilsener was of particular note as a high ABV beer (8%) retaining an excellent pilsener character. Moab Arnie is a refreshing cream ale take-off on the taste of an Arnold Palmer soft drink that is a collaborative brew with 2 Row Brewing in the Salt Lake area.

A distillery was added in 2017. Winter is the off-season for tourism, and 90% of the winter business comes from locals. In peak tourism season, that drops to 10–20%. Moab Brewery is heavily involved in area events, including rodeo, marathon, climbing, and other running events.

CONTACT INFORMATION

Arches National Park
PO Box 907
Moab, UT 84532
(435)-719-2299

BREWERY/RESTAURANT

Moab Brewery
686 S. Main St.
Moab, UT 84532
Distance from trailhead: 19 miles

WATCHMAN LOOKOUT

ZION BREWS AND CANYON VIEWS

STARTING POINT	OBJECTIVE
ZION CANYON BREWPUB	WATCHMAN LOOKOUT
BEER	HIKE TYPE
SPRINGDALE AMBER	MODERATE
FEES	SEASON
NATIONAL PARK ENTRY FEE	SPRING–FALL
MAP REFERENCE	DOG FRIENDLY
POSTED AT ZION NP VISITOR CENTER	NO
DURATION	LENGTH
2 HOURS	3.6 MILES
LOW POINT / HIGH POINT	ELEVATION GAIN
3,914 FEET / 4,420 FEET	650 FEET

ALCOHOL 4.0% CONTENT

RED ALE

AMBER-RED

HINT OF BREAD

TOASTED MALT WITH A FAINT FRUITINESS

BITTERNESS
IBU: 21

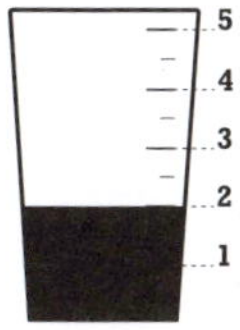

SWEETNESS

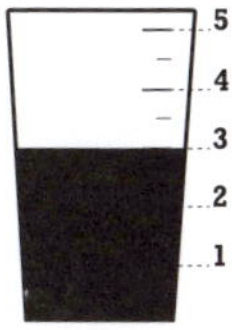

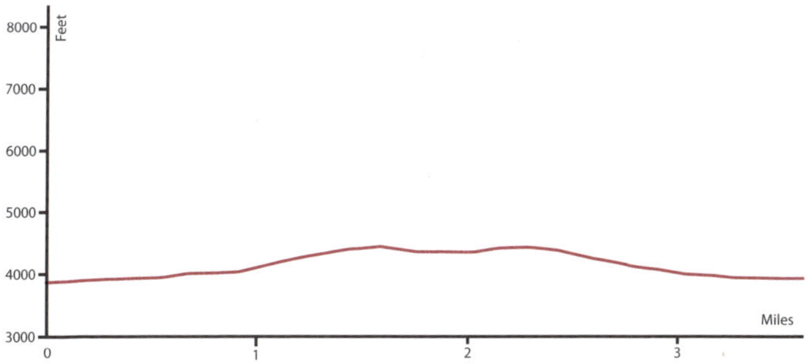

HIKE DESCRIPTION

After experiencing breathtaking panoramic views of Zion Canyon on the Watchman Trail, a moderately challenging hike, treat yourself to a well-deserved craft beer at the Zion Brew Pub, a local favorite celebrated for its handcrafted brews and inviting atmosphere.

The Watchman Lookout Trail near the south entrance of Zion National Park can be overlooked by the crowds who flock to more famous hikes further up the canyon. Making it part of a beer hike offers its advantages, though. For one, a hike that incorporates the trail can be started and ended at the Zion Brew Pub, home of Zion Brewing Company. I love beer hikes that I can start and end at the brewery instead of wasting time in the car. Second, the crowds are a problem at Zion, and a Watchman hike is downright lonely compared to many other places that give visitors a sense of Zion's grandeur.

Adjacent to the Zion Brew Pub in Springdale is a pedestrian bridge over the Virgin River and a pedestrian entry station into the National Park. It allows for a quick way into the park while others sit in a traffic jam at the vehicle entry. More than enough signs guide you to the Park Visitor Center, which is well worth a stop to learn about the flora, fauna, and history of Zion Canyon and to check out the map displays and tourist gear on sale. You'll also pass the shuttle bus station with long, snaking lines of people cooling their heels and waiting for a ride up the canyon.

The Watchman Lookout Trail follows the river across a grassy flat before beginning an ascent of a side canyon. Hardy shrubs and evergreen trees provide occasional shade along the way, and prickly pear cactus is common, as are wildflowers in season. The trail climbs the north wall before crossing a small stream and continuing a gentle climb on a bench on the south side. Eventually, the trail crests a ridge, the hike's highest point, and then drops to the Watchman Lookout.

While the trail doesn't lead to the summit of Watchman Peak, the views from the Lookout are breathtaking. Watchman Peak rises 2,200 feet to the south above the overlook. It is part of the same formation as Bridge Mountain to the north. The canyon stretches before you, a vast expanse of red rock sculpted by time. The Virgin River is a ribbon of silver, snaking through the canyon floor. There are views of Zion Canyon, the Watchman, Temples and Towers, lower Zion Canyon, and Springdale. To the west, the towering peaks of the Kolob Canyons remind you of the park's immense scale.

After soaking in the panoramic views, the overlook features a short loop trail that follows the edge of the Watchman bench, offering even more scenic views. Take your time to appreciate the diverse ecosystem surrounding you. The imposing bulk of Bridge Mountain stands tall to the north of the Watchman Spire. Once you complete the short loop, descend the trail taking the same reverse route, and return to the Zion Brew Pub.

TURN-BY-TURN DIRECTIONS

1. Facing the Zion Brew Pub entryway, go left about 200 feet between the buildings until you see a pedestrian bridge over the river. Proceed across the bridge.
2. At 0.1 miles, just across the river is a pedestrian entry station into Zion National Park. If it is attended, pay the fee or show your annual pass if you have one. Proceed through the station and follow the signage to the Park Visitor Center.
3. At 0.2 miles, proceed past the Visitor Center and the adjacent shuttle bus stop toward the river. Numerous signs point the way to Watchman Trail.
4. At 0.3 miles, follow the route across the road and along the river.
5. At 0.6 miles, cross a Park service road and follow the trail as it begins ascending a side canyon.
6. At 1.7 miles, crest a ridge and bear right onto a trail leading down to the Watchman Lookout point.
7. At 1.8 miles, from Watchman Point continue on the loop back to the intersection with the main trail.
8. At 2.1 miles, turn right onto the main trail and follow the same route you hiked up on back to the Zion Brew Pub.

FIND THE TRAILHEAD

From the Harrisburg Junction exit on I-15 (Exit 16), take Utah State Highway 9 East (UT-9E) 32.5 miles to Springdale. Turn right into the Zion Brew Pub parking lot just before the highway enters Zion National Park.

ZION BREWING COMPANY

I can't think of a brewery with a more stunning backdrop than Zion Brewing Company, with Watchman Peak soaring above. The brewery was founded in 2006 as the first craft brewer in southern Utah. One side of the brewpub is a restaurant, and the other is a taproom with a terrace along the river. The taproom has tavern fare for snacks and the restaurant offers burgers, sandwiches, salads, and comfort foodish dishes.

The nine faucets in the taproom pour a variety of brews with names like Springdale Amber, Kinesava Kolsch, Engel Landen Pilsener, Ascender Hefeweizen, Zion Pale Ale, Echo IPA, Burnt Mountain Brown, and Conviction Stout. The head brewer has been in place for more than a decade and has grown production to 1,500 bbl annually. Zion bottled earlier in

its history but now sells all draft beer from the brewpub and a satellite taproom in St. George. It's a busy place adjacent to the National Park. The terrace was a fine place for a refreshing beer at the end of the hike—brew with a view!

CONTACT INFORMATION

Zion National Park
1 Zion Park Blvd.
Springdale, UT 84767
+ 1 (435)-772-3256

BREWERY/RESTAURANT

Zion Brewery
95 Zion Park Blvd,
Springdale, UT 84767
Distance from trailhead: 0 miles

TURTLE WALL

RED ROCK CANYONS TO PARADISE RIM

STARTING POINT	OBJECTIVE
TURTLE WALL TRAILHEAD	PARADISE RIM
BEER	HIKE TYPE
MAS FUEGO RAUCHBIER	EASY
FEES	SEASON
$15 PER VEHICLE DAY USE FEE	YEAR-ROUND, ALTHOUGH HOT IN SUMMER
MAP REFERENCE	DOG FRIENDLY
POSTED AT THE TRAILHEAD	LEASHED
DURATION	LENGTH
2 HOURS	3.94 MILES
LOW POINT / HIGH POINT	ELEVATION GAIN
2,979 FEET / 3,309 FEET	463 FEET

ALCOHOL 5.0% CONTENT

RAUCHBIER

DARK BROWN

SMOKY NOSE

CLEAN, MALTY, SMOKY

BITTERNESS
IBU: 25

SWEETNESS

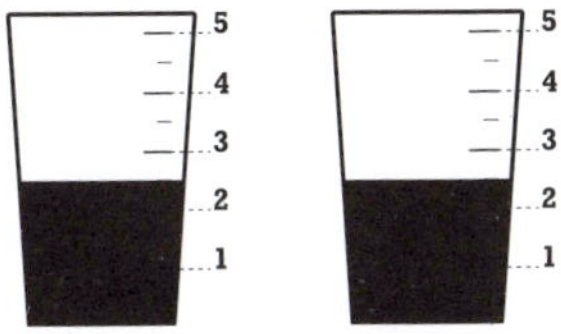

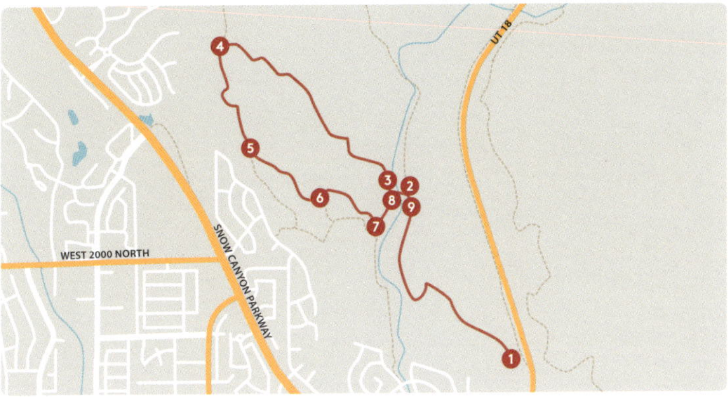

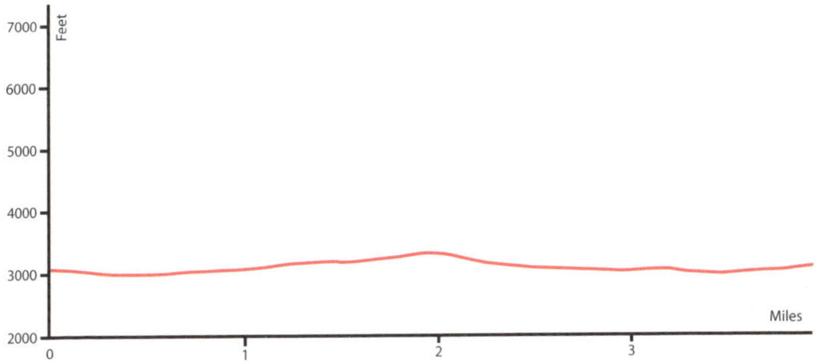

HIKE DESCRIPTION

Hike in red rock canyons with the tease of desert tortoise and lizard sightings, followed by a cold one (or two) at Silver Reef Brewing.

The Turtle Wall Loop Hike uses segments of the Chuckwalla, Turtle Wall, and Paradise Rim trails in Snow Canyon State Park near St. George, Utah. Starting at the Chuckwalla Trailhead, the terrain makes for easy hiking and stunning views of the surrounding desert. The route winds through a series of red rock canyons where, if you are there at the right time of year and you are lucky, you might catch glimpses of wildlife like desert tortoises and lizards.

The Snow Canyon State Park is a 7,400-acre scenic park, once a thriving prehistoric lake bed. Over millions of years, wind, water, and time sculpted the red sandstone cliffs and canyons of today. It is a place of majestic views where the subtle interplay of light, shadow, and color dances across the canyon walls. There are more than 38 miles of hiking trails, a three-mile paved walking/biking trail, and over 15 miles of equestrian trails in the park and adjacent preserve lands.

Evidence suggests human presence in the canyon as early as 10,000 years ago. Puebloan culture was present from about 250 to 1200 AD, and this was the land roamed by the Southern Paiute until the arrival of Mormon settlers in the mid-1800s. Some say the park's name is derived from the contrasting view of snow-capped peaks to the north encountered by early settlers. Others told me it is named for early Mormon settlers Lorenzo and Erastus Snow.

Starting on the Chuckwalla Trail, the initial segment takes you through a narrow canyon with heavy undergrowth in places. Emerging from the canyon, the route follows the Turtle Wall, a series of rounded sandstone formations resembling turtles' backs. Reaching Paradise Rim Trail there is a sweeping vista of the valley below. The loop back to to trailhead traverses an up-and-down desert landscape. Vegetation is thick in the ravines and includes desert plants like creosote bush, yucca, sage, scrub oak, and desert willow.

The desert tortoise lives in Snow Canyon State Park, but count yourself lucky if you spot any. We didn't, although we spoke with locals along the trail who told us that they had seen them many times. They are said to be more active in the early morning or late afternoon. The tortoise is adapted to the local environment and plays a crucial role in the ecosystem. Desert tortoises are said to grow to be between 8 and 15 inches long and weigh up to 15 pounds. It's important to note that they are a protected species, and their habitat is fragile. If you're lucky enough to spot one, please observe it from a distance and avoid disturbing it. Although I class this as an easy hike, don't take preparations lightly. Bring plenty of water for a hike in the desert. Sun protection is essential.

TURN-BY-TURN DIRECTIONS

1. From the trailhead kiosk, follow the Chuckwalla Trail.
2. At 0.8 miles, turn left at the junction onto Turtle Wall Trail.
3. At 0.9 miles, keep right on Turtle Wall Trail.
4. At 1.8 miles, turn left at the T junction with Paradise Rim Trail.
5. At 2.2 miles, bear left and continue on Paradise Rim Trail.
6. At 2.6 miles, bear left and continue on Paradise Rim Trail.
7. At 2.9 miles, turn left at the junction onto Halfway Wash Trail.
8. At 3.0 miles, turn right at the junction onto Turtle Wall Trail.
9. At 3.1 miles, turn right on Chuckwalla Trail to return to the trailhead.

FIND THE TRAILHEAD

From the St. George Blvd. (I-15 Business) exit on I-15, exit onto E St. George Blvd and travel 0.1 miles to N 1000 E (first cross street); turn right and travel 0.2 miles to E. Red Hills Parkway; turn left and travel 3.4 miles to Utah Highway 18 N; turn right and travel 0.4 miles to the left turn into the Chuckwalla Trailhead parking area.

SILVER REEF BREWING COMPANY

Silver Reef Brewing Company is located in an industrial area on the south side of town. It has an industrial-chic vibe that combines the taproom and brewhouse into one big, open warehouse space. There are plenty of seating options, both indoors and outdoors. It is relaxed and inviting, and the staff was friendly and helpful.

The brewery is named after the historic mining town of Silver Reef, which can be visited about fifteen miles to the northeast. It is now a ghost town. Silver Reef Brewing has an interesting backstory. It traces its history to Las Vegas, about 120 miles south in Nevada. The Ellis Island Brewery and Casino in Las Vegas back in the 90s was once said to be the largest brewpub in the Mountain West region (Arizona, Colorado, Idaho,

Montana, Nevada, New Mexico, Utah, and Wyoming). In 2018, more capacity was needed, and the Silver Reef Brewing Company was started by the casino's ownership in St. George. On-site brewing was suspended in Las Vegas in 2022, and since that time, the casino's beer has been supplied from the Silver Reef operation. The brewery is part of a family of brands including distilled spirits and a nearby winery operation.

Silver Reef Brewery offers a rotating selection of beers from a dozen taps with names like Agua del Diablo (Mexi-lager), Little Foot Amber Ale (American amber), Koval Pilsener (Czech-style), Cold Hearted Woman Love IPA (cold IPA), Mas Fuego Rauchbier (smoked lager), Black Hill Schwartzbier, and Guavaloo (fruited Berliner Weisse). I'm a sucker for a good Rauchbier when I have a chance, and I enjoyed a couple of other beers as well—a nice Hefeweizen and a Downwinder (West Coast IPA). Due to the peculiarities of Utah laws, I had to get the Downwinder in a can. By law, beers above 5% ABV can't be served on draft, so are only offered in cans. Silver Reef offers several styles of these "high-point" beers in cans ranging from 6.8 to 8% ABV. Everything I tried was solid beer.

LAND MANAGER

Snow Canyon State Park
1002 Snow Canyon Drive
Ivins, UT 84738
+ 1 (435)-628-2255

BREWERY/RESTAURANT

Silver Reef Brewing Company
4391 Enterprise Drive
St. George, UT 84790
Distance from trailhead: 10 miles

ARIZONA

SANDYS CANYON

THE ARIZONA TRAIL MEETS A BEAUTIFUL ARIZONA BEER

STARTING POINT	OBJECTIVE
CANYON VISTA TRAILHEAD	ARIZONA TRAIL
BEER	HIKE TYPE
TOWER STATION IPA	EASY
FEES	SEASON
NONE	SPRING-FALL
MAP REFERENCE	DOG FRIENDLY
POSTED AT TRAILHEAD	YES
DURATION	LENGTH
2.5 HOURS	6.25 MILES
LOW POINT / HIGH POINT	ELEVATION GAIN
6,618 FEET / 6,951 FEET	426 FEET

ALCOHOL 7.3% CONTENT

AMERICAN IPA

COPPER-ORANGE

PINEAPPLE-TANGERINE

SMOOTH, HOPPY, HINT OF FRUIT

BITTERNESS
IBU: 70

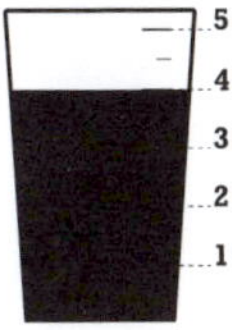

SWEETNESS

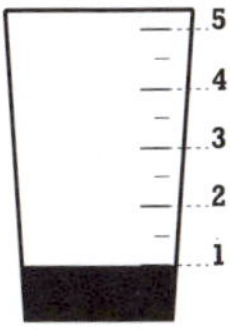

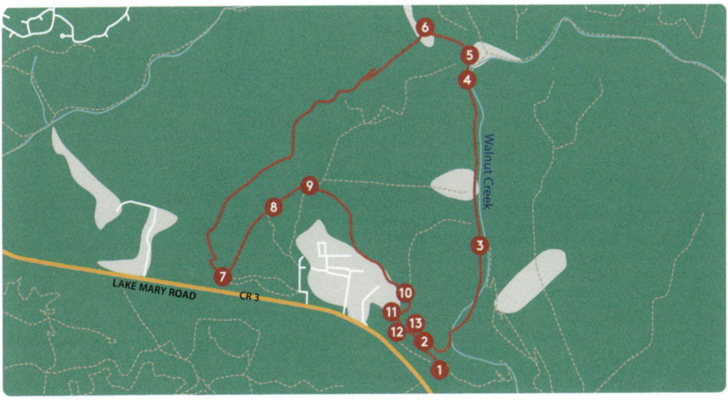

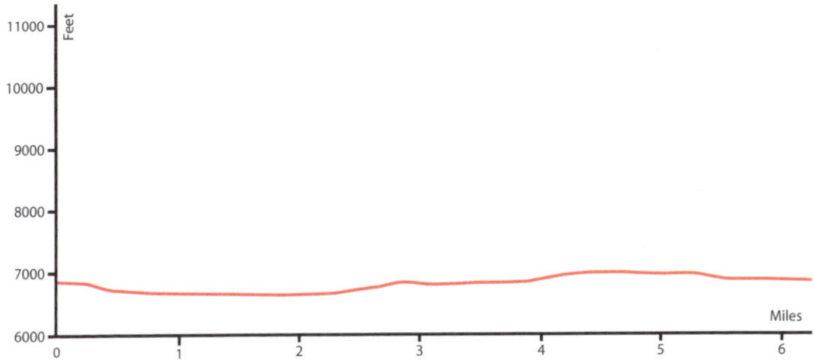

HIKE DESCRIPTION

This easy loop route takes hikers through varied terrain to Fisher Point—a unique 100-foot cliff over a cave—while traversing a section of the historic Arizona Trail.

The route begins at the Canyon Vista trailhead and quickly descends into Sandys Canyon, following a creek bed (dry when we visited) through a shaded forest. The trail intersects with the Arizona Trail (AZT) and continues up a pleasant valley called the Walnut Canyon Passage. Intermittent patches of forest offer shade as the route passes through several flat, grassy meadows.

At Fisher Point, the trail splits, with one way leading east into Walnut Canyon and Walnut Canyon National Monument, and the other continuing north toward Fay Canyon and eventually Flagstaff. Fisher Point features a striking 100-foot cliff rising from the valley floor. It's worth exploring the shallow cave below the cliff.

If you haven't heard of it, the Arizona Trail (AZT) is an 800-mile non-motorized trail from Utah to Mexico connecting Arizona's desert, mountain, canyon, and forest landscapes and passing through many communities. It was envisioned by a hiker named Dale Shewalter in the 1970s. He first walked the route in 1985 to demonstrate its feasibility. The idea stuck, and since the 1990s, the Arizona State Park system and the non-profit Arizona Trail Association have partnered in the stewardship of the trail. Some consider AZT one of the country's premier long-distance trail experiences. It was designated by Congress as a National Scenic Trail in 2009, one of 11 National Scenic Trails in the U.S.

Fay Canyon is a path less traveled, with a narrower trail in a narrower valley. Eventually, the trail climbs through dense forest and reaches a system of forest roads on a fairly flat mesa top. Some of the roads branch back to small housing neighborhoods near Lake Mary Road, while others dead end at the canyon rim. The suggested route passes through a pleasant forest and eventually loops back to the starting point.

There are plenty of possible route variations and more hiking opportunities throughout the area. The trail split at Fisher Point is, in fact, two variants of the AZT, one that leads through the city of Flagstaff and the other leading into Walnut Canyon, through the National Monument, before heading north and bypassing the city. Walnut Canyon National Monument preserves and presents a system of ancient cliff dwellings built centuries ago by people known as the Sinagua. There are numerous cliff dwellings carved into the sandstone walls. The AZT travels through the park and offers a unique opportunity to experience both ancient cliff dwellings and the broader natural beauty of the surrounding landscape.

TURN-BY-TURN DIRECTIONS

1. From the trailhead kiosk, follow the pathway to the Sandys Canyon trail.
2. At 0.2 miles, turn right at the trail junction and descend into the canyon (this is the point where the loop hike will return).
3. At 1.0 miles, bear left at the intersection with the Arizona Trail.
4. At 1.8 miles, bear left and stay on the Arizona Trail. The trail to the right is a shortcut to Walnut Canyon Trail.
5. At 2.0 miles, reach Fisher Point. Keep left on the Arizona Trail route heading toward Flagstaff.
6. At 2.3 miles, turn left onto the Fay Canyon Trail and proceed into Fay Canyon.
7. At 4.2 miles, emerge from Fay Canyon onto a dirt road cutting through the forest. Turn left onto an intersecting road leading onto the forested mesa.
8. At 4.7 miles, continue straight at an intersection with a forest road to the right.
9. At 4.9 miles, continue straight through a crossroad of trails. From this point, the route begins descending through the forest, skirting a neighborhood of homes.
10. At 5.7 miles, bear right at the intersection with a forest road.
11. At 5.8 miles, turn left at the T-intersection with a forest road.
12. After 100 yards, bear left on a forest pathway leaving the road.
13. At 6.0 miles, turn right at the trail intersection onto the spur to return to the trailhead.

FIND THE TRAILHEAD

From Flagstaff, travel south on Lake Mary Road (County Road CR3) for 5 miles and turn left at the sign for Canyon Vista–CR 9478Y onto a well-graded dirt road. Within 100 yards, turn right onto a well-graded dirt road leading to the Canyon Vista trailhead parking area.

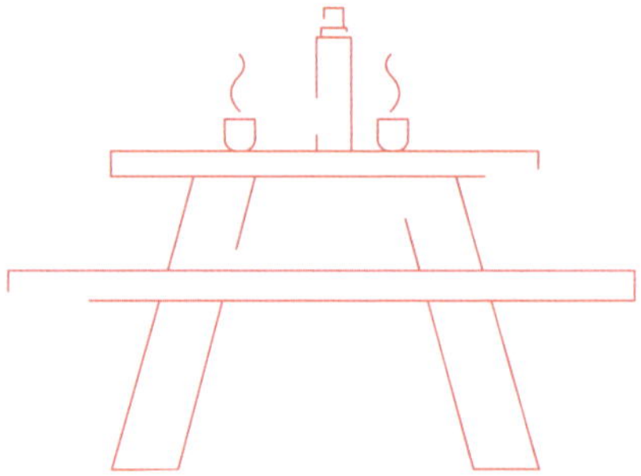

MOTHER ROAD BREWING COMPANY

The sun was setting over the San Francisco Peaks, casting a warm glow on the iconic Route 66 signs along the streets of Flagstaff, Arizona. Nestled in a pedestrian-friendly area between the old center of town and the campus of Northern Arizona University is the taproom of Mother Road Brewing Company. I ordered up a flagship Tower Station IPA. The names of other beers from the fourteen taps evoke Flagstaff's Route 66 heritage. Turbo Tower Mango Imperial IPA, Sunday Drive American Lager, Lost Highway Black IPA, Daily Driver Juicy IPA, and Limited Visibility (hazy IPA) are examples of other regular offerings. Several taps are dedicated to limited-release beers like a festbier, a couple of saisons, and an oatmeal stout.

The taproom was abuzz. Locals, student types, and tourists filled the rustic-industrial decor, sharing dinner, stories, laughter, and pints. Families, some with children, were sprinkled throughout the outdoor seating area. Mother Road prides itself on being a community-minded place. The menu is limited but interesting. I went for the black bean bowl. The brewery had been co-located with the taproom the last time I was here, but since has expanded to a larger nearby location. Mother Road beers are now available in bars, restaurants, and liquor stores throughout Arizona.

As we savored our beers, we couldn't help but feel a connection to the spirit of the Mother Road, the iconic Route 66 that runs through the heart of Flagstaff. Just as the highway once brought travelers from all walks of life together, Mother Road Brewing Company was doing the same, fostering a sense of community and shared experience over a love of craft beer.

Mother Road Brewing Company drew inspiration for its name from Flagstaff's location along the historic Route 66, nicknamed the Mother Road in John Steinbeck's 1939 novel *The Grapes of Wrath*. Parts of the original Route 66 alignment still exist in Flagstaff, and the city has worked to preserve its Route 66 legacy. "Flag" as it is called, was one of several oases along the Mother Road providing fuel, places to stop over, and repair shops for travelers making the cross-country journey.

Craft beer has been a thing in "Flag" since the 1990s, and there are several other local breweries close by, including Flagstaff Brewing Company, Beaver Street Brewery, Lumberyard Brewing Co., Wanderlust Brewing Co., Historic Brewing Company, Grand Canyon Brewing Co., and Dark Sky Brewing. Mother Road Brewing Company came on the scene in 2011 and has grown to its current 27,000 bbl capacity. A "Flagstaff Brewery Trail" encourages visitors to visit and explore them all.

CONTACT INFORMATION

Coconino National Forest
1824 S. Thompson St.
Flagstaff, AZ 86001
+ 1 (928) 527-3600

BREWERY/RESTAURANT

Mother Road Brewing Company
7 South Mikes Pike
Flagstaff, Arizona 86001
Distance from trailhead: 8 miles

THUNDER MOUNTAIN

RED ROCKS AND AMBER BEER IN THE VORTEX

STARTING POINT	OBJECTIVE
THUNDER MOUNTAIN TRAILHEAD	THUNDER MOUNTAIN
BEER	HIKE TYPE
RED ROCK AMBER LAGER	MODERATE
FEES	SEASON
NONE	LATE SUMMER THROUGH SPRING
MAP REFERENCE	DOG FRIENDLY
POSTED AT TRAILHEAD	YES, LEASH REQUIRED
DURATION	LENGTH
2.5 HOURS	4.25 MILES
LOW POINT / HIGH POINT	ELEVATION GAIN
4,522 FEET / 4,877 FEET	594 FEET

ALCOHOL
6.0%
CONTENT

AMBER LAGER

AMBER

CLEAN,
SLIGHT MALT NOSE

LIGHT, MALTY, WITH JUST
A TOUCH OF HOPPINESS

BITTERNESS
IBU: 20

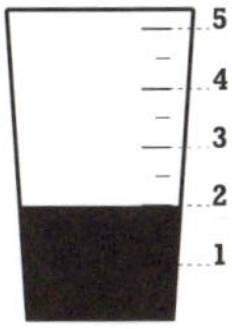

SWEETNESS

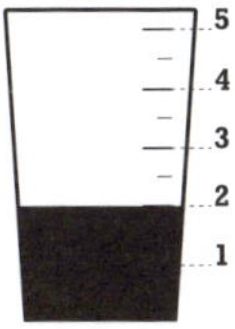

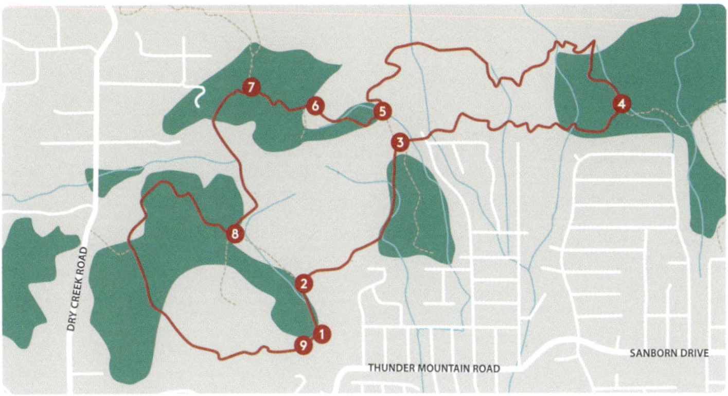

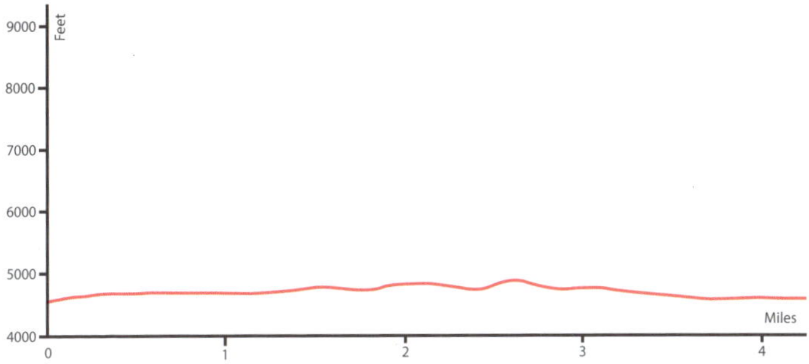

HIKE DESCRIPTION

A stunning hike in the red rocks and a refreshing beer at Sedona Beer Company take center stage on a visit to the famous desert town.

Sedona attracts plenty of attention for its luxury resorts in the midst of a striking red rock landscape, together with a New Age reputation as a swirling center of positive energy with meditative and self-exploratory properties—vortices. If you ask me, scenic hiking paired with good beer is enough reason to pay a visit.

The Coconino National Forest surrounds the town of Sedona in the northern Verde Valley region of Arizona. A thick layer of red-to-orange sandstone called the Schnebly Hill Formation is a distinctive and colorful natural feature throughout the area. A thousand years ago, Native American hunter-gatherers, now called the Sinagua, inhabited the area. A handful of homesteaders put down roots in the 1870s, starting a fruit farming and ranching era. Sedona was named after Sedona Schnebly, wife of one of the homesteaders and the first postmaster. In the 1950s tourism development got underway to evolve into the tourism and getaway destination of today. Now Sedona attracts more than 3 million visitors annually.

The Thunder Mountain Loop hike uses trails that wind around and beneath prominent features called Little Sugarloaf, Chimney Rock, and Capitol Butte (a.k.a. Thunder Mountain). The 4.25-mile loop hike starts at an elevation of 4,523 feet (1,378 m) and provides inspiring vistas, varied terrain, and great photography opportunities. Throughout the hike, you're immersed in the beauty of Sedona's red rock formations. Short but steep climbs from the route lead to the upper base of Chimney Rock and the summit of Little Sugarloaf, offering even more panoramic views of Sedona's surrounding landscape. Part of the route crosses into the Secret Mountain Wilderness Area, which covers approximately 47,194 acres (191 square kilometers).

More than 400 miles of recreational trails provide many opportunities for hikers, mountain bikers, and equestrians. The Sedona Red Rock Trail Fund is a prominent volunteer organization that partners with the Forest Service to maintain the trail system. An interesting innovation you'll see at Sedona Beer Company after the hike is an "off-the-trail trailhead" with great information about local hiking options.

Sedona can be damn hot, especially during the summer months. While you can hike in Sedona year-round, it's important to tune in to weather conditions before the hike. The best time of year for hiking here is during the spring (March–May) and fall (September–November) seasons. Early morning or late afternoon hikes can help beat the heat. Carry plenty of water.

TURN-BY-TURN DIRECTIONS

1. From the trailhead kiosk, follow the dirt, single-track Thunder Mountain Trail to the right.
2. At 0.1 miles, bear right on Thunder Mountain Trail at the junction with Lower Chimney Rock Loop Trail.
3. At 0.6 miles, bear right toward the Andante Trailhead and continue on the Andante Trail.
4. At 1.3 miles, bear left on the Andante Trail at the junction with the Teacup Trail.
5. At 2.4 miles, bear right and ascend Chimney Rock Pass Trail at the junction with Thunder Mountain Trail.
6. At 2.6 miles, catch the view at Chimney Rock Pass before continuing on the trail.
7. At 2.8 miles, bear left on Chimney Pass Trail at the junction with the Summit Route Trail.
8. At 3.2 miles, bear right on Lower Chimney Rock Loop Trail at the intersection with the Andante West Trail to Little Sugarloaf Summit.
9. At 4.2 miles, return to the Thunder Mountain Trailhead kiosk.

FIND THE TRAILHEAD

From Sedona Beer Company Basecamp, head northwest on Dry Creek Road 0.4 miles. Turn right onto Thunder Mountain Road and travel 0.6 miles to the entry to Thunder Mountain Trailhead on the left.

SEDONA BEER COMPANY

Sedona Beer Company is a locally owned craft brewery with brewing operations at its Basecamp location as well as a taproom and pub in the center of the town (called "uptown" locally). The business was started in 2018 and added the Basecamp location in 2024. The Basecamp is a modern, relaxed space with a big outdoor patio. A small variety of pub food is prepared and served out of a trailer on the patio.

A variety of beers flow from the sixteen taps, including a few guest taps. The styles and names are eclectic—Sedona Sunrise (light lager), Hat-erade (fruited sour), Beach Please! (dank IPA), Unsupervised Children (hazy IPA), Where's the Vortex (hazy DIPA), Monsoon Nights (choco-late porter), Sinagua Serendipity (9.5% imperial brown ale), and a fine Oktoberfest were some of the offerings. The taps rotate frequently and seasonally.

Sedona Beer exhibits a strong commitment to sustainability and community engagement. All of their beers are made with local malted barley from Sinagua Malt, an interesting public benefit enterprise dedicated to water conservation in the Verde Valley. Sinagua Malt works with farmers in the Verde Valley to grow barley that requires less water than their traditional crops. The result is savings of millions of gallons of Verde River water and great-tasting, unique beers.

Kali Gajewski, a lifelong local with a social work background, founded Sedona Beer with her husband, the brewer. Kali told me that Sedona Beer partners with the Red Rock Trail Fund and regularly hosts events and fundraisers to support local causes. They are all about sustainability and providing a welcoming space for both locals and visitors.

CONTACT INFORMATION

Coconino National Forest
8375 State Route 179
Sedona, AZ 86351
+ 1 (928) 203-2900

BREWERY/RESTAURANT

Sedona Beer Company Basecamp
70 Dry Creek Road
Sedona, AZ 86336
Distance from trailhead: 1.2 miles

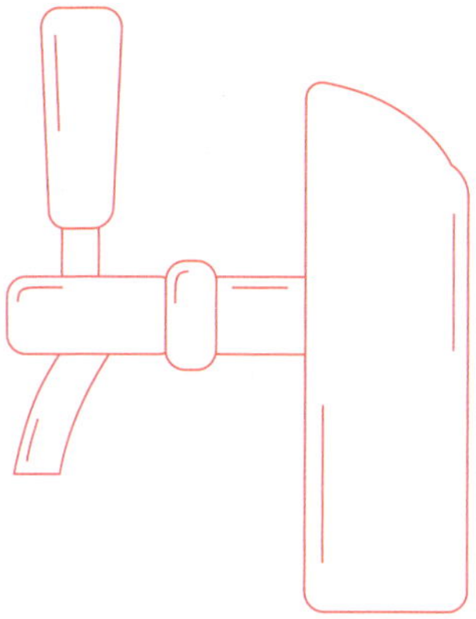

WOODLAND LAKE

FROM TOWERING PINES TO A MOUNTAIN LAKE

STARTING POINT	OBJECTIVE
BIG SPRINGS TRAILHEAD	**WOODLAND LAKE**
BEER	HIKE TYPE
BLONDE	**EASY**
FEES	SEASON
NONE	**SPRING TO FALL**
MAP REFERENCE	DOG FRIENDLY
POSTED AT TRAILHEAD	**YES**
DURATION	LENGTH
2 HOURS	**5 MILES**
LOW POINT / HIGH POINT	ELEVATION GAIN
6,722 FEET / 6,909 FEET	**248 FEET (75 M)**

ALCOHOL 7.3% CONTENT

BELGIAN-STYLE BLOND ALE

GOLDEN

MAIL WITH HINTS OF FRUIT AND SPICINESS

CLEAN, CRISP, BALANCED

BITTERNESS
IBU: 31

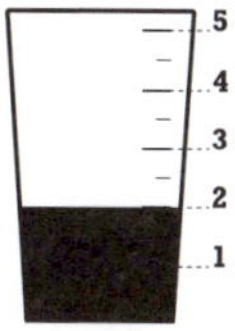

SWEETNESS

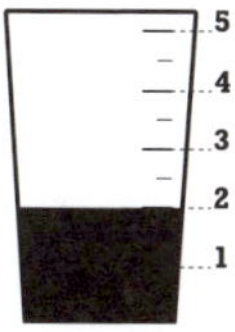

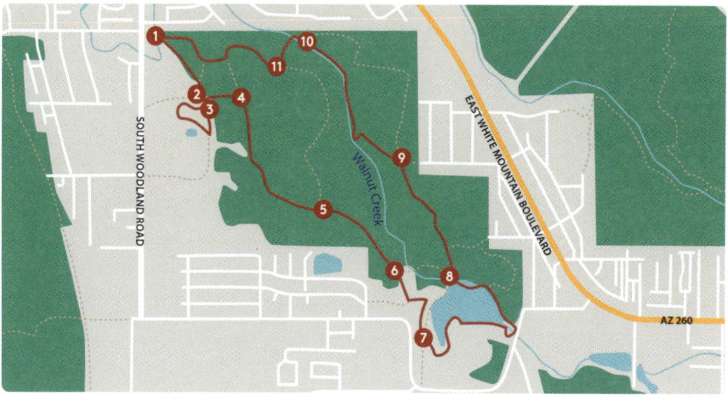

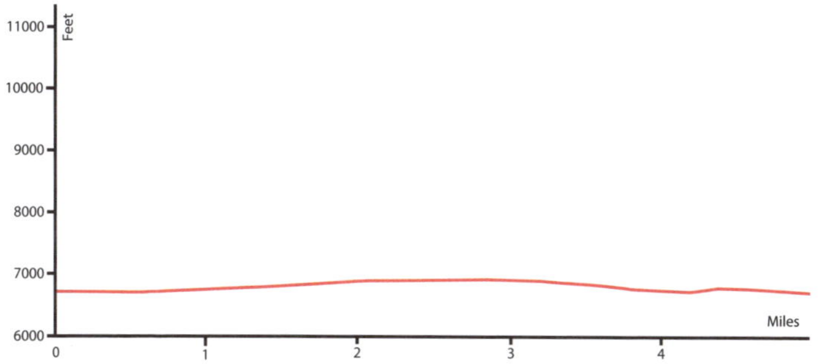

HIKE DESCRIPTION

"Small Town, Big Beers" is the perfect motto for a day in Pinetop: after wandering below towering pines to a mountain lake, head for high-ABV Belgian-inspired craft brews near the finish.

This is an easy five-mile route through a section of Apache-Sitgreaves National Forest that is embedded within the small community of Pinetop. Several trails lace through the area, offering multiple options for longer (or shorter) loops. Several trailheads are potential starting points around the periphery.

Our hike starts at Big Springs Trailhead, a well-marked parking area away from the Pinetop commercial strip. Maps and trailhead signs indicate that this is the Big Springs Environmental Study Area, a collaborative project involving the local community, school system, Arizona Game and Fish Department, and the Forest Service. Adjacent to the trailhead is a large wetland area with ponds and wetland habitat.

A small loop on a trail identified as Bog Springs Trail passes through the wetland before meeting the Hitching Post Trail over to Woodland Lake. A developed, paved trail segment circles the lake before intersecting with the Turkey Track Trail. A side trail following Walnut Creek eventually connects to the Hitching Post Trail and then returns to the trailhead.

The gentle trail passes along a creek and through wetlands, forests, and meadows on its way to a mountain lake. Woodland Lake is a small lake (18 acres) where people fish, kayak, and boat (non-motorized).The trails, mostly natural-surfaced single-track, are well-maintained and marked. The wildlife we encountered was mostly waterfowl, although there are plenty of other kinds of wildlife and birdlife in the area. Keep an eye out for deer, elk, and various bird species. Abundant wildflowers adorn the path. If you're lucky enough to time your visit in the fall, you're in for a show with all the foliage.

Pinetop is situated in the White Mountains, a range that straddles the Arizona-New Mexico border. Situated at 6,805 ft (2,074 m) elevation, it has long been a vacation refuge for Arizona desert dwellers seeking reprieve from the heat—and the promise of a local ski area. The small community of about five thousand people is a great place to set out for outdoor activities, including hiking, mountain biking, fishing, and skiing. The White Mountain Trail System (WMTS) offers hundreds of miles of trails in the vicinity. TRACKS, a volunteer trails organization, works to develop, maintain, and promote these trails.

TURN-BY-TURN DIRECTIONS

1. From the trailhead kiosk, cross the footbridge, then turn right along the rocky path.
2. At 0.4 miles, bear right to take a small loop detour in the wetland area.
3. At 0.8 miles, complete the loop and turn right on the connector trail to the Hitching Post Trail.
4. At 1.0 miles, turn right on the Hitching Post Trail.
5. At 1.5 miles, bear right and continue on the Hitching Post Trail
6. At 1.9 miles at the intersection with Meadowview Trail, bear right and continue on the Hitching Post Trail.
7. At 2.3 miles, reach the junction with the Woodland Lake Trail; bear right to traverse the lake counterclockwise.
8. At 3.1 miles, turn right and follow the Turkey Track Trail.
9. At 3.5 miles, turn left and follow the Walnut Creek Trail.
10. At 4.2 miles, bear left on a connector trail back to the Hitching Post Trail.
11. At 4.6 miles, turn right on the Hitching Post Trail and follow it back to the trailhead.

FIND THE TRAILHEAD

From Pinetop Brewing Company in the center of the Pinetop commercial strip, turn left (north) onto Arizona Highway 260 (W. White Mountain Blvd) for 1.0 mile. Turn left onto Woodland Road and travel 0.6 miles. Turn left into the Big Springs Trailhead parking area.

PINETOP BREWING COMPANY

Pinetop Brewing Company is a small brewery that got its start as part of a local BBQ restaurant but has since expanded into its own modern brewery and taproom space on the main drag. Belgian-style beers dominated the tap list of eight of their beers, though they also have a number of guest taps featuring regional and national beers. In addition to the flagship Blonde, they were pouring a Saison, a Dubbel, a Trippel, an Amber, Grand Cru (dark amber), and Abbot (Belgian quad). Every one of these are strong beers ranging from 6.8 to 8.5% ABV. Their tagline, "Small Town, Big Beers," fits.

Pinetop Brewing Company has a generally rustic ambiance set among some big pines. A small outdoor seating area is jammed together with a tight parking lot out front. The food menu is eclectic. The brewhouse is a 10bbl (310-gallon) steam-fired brewing system. They pride themselves on using traditional European brewing techniques, such as step-mashing and the use of Belgian "candi" sugar—an unrefined beet-derived brewing sugar. All of the beers appear to be served in stemmed goblet glassware.

Another interesting local beer venue is Munich Haus Grill-n-Beergarden, just down the street. This is not a brewery but a place with multiple German beers available to match the German-inspired menu.

LAND MANAGER

Apache-Sitgreaves National Forest
2022 W White Mountain Blvd.
Lakeside, AZ 85929
+1 (928) 368-2100

BREWERY/RESTAURANT

Pinetop Brewing Company
159 W White Mountain Blvd,
Lakeside, AZ 85929
Distance from trailhead: 2 miles

FAT MAN PASS

WILDERNESS HIKING, WILDERNESS BEER

STARTING POINT	OBJECTIVE
PIMA CANYON TRAILHEAD	FAT MAN PASS /HIDDEN VALLEY
BEER	HIKE TYPE
DON'T F#%K IT UP BLONDE ALE	MODERATE
FEES	SEASON
NONE	SEPTEMBER–MAY
MAP REFERENCE	DOG FRIENDLY
POSTED AT TRAILHEAD; USGS 805654	YES, LEASHED
DURATION	LENGTH
3 HOURS	6 MILES
LOW POINT / HIGH POINT	ELEVATION GAIN
1,392 FEET / 2,222 FEET	1,161 FEET

ALCOHOL 5.5% CONTENT

BLONDE ALE

GOLDEN

LIGHT, MALTY

CLEAN, DRY,
HINT OF HONEY

BITTERNESS
IBU: 15

SWEETNESS

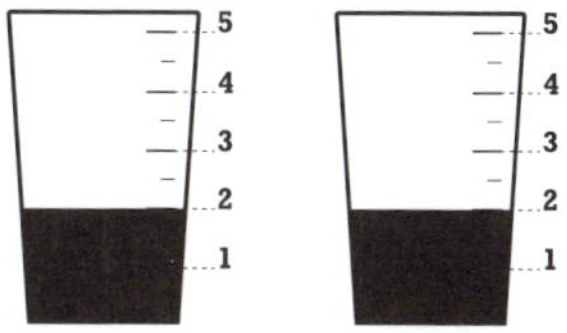

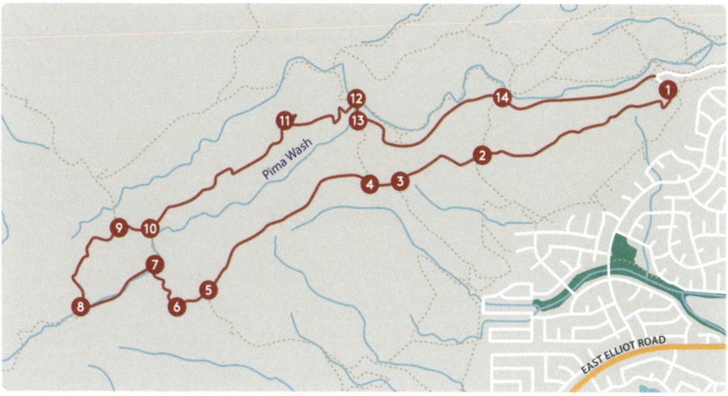

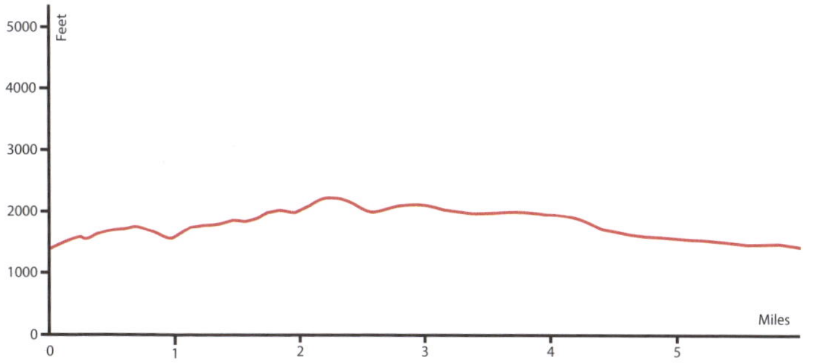

HIKE DESCRIPTION

Can you fit through Fat Man Pass?

Phoenix is a huge urban area in a basin with mountains rising on all sides. South Mountain Park is one of the largest city parks in the country, including three mountain ranges and covering more than twenty-five square miles. There are several access points, but we chose the Pima Canyon Trailhead, being the closest to our after-hike beer. These are rocky mountains with rough terrain and classic Sonoran Desert vegetation. There are saguaro, cholla, barrel, and other cactus species, palo verde and mesquite trees, and wand-like ocotillo, although the stress of the urban area on the plant life is obvious. The park has a network of more than 100 miles of trails for hikers, mountain bikers, and horseback riders to share.

Our loop hike to Fat Man Pass starts on the Marcos de Niza trail, transitions to a trail known as Midlife Crisis, reaches the pass through Hidden Valley, and then loops back on National Trail, a designated National Recreation Trail. The ascent on Marcos de Niza and Midlife Crisis climbs a rocky ridge with false summit after false summit. It was a relief to turn onto the descent into Hidden Valley, a long rift between two mountain ridges. A bit of bouldery scrambling takes you to the wash at the bottom. A short walk up the ravine leads to Fat Man Pass, a narrow slot between tumbled boulders that is a tight squeeze for a somewhat portly guy like me.

The descent is interesting as well. A unique feature is a long, natural tunnel leading out of Hidden Valley. National Trail descends another ridge closer to the city and provides dramatic skyline and distant mountain views for most of the way down. Piestewa Peak, Camelback Mountain, and Four Peaks (the highest mountains in the area) are the most prominent. The trails are generally well-marked, but junctions can be confusing, so pay close attention to the signs.

Throughout your hike, you will experience the park's diverse wildlife. You might see coyotes, quail, chipmunks, and hummingbirds. Bees are also common, often nesting in the canyons, and rattlesnakes, scorpions, tarantulas, and Gila monsters are also present, so it is essential to be aware of your surroundings. The terrain is rocky with varying difficulty, including some steep inclines and declines. The hike can be hot, even when temperatures are moderate.

When hiking in the Sonoran Desert, keep in mind that it's important to bring plenty of water. Temperatures can be very high, especially during the summer, and it's best to avoid hiking during the hottest part of the day. It is also important to stay on designated trails to avoid damaging the fragile desert environment. Trail traffic was light during our visit. We encountered mostly hikers, but there were a few mountain bikers and a couple of horses on National Trail. It is an urban area, though, so don't be surprised to be sharing the trail.

There are plenty of other hiking options in the Phoenix area, including ascents of Camelback Mountain, Piestewa Peak (formerly called Squaw Peak), Four Peaks Wilderness Area, the White Tank Mountains, Sierra Estrella Mountains, and the Superstition Mountains and Wilderness Area.

TURN-BY-TURN DIRECTIONS

1. Locate the Marcos de Niza trailhead on the south edge of the parking lot; follow the trail up the hill into the park.
2. At 0.9 miles, continue straight at the junction with Beverly Canyon Trail.
3. At 1.3 miles, continue straight at the junction with Chihuahua Ridge Trail.
4. At 1.4 miles, continue straight on the Midlife Crisis Trail at the junction with an unnamed trail to the right.
5. At 2.2 miles, continue straight on the Midlife Crisis Trail at the junction with Young Man Trail to the left.
6. At 2.3 miles, turn right onto Hidden Valley Trail and descend into the wash.
7. At 2.5 miles, you reach the bottom of the wash. Turn left and proceed up the wash.
8. At 2.9 miles, you reach Fat Man Pass. Squeeze through (or scramble around) and turn right onto National Trail.
9. A 3.3 miles, continue straight to stay on National Trail at the junction with Mormon Trail.
10. At 3.5 miles, continue straight to stay on National Trail at the junction with Hidden Valley Trail. A short side trip on Hidden Valley Trail leads to the natural tunnel.
11. At 4.2 miles, begin a steep descent to a switchback.
12. At 4.6 miles, turn sharply at the right to stay on National Trail at the junction with Pima Wash Trail.
13. At 4.7 miles, bear left on National Trail at the old stone house ruin.
14. At 5.3 miles, continue straight at the junction with Beverly Canyon Trail to return to the parking area.

FIND THE TRAILHEAD

From the Baseline Road exit on I-10, travel west on Baseline Road 1,110 feet to Arizona Grand Parkway. Turn left on Arizona Grand Parkway and travel 600 feet to a traffic circle. Take the first exit onto Pointe Parkway W and travel 0.4 miles to another traffic circle. Take the 2nd exit onto South Pointe Parkway E and continue 0.6 miles to East Guadalupe Road. Travel 1,100 feet to South 48th Street and turn right. After 250 feet, turn left onto East Pima Canyon Road, which ends after 650 feet in the Pima Canyon Trailhead parking area.

ARIZONA WILDERNESS BREWING COMPANY

A visit to Arizona Wilderness Brewing Company in Gilbert promises more than just some great-tasting beers and food. You are at a place that is deeply invested in sustainability, and whose owners are deeply committed to the Arizona Wilderness experience. From the outside, the brewery looks like just another restaurant on a suburban street (Gilbert is a town that the Phoenix urban area has overtaken). The inside is colorful and relaxed, with a friendly neighborhood feel supplemented by shady outdoor spaces.

Co-founder Jon Buford's passion for the Arizona wilderness is evident in the restaurant and tap room. The shape of the logo evokes signage used in wilderness areas throughout the country. Wilderness maps and photographs are on display throughout. A big bulletin board is provided as a place for patrons to post photos of their wilderness experiences. Jon told me that there are 90 designated wilderness areas in Arizona and that he has visited every one of them. He is an accomplished outdoors photographer, and soon after my visit he will have a book of his Arizona wilderness photography published by *Arizona Highways* magazine. The vibe I got from Jon was an interesting combination of laid-backness and intensity.

Inspired after a backpacking trip in Arizona's Chiricahua Wilderness, Jon and his partner Patrick founded the brewery in 2013 with the idea of infusing the essence of Arizona Wilderness into their brand. Connecting with the community was another part of the vision, and initial financing came from a successful Kickstarter campaign. Notoriety came quickly as Arizona Wilderness was named as the "Best New Brewery in the World" by RateBeer.com soon after opening. Another key part of the vision is to be a "cause-based business" that seeks out high-quality local ingredients and employs sustainable practices throughout the enterprise.

This goes far beyond mere lip service. Jon told me that the restaurant showcases local agriculture and farmers sourcing local meats, produce, and other ingredients from more than forty Arizona farms and producers. About 50% of what they buy is locally sourced. Menu descriptions highlight the sources and tell their stories. Food waste is composted through a local program that then provides produce back to the restaurant, creating a circular supply chain. Their zero-waste approach incorporates composting and recycling with no single-use plastics. I chose the "After Hike Burger," which featured Arizona grass-fed beef, pork belly brisket, and avocado on a locally baked bun. The menu features appetizers, burgers, sandwiches, salads, and tacos. Jon told me that their loyal customers are as likely to come for the food as the beer.

The brewery uses Arizona-grown-and-made malts from Sinagua Malts in nearly all of the beers they make. Sinagua is an interesting initiative that has diverted Arizona farmers from growing water-thirsty crops like corn and alfalfa to drought-resistant grains that make great beers. A lot of water is being saved. Arizona Wilderness is Sinagua Malt's largest customer. Other local ingredients that have found their way into the beer are things like mesquite pods and spruce tips foraged from the Arizona wilderness, and local honey, strawberries, and catnip. Jon told me that they have brewed dozens of beers that have used foraged ingredients. Ninety percent of their brewing ingredients are sourced in Arizona.

Arizona Wilderness was the first brewery to use Sonoran white wheat, a grain grown in the desert of the Southwest, and they use it in all of their witbiers and saisons. I tried out a tasty lager made with Kernza, a drought-tolerant perennial grain that is great for soil conservation and carbon sequestration. Arizona Wilderness even specifies recycled materials (recycled water bottle content) for their T-shirts and uses soy ink for their can printing, making the cans 100% recyclable. Who would've thunk it?

The Arizona Wilderness range includes their flagship Don't F#%k It Up (a blonde ale), Cactus Juice (fruited sour), Refuge IPA, and La Ciudad (hazy IPA). Don't F#%k It Up is a bow to a big rule for beer hikers and others out on the trail – Leave No Trace. Seasonal offerings carry names like AZ Dreamsicle (imperial IPA), American Presidential (imperial stout), July 11th (IPA), and Pecan Pie Brown Ale. Funky stuff includes Camp Coolship (lambic-inspired beer brewed using their portable coolship), Sonoran Prince (peach sour), and Terroir Project (barrel-aged sour).

Arizona Wilderness has two other locations, a large European-style beer garden with a bar in downtown Phoenix, and Woodnotes Cellar, a cozy spot near the Gilbert brewery that focuses on spontaneous fermented and barrel-aged beers. The Phoenix area has plenty of breweries scattered around the metro area to support all of your beer hiking needs. I counted more than 50 before I gave up.

CONTACT INFORMATION

Phoenix Parks and Recreation Department
200 W. Washington Street
Phoenix, AZ 85003
+ 1 (602) 262-7393

BREWERY/RESTAURANT

Arizona Wilderness Brewing Company
721 N Arizona Ave
Gilbert, AZ 85233
Distance from trailhead: 9 miles

BREN MOUNTAIN

TUCSON MOUNTAINS CHAOS AND DRAGOON BREWERY

STARTING POINT	OBJECTIVE
GATES PASS SCENIC VIEWPOINT	BREN MOUNTAIN
BEER	HIKE TYPE
FALL FOR YOU (BLACK IPA)	MODERATE
FEES	SEASON
NONE	SEPTEMBER–MAY
MAP REFERENCE	DOG FRIENDLY
POSTED AT TRAILHEAD; USGS 738142	NO
DURATION	LENGTH
2.5 HOURS	3.8 MILES
LOW POINT / HIGH POINT	ELEVATION GAIN
2,858 FEET / 3,356 FEET	863 FEET

ALCOHOL 6.0% CONTENT

BLACK IPA

BLACK

HOPPY WITH PINEY TRACE

ROASTY, HOPPY

BITTERNESS
IBU: 35

SWEETNESS

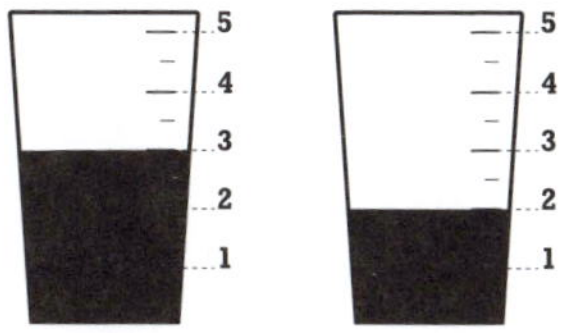

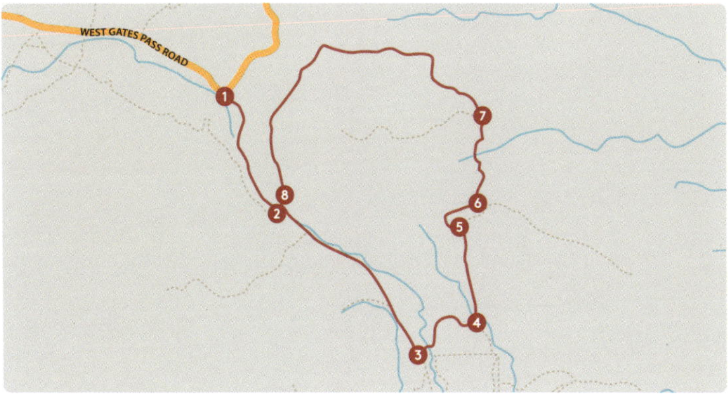

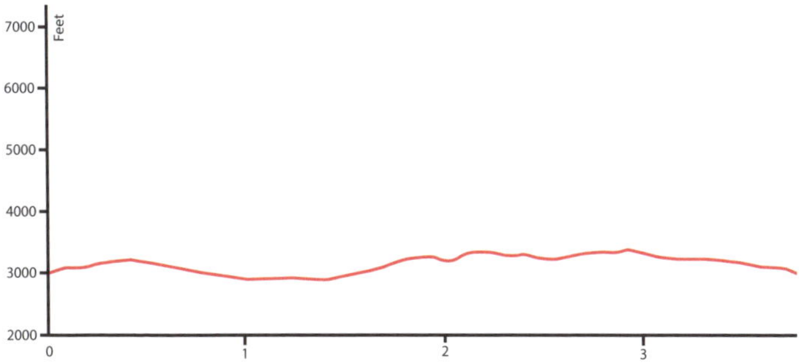

HIKE DESCRIPTION

Challenging terrain, breathtaking views, and jumping cholla!

The Bren Mountain Loop Around hike in Tucson Mountain Park is an immersion into Sonoran Desert scenery, challenging terrain, and what some geologists call the "Tucson Mountain Chaos," a jumble of different rock types including limestone, volcanic tuff, rhyolite, granite, and schist. This is rugged landscape compared to more well-traveled trails in nearby areas. Bren Mountain, sometimes called "Brens Better," is well known to Arizona peak baggers who scramble to the top on a rough spur trail from the backside of the loop.

The trailhead is at a scenic viewpoint and parking area just below Gates Pass. Tucson Mountain Park is a preserve encompassing a diverse landscape and several hiking trails, some also appropriate for mountain bikes and horses. Dogs are not permitted on most of the trails. The park's vegetation is typical of the Sonoran Desert, with various types of cacti, including saguaro, cholla, and barrel cactus, as well as palo verde trees. The park is also home to local wildlife, like bighorn sheep and lizards. Just to the north is a large unit of Saguaro National Monument, which also offers rugged hiking options.

The hike begins on the David Yetman Trail, a rocky single track that runs through a pass between Golden Gate Mountain and Bren Mountain. Soon after the pass, the loop route splits off onto an unnamed, less traced pathway. There is some up and down through a series of arroyos cutting down from the peak before ascending a steep slope to the summit ridge. There are more ups and downs as you loop around the peak, and you can catch some great views of the surrounding mountain systems, including the Tucsons, Rincons, Santa Catalinas, Santa Ritas, and Tortolitas.

The desert climate is hot and dry, particularly during the summer, making it essential to carry plenty of water and take precautions against heat exposure. Summer hikers need to be aware of the monsoon season, with its potential for storms and flash floods. The abundant, towering saguaros along the way present little hazard, but watch out for those jumping cholla. They don't actually jump, but their spines detach easily and latch onto whatever gets too close, giving the impression of jumping. This is one of nature's mechanisms to support spreading and reproduction.

There are loads of hiking options in the Tucson area, offering a variety of hiking experiences, from easy strolls to challenging climbs. Another popular area is Sabino Canyon in the Santa Catalinas The canyon features soaring rock walls, sycamores and cottonwoods, cascading waterfalls, and water that flows year-round. Mount Lemmon, the highest part of the Santa Catalina range, offers riparian trails in a subalpine forest, making it a great area to beat the heat. Saguaro National Park not only features huge stands of massive saguaros but also features hikes past abandoned mines and through flats that display abundant wildflowers following rains. This area has a rich history of human habitation, with evidence of Hohokam Indian presence. The area was also part of the Old West, and the nearby Old Tucson movie studio is a reminder of this era.

TURN-BY-TURN DIRECTIONS

1. From the trailhead kiosk, follow the David Yetman trail.
2. At 0.4 miles, continue straight on the David Yetman Trail (the unnamed intersecting trail to the left is your return route).
3. At 1.1 miles, there is an intersection of several trails. Turn left on the first trail at the intersection.
4. At 1.3 miles, turn left at the T junction on an unnamed path to proceed uphill.
5. At 1.6 miles, veer left at the junction and continue to climb.
6. At 1.8 miles, stay left and continue on the unnamed trail.
7. At 2.2 miles, continue straight at the junction with a rough path to the left that scrambles up to Bren Peak, 0.5 miles up if you want to check it out.
8. At 3.4 miles, turn right on the David Yetman Trail to return to the trailhead and parking area.

FIND THE TRAILHEAD

From the W Grant Road Exit on I-10, travel west on W Grant Road for 1.25 miles, where the name changes to W Ironwood Hill Drive. Travel 2.8 miles to N Camino De Oeste and turn left. Travel 1.1 miles to W Gates Pass Road and turn right. Travel 3 miles, and Gates Pass Scenic Viewpoint, Trailhead, and parking area are on the left.

DRAGOON BREWING COMPANY

Dragoon Brewing Company is a no-nonsense brewery somewhat secluded in an industrial park on the northwest side of the city. A spacious, well-appointed taproom is connected to the modern brewhouse. Guests can watch the beer ripening through a series of viewing windows while enjoying a beer. The vibe-is laidback, and I'd venture the clientele leans toward regulars.

Operations Manager Wes McCanse was kind enough to take me around the back of the house to get a closer look. This brewery is focused on beer—no restaurant. Food trucks occasionally come and go. Dragoon's beers are broadly distributed in the Tucson area and across Arizona, so there are healthy kegging and canning operations. Wes told me the owners are a trio of guys who started as home brewers in the 90s and came together to open Dragoon in 2012. Wes feels that the dedication of the people and the team are the key to their success. There is a lot of stability and passion involved. For example, Wes grew up in Tucson, has worked at Dragoon since its beginning, and has worked his way from the bottom up. He said there are a lot of similar stories across the staff of 20.

The taproom had eleven taps pouring an interesting variety of styles. Dragoon IPA, Dragoon Pils, Santa Cruz'r (golden ale), Dragoon Amber (amber ale), Florecita (juicy IPA), Salem (dunkel), Stoutstanding, Sibling Rivalry (hoppy lager), Fall For You (black IPA), The Dos (Russian imperial stout), and Baldur (barrel-aged barleywine) are some of the beers you might encounter. They also produce and bottle some barrel-aged sours. Wes told me that Dragoon typically brews about 30 different beers during a year.

There is a nice craft beer scene in Tucson with a mix of established breweries and newer, experimental operations. Tucson has a laid-back, college-town feel that contrasts sharply with the feel of Big Brother Phoenix to the north. A premium is placed on "local" and unique, which comes through in the brewery scene. Other breweries to check out if you have the time include Barrio Brewing Company, 1912 Brewing Company, BlackRock Brewers, Borderlands Brewing Company, Brick Box Brewery,

Button Brew House, Corbett Brewing Company, Crooked Tooth Brewing Company, Dove Mountain Brewing Company, Firetruck Brewing Company, Harbottle Brewing Company, Pueblo Vida Brewing Company, Screwbean Brewing, and Slow Body Beer Company. There are more than 20 to choose from.

CONTACT INFORMATION

Tucson Mountain Park
Pima County Conservation Lands and Resources
201 N Stone Ave.
Tucson, Arizona 85701-1207
+ 1 (520) 724-5000

BREWERY/RESTAURANT

Dragoon Brewing Company
1859 W Grant Rd #111
Tucson, AZ 85745
Distance from trailhead: 8 miles

NEW MEXICO

DRAGONFLY LOOP

ANCIENT PETROGLYPHS, DESERT VISTAS, AND A MEETING PLACE FOR BEER HIKERS

STARTING POINT	OBJECTIVE
DRAGONFLY TRAILHEAD	MIMBRES-MOGOLLON PETROGLYPHS
BEER	HIKE TYPE
NM-15 HAZY IPA	EASY
FEES	SEASON
NONE	YEAR-ROUND
MAP REFERENCE	DOG FRIENDLY
POSTED AT TRAILHEAD; USGS 817802	YES
DURATION	LENGTH
2 HOURS	3.5 MILES
LOW POINT / HIGH POINT	ELEVATION GAIN
6,106 FEET / 6,283 FEET	233 FEET

ALCOHOL
7.5%
CONTENT

HAZY PALE IPA

CLOUDY STRAW

FLORAL

CITRUSY

BITTERNESS
IBU: 40

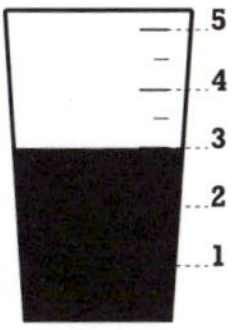

SWEETNESS

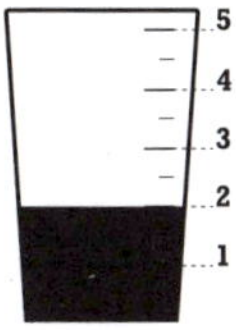

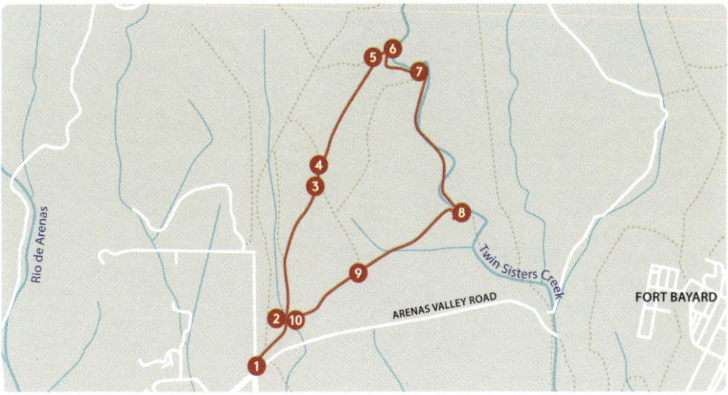

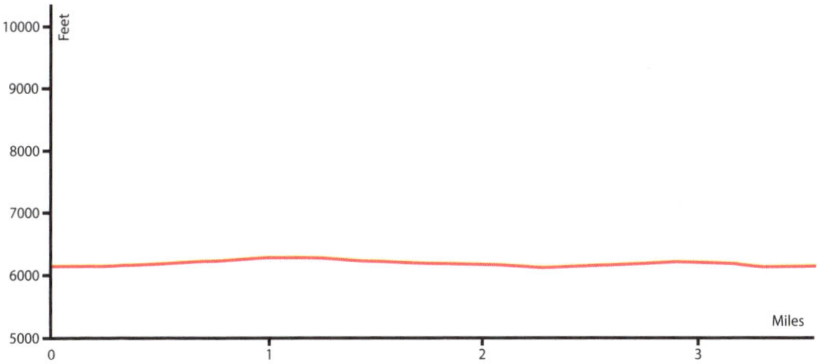

HIKE DESCRIPTION

Hear whispers of the past as you explore the Dragonfly Loop.

The Dragonfly Loop is a beautiful three-and-a-half-mile hike located near Silver City, New Mexico, and the Open Space Brewery. The route takes you through a basin in the Gila National Forest, where you can enjoy stunning desert scenery. The route winds through a landscape dominated by piñon and juniper trees, some offering welcome shade. Open meadows of yellow grass are interspersed with trees and interesting rocky outcrops. But the real highlight of the trail is the collection of petroglyphs—ancient rock carvings created by native people hundreds of years ago.

The terrain is gentle and easy to walk, making it a great option for hikers of all levels. As you hike, keep an eye out for desert cottontail rabbits, lizards, deer, and even the occasional dragonfly (especially during the summer months). If you are a birder, the area won't disappoint.

The most fascinating part of the hike comes about two miles in, where a collection of petroglyphs are scratched onto the dark rocks, forming an area of steep walls along Twin Sisters Creek. The carvings will have you imagining the lives of the Mimbres-Mogollon people who lived in the area more than a thousand years ago. They depict animals, geometric shapes, and even some human-looking figures. And of course, the namesake dragonfly. It's a humbling experience to see these ancient works of art and contemplate the people who created them. Search, find, look, photograph, but please don't touch.

The Dragonfly Loop Trail is part of the larger Fort Bayard Trail system, which features many crisscrossing paths and the opportunity to make your own loops of varying lengths. Although not a formal trailhead, the system can be accessed by a pathway that connects directly to the beer garden at Open Space Brewing Company. Fort Bayard is a historic military fort established in the 1800s that protected nearby mining operations from Apache raiders. In its later history, it was used as a sanitarium and veterans' hospital. The fort, a national historic landmark, is a sprawling site of quiet lanes lined with vacant buildings, a small museum, and a historic cemetery. This was once home to Buffalo Soldiers, some of the nation's first African American enlistees.

Along the hike, there are glimpses of a prominent rock formation to the east called the Kneeling Nun. A source of local legend for centuries, the formation resembles a kneeling woman at the altar of a massive cliff face. Numerous variations of the legend exist, but the common version involves a nun who breaks her vows and falls in love. As punishment, she is turned to stone and forever kneels in penance.

Prepare for the desert environment with plenty of water and sun protection. Thunderstorms are common during the summer months, so check the weather report and prepare accordingly. The Silver City area offers a wealth of hiking options, although I found I had to dig a bit to sort them out. The proprietors of Open Space Brewing are hikers themselves (more about that below), and you will find them an excellent resource. Silver City has a rich history dating back to the 1870s, when there was a local silver strike. Historical figures like Geronimo, Billy the Kid, Butch Cassidy, and "Dangerous Dan" Tucker feature in local lore. The present town has a small university, a historic center, and a vibrant creative scene, and it is a popular destination for outdoor enthusiasts. Silver City is also an important stop for hikers on the Continental Divide Trail, the 3,000-mile long-distance trail from Mexico to Canada.

TURN-BY-TURN DIRECTIONS

1. From the Dragonfly trailhead kiosk, follow the Dragonfly Trail.
2. At 0.2 miles, bear left at the junction (to the right is your return route).
3. At 0.8 miles, continue straight on the Dragonfly Trail where it intersects with an unnamed trail to the right.
4. At 0.9 miles, continue straight on the Dragonfly Trail where it intersects with an unnamed trail to the left.
5. At 1.4 miles, bear right at an intersection with an unnamed connector trail to descend toward Two Sisters Creek.
6. At 1.5 miles, turn sharply to the right at an intersection to follow the creek into a small canyon. The trail to the left is a connector to the Servis Corrals Trail.
7. At 1.7 miles, reach an outcrop above the creek, which is the general area where petroglyphs can be found. Beaten paths provide clues for where to look. Bear left, following the creek, at the T junction with an unnamed trail to continue the loop hike.
8. At 2.4 miles, turn right at the junction with Twin Sisters Creek trail and proceed uphill from the creek.
9. At 2.9 miles, bear left at the junction with an unnamed trail to the right.
10. At 3.3 miles, bear left at the junction to return to the trailhead.

FIND THE TRAILHEAD

From the junction of US Highway 180 and NM Highway 90 in Silver City, travel 4 miles east to Arenas Valley Road. Turn left on Arenas Valley Road and travel 1.6 miles to Elias Road. Turn left and the Dragonfly Trailhead parking area is 300 feet ahead on your right.

OPEN SPACE BREWING

Open Space Brewing opened its doors in October 2023 as the realization of a dream for its owners. The brewery's mission is to be a gathering place for the local community and the lovers of the area's outdoor resources. The owners, Matt Leef and Alexa Tubbs, are a couple who first met while they were thru-hiking on the Continental Divide Trail (CDT) in 2019. They discovered they share a love of open spaces, hiking, and a good beer along the way.

Matt is a West Coast guy who goes by the trail name Brewhiker. He holds a degree in fermentation sciences and learned practical brewing as a home brewer (he was an active member of Quality Ale and Fermentation Fraternity (QUAFF), a prominent San Diego brew club) and during a stint with Boston Beer Company. Alexa is an easterner with a degree in the business of art who traveled west to take on the CDT from north to south. Matt is the brewer, and Alexa is the creative entrepreneur. The couple met while sharing a can of Moose Drool, a Montana brown ale, at an overnight stop on the trail in Glacier National Park. As they hiked, their bond developed and a vision started to form. Following their CDT adventure, a friend invited them back to the Silver City area, and their vision became entwined in the place.

Matt was living up to his handle, brewing pint batches of beer as he hiked the trail incorporating foraged bittering ingredients, including pine cones, pine needles, and crumbled sage. Berries provided another source of flavoring. He started figuring out how to do this on a prior long-distance hike on the Pacific Crest Trail. Matt showed me his fermenter, an old plastic pop bottle that is encrusted with the remnants of the hearty yeast strain that has traveled with him for thousands of miles of brewing on the trail. As someone who dabbles in home brewing, I plan to give it a try myself.

Open Space Brewing is housed in the motor pool bay of a former National Guard facility in an area locally known as "the Mining District." Although close to Silver City, Alexa told me that they closely identify with the village of Santa Clara and that the village is their landlord. This is an old-school mining area that has seen Native American, Spanish, Mexican, and American mining activities to this day. The nearby Santa

Rita open-pit copper mine is one of the largest in the world. The brewhouse sits in a roped-off part of the open space. Huge roll-up doors on both ends allow the space to be opened to the great outdoors.

The mellow atmosphere had a buzz to it. Vintage tables and chairs were collected around a bartop fashioned from a massive, knotty slice of a ponderosa pine. The crowd was mostly congenial locals who were chatting it up with Alexa. Matt seemed to stay mostly focused on pouring and talking beer. No food is served, but sometimes there are food trucks on site.

Alexa told me they frequently see CDT thru-hikers in the brewery, whose story has become part of the conversation on thru-hiker forums. You can even "pay it forward" by buying a "trail magic" beer for the next thru-hiker to show up, and we gladly did so. Open Space has partnered with groups like the Continental Divide Trail Coalition, the New Mexico Wilderness Alliance, the Gila Back Country Horsemen, and the local community hosting events and sharing proceeds to support the partners.

The brewery's beer range reflects the brewery's vision and Matt's interesting brewing experiences. The lineup rotates, but we tasted the NM-15 Hazy IPA (the brewery's flagship, named for the curvy scenic highway through the nearby Black Mountains), La Chancla (porter), Waterworks (pale ale), Meet Me In the Mountains (barleywine), Bushwhacker (Belgian blonde), Cartography (stout), Garden Day Saison (sage-infused), and a house-made root beer called "The Lonely Boot."

There are two other small breweries in the area. Little Toad Creek Brewery & Distillery is located in the historic center of Silver City, and the rustic Ravenswing Farm is in the Mule Mountains to the southwest. Ravenswing brews "wild cerveza." Wild cerveza is a high-ABV sour beer made with wild yeasts and bacteria native to the Gila National Forest.

CONTACT INFORMATION

Gila National Forest
3005 E. Camino del Bosque
Silver City, NM 88061
(575) 388-8201

BREWERY/RESTAURANT

Open Space Brewing
11990 US-180
Santa Clara Armory,
Santa Clara, NM 88026
Distance from trailhead: 5 miles

SOLEDAD CANYON

SOLITARY DESERT HIKING CHASED BY AN ICEHOUSE-BREWED BEER

STARTING POINT	OBJECTIVE
SOLEDAD CANYON TRAILHEAD	INTERMITTENT WATERFALL, ABANDONED RANCH
BEER	HIKE TYPE
BLACK ICE LAGER	EASY
FEES	SEASON
NONE	YEAR ROUND
MAP REFERENCE	DOG FRIENDLY
POSTED AT TRAILHEAD; USGS 818420	YES
DURATION	LENGTH
2.5 HOURS	3.8 MILES
LOW POINT / HIGH POINT	ELEVATION GAIN
5,613 FEET / 6,210 FEET	738 FEET

ALCOHOL 5.1% CONTENT

LAGER

BLACK

HINTS OF CARAMEL, CHOCOLATE, AND COFFEE

MALTY, ROASTY

BITTERNESS

IBU: 20

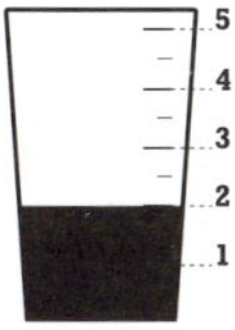

SWEETNESS

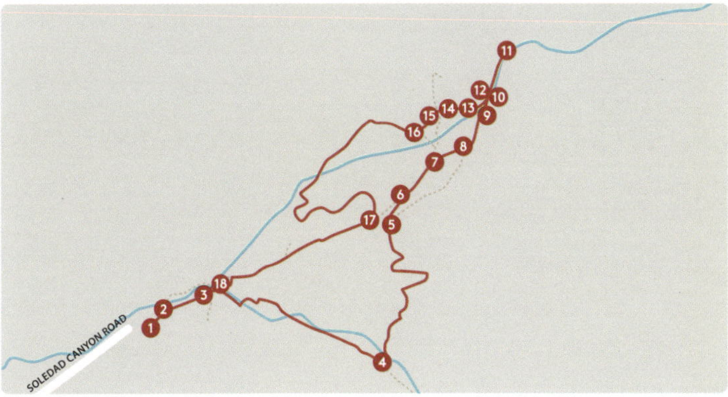

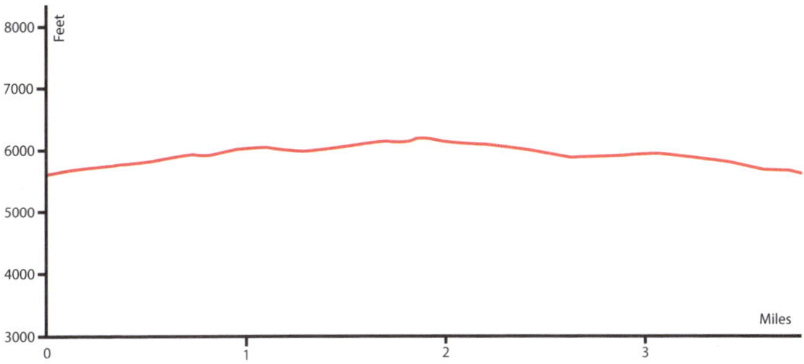

HIKE DESCRIPTION

Finding Solitude in Soledad Canyon

Soledad translates to solitary—or solitude. And that's exactly what you might feel as you wander a loop through Soledad Canyon in the Organ Mountains. This isn't the kind of loneliness that makes you feel lost or afraid, though. It's the peaceful solitude of the desert, where the only sounds are the whisper of the wind through the creosote and the distant call of a hawk.

This area, part of the vast Chihuahuan Desert, is a tapestry of life. Imagine yourself walking through a landscape painted with vibrant greens of agaves, the sharp points of prickly pear cacti, and the delicate blooms of desert wildflowers. Scrub oaks and small pine trees offer shade as you increase elevation, while agave and mountain mahogany are on display along the route. It's a harsh beauty where life finds a way to thrive in the face of extreme heat and limited water.

Soledad Canyon itself is a gem. Located about ten miles east of the center of Las Cruces, it offers a taste of the raw, untamed beauty of the Organ Mountains. The area is situated at the juncture of Bar Canyon and Soledad Canyon, an area known for its scenic vistas of the central Organ Mountains and the southern Mesilla Valley. The dramatic peaks of the Organs, named for their resemblance to the pipes of a pipe organ, rise dramatically from the desert floor. They're composed of igneous rock, primarily granite and rhyolite, giving them a rugged, almost otherworldly appearance.

The route meanders up a desert wash, with the towering Organ Mountains providing a constant backdrop. Canyon walls have a reddish hue from the rhyolite rock, and the various trails pass through areas of loose sand and gravelly uplands. Impressive specimens of yucca are everywhere with their feathery plumes reaching for the sky. Eventually, the canyon narrows, and you'll find yourself in a steep, narrow gorge leading to a seasonal waterfall that cascades down a rock face. A manmade dam at the base of the falls appears to be a catchment that once provided water for a nearby ranch site. Further along, the ruins of an old ranch house conjure imaginings of tough people tending their livestock in this rough, unforgiving land.

Soledad Canyon is just one of many possible hiking adventures waiting to be discovered in the Organ Mountains-Desert Peaks National Monument. The vast expanse of protected land encompasses not only the dramatic Organ Mountains but also the volcanic Potrillo Mountains and the rugged Robledo and Doña Ana Mountains. The Organs reach upward of 9,000 feet and have been climbed since the 1890s. Dripping Springs is another popular hiking destination in the Organs. The Potrillos feature unique volcanic landscapes and otherworldly formations.

TURN-BY-TURN DIRECTIONS

1. From the trailhead kiosk, follow the Soledad Canyon Trail.
2. After 250 feet, bear right at the junction with an unnamed trail to the left and continue.
3. At 0.1 miles, take the right fork at the junction to follow Soledad Canyon Road, a gravelly trail that ascends into the canyon.
4. At 0.7 miles, turn left onto an unnamed trail.
5. At 1.3 miles, bear left at the junction with an unnamed trail.
6. At 1.4 miles, turn right onto the Soledad Canyon Trail and continue to ascend.
7. At 1.5 miles, turn right onto an unnamed trail into a small meadow.
8. At 1.6 miles, continue straight at the junction with an unnamed trail to the right.
9. At 1.7 miles, continue straight at the junction with an unnamed trail to the left.
10. At 1.8 miles, continue straight as the canyon narrows. To the left is the trail you will take to continue the loop when you come back down the canyon.
11. At 1.9 miles, you reach the turnaround point at a waterfall that drops into a dammed pool. Descend back the way you came.
12. At 2.0 miles, bear right at the junction with the trail you came on.
13. At 2.1 miles, continue straight at the junction with an unnamed trail to the left.
14. At 2.2 miles, you reach the remnants of stone buildings that were once a ranch. After looking around, continue straight, crossing an unnamed intersecting trail.
15. At 2.3 miles, bear right at the junction with an unnamed trail to the right.
16. At 3.1 miles, turn right onto the Soledad Canyon Trail to descend back to the trailhead.
17. At 3.6 miles, continue straight to the trailhead and parking area.

FIND THE TRAILHEAD

The Soledad Canyon Trailhead (also known as Bar Canyon Day Use Area) is located on the west at the foot of the Organ Mountains, 10 miles east of Las Cruces. From Exit 1 on Interstate 25, take University Avenue/Dripping Springs Road east for about 4.5 miles, then turn right (south) on the Soledad Canyon Road. That road takes a sharp left turn (east) in a mile; follow it all the way to where it ends at the parking area and trailhead.

ICE BOX BREWING COMPANY

The Icebox Brewing Company brewery and taproom is housed in a former ice plant building on US Highway 70, the main east-west highway through this part of the country before the arrival of the Interstate Highway System. Co-founder and General Manager Brian Weidauer explained that the "Icebox" name comes from the building's history. Brian explained that in former days, trucks hauling produce cross-country would stop at strategically placed icehouses positioned across the country, and this was the stop in Las Cruces. For obvious reasons, an icehouse has some attractive attributes for conversion to a brewery. The brewery maintains the building's industrial bones with exposed ductwork, concrete floors, and photographs of its past life as City Ice

Service. The brewery is open to the large, no-frills taproom. Brian said that the desire is to foster an inviting atmosphere for patrons to gather and socialize.

Brian describes Las Cruces as a "Bud Light" kind of beer culture. As a result, he said that Icebox focuses on crafting approachable beers that appeal to both craft beer enthusiasts and casual drinkers. Icebox Light, their best seller, is a light lager designed to be a gateway to craft beer for mass-produced-domestic-beer drinkers. However, the brewery also offers a diverse range, with eight core styles available year-round, along with four to six rotating seasonal or specialty beers. Mexican Lager, Green Chile Blonde Ale, All Dogs Go To Hefen (hefeweizen), Black Ice Lager (schwarzbier), Emperor Stout, Arctic Amber Ale, Wright of Passage Scottish Ale, Hopsicle Hazy IPA, Chief Edgar IPA, Grassy Knoll IPA, and Frostbite IPA are some of the other beers you may encounter.

Icebox Brewing, founded in 2019, is an ambitious enterprise that operates additional locations. Three more are in Las Cruces, and one is up in Hatch, home of the world's best green chile farms. Icebox is involved in the local community, and they partner with local non-profit organizations. Brian told me that the taproom at the brewery has become a popular spot for locals. A raucous session of "Singo," a fun take-off on bingo, was in full swing while we were there.

In addition to the Ice Box Brewing locations, the craft beer scene in Las Cruces provides a good number of options befitting a university town. Picacho Peak Brewery and Spotted Dog Brewery brew locally. Silver City's Little Toad Creek Brewery and Distillery, and Albuquerque-based Bosque Brewing also operate craft beer venues in the community.

CONTACT INFORMATION

Organ Mountains-Desert Peaks National Monument
Bureau of Land Management (BLM)
1800 Marquess St.
Las Cruces, NM 88005
+1 (575) 525-4300

BREWERY/RESTAURANT

Ice Box Brewing Company
2825 W Picacho Ave.
Las Cruces, NM 88007
Distance from trailhead: 18 miles

GRINDSTONE CANYON

UNPLUG, UNWIND, AND DOWNSHIFT IN RUIDOSO

STARTING POINT	OBJECTIVE
GRINDSTONE TRAILHEAD	GRINDSTONE LAKE
BEER	HIKE TYPE
HIKIN' BEER	MODERATE
FEES	SEASON
NONE	APRIL TO NOVEMBER
MAP REFERENCE	DOG FRIENDLY
POSTED AT TRAILHEAD; USGS 818627	YES
DURATION	LENGTH
2.5 HOURS	6.5 MILES
LOW POINT / HIGH POINT	ELEVATION GAIN
6,882 FEET / 7,376 FEET	755 FEET

ALCOHOL
5.2%
CONTENT

VIENNA LAGER

AMBER

CARAMEL AND FLORAL HOPS

TOASTED MALT, CLEAN FINISH

BITTERNESS
IBU: 25

SWEETNESS

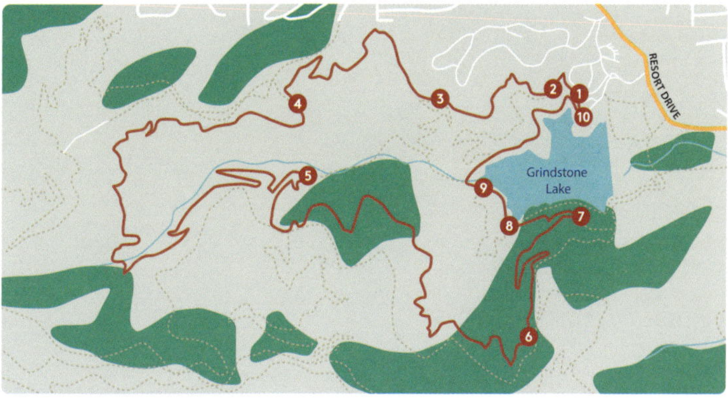

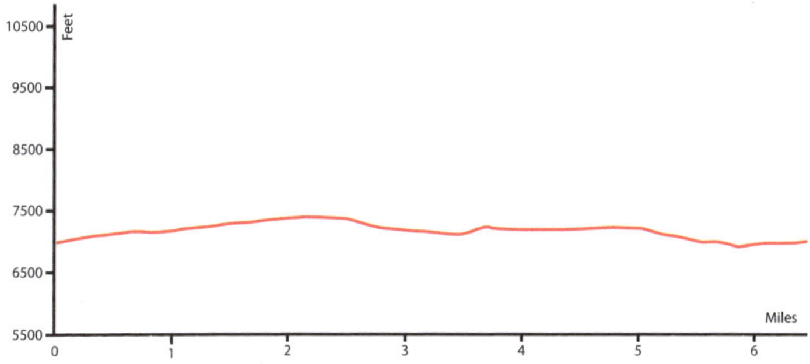

HIKE DESCRIPTION

Mountain trails and a serene lake in the heart of the Sierra Blancas.

Grindstone Canyon is a major side canyon and watershed bordering the southwestern edge of the village of Ruidoso in the Sierra Blanca mountains of southern New Mexico. A dam was built in the canyon in 1987 to capture surface water to supply the village and to deal with flooding issues downstream. Since that time, a multi-use trail system has continued to be improved in the upper reaches of the canyon that cradles the lake. There is a system of five trails in the canyon totaling 18 miles. They are used for hiking, mountain biking, and horseback riding.

The lake is easily accessible from Ruidoso. Grindstone Trailhead is located adjacent to a large parking area perched above the lake. The loop route climbs to a high contour arcing around the lake. The emerald water surface comes in and out of view down the many drainages crossed along the way. Eventually, a series of switchbacks descend back down to lake level, and the last part of the hike follows the shore back around to the starting point.

Beginning at about 7,000 feet (2,130 m.) elevation, you are in a pine forest for nearly all of the hike. Ponderosa pines tower above. On the first part of the hike are groupings of huge alligator junipers, much bigger than I'm used to seeing so many in a small area. The occasional agave (also known as the century plant) and cactus remind you that you are in a high desert. The birdlife is plentiful, and we encountered several groups of deer along the way. There are occasional views to the mountain peaks above, which rise to 12,000 feet (3,650 m).

Multiple intersecting trails in Grindstone Canyon create the opportunity to shorten or lengthen the hike to fit your interests. There are plenty of other hikes of all distances and difficulty levels available in the area as well. Check out Moon Mountain, Lookout Mountain, Sierra Blanca Crest, and the White Mountain Wilderness Area. Recent wildfires have prompted closures in some areas, so make sure to do your research.

Ruidoso is actively positioning itself as a destination for outdoor adventure activities and events. The Wild West MTB Fest is an annual mountain bike festival held in the fall that features multiple races, clinics, and entertainment. Grindstone Canyon will be the site of an XTERRA World Championship qualifying event in 2025 and will become part of the XTERRA Americas Tour. The August events include a full-distance triathlon, a 10K trail run, a kids' race, and a sprint distance triathlon. A mile-long Eurostyle mountain coaster and zipline attractions located near the local ski area cater to outdoor adrenaline junkies.

TURN-BY-TURN DIRECTIONS

1. From the trailhead kiosk, take Grindstone Canyon Loop Trail, a single track with a dirt surface.
2. At 0.1 miles, bear right at the junction with the T96 trail.
3. At 0.5 miles, continue straight at the junction with an unnamed trail that descends to the left.
4. At 1.3 miles, bear left at the junction with the Alfred Hale Connector Trail.
5. At 3.4 miles, bear right at the junction with an unnamed trail that descends into the ravine.
6. At 4.9 miles, bear left at the junction with the Grindstone Ridge Trail (T97).
7. At 5.6 miles, reach a junction with an unnamed trail on the right and continue straight onto a switchback descending toward the lake.
8. At 5.8 miles, continue straight at the junction onto the Fisherman's Trail.
9. At 5.9 miles, continue straight at the junction onto the Grindstone Loop Trail following the edge of the lake.
10. At 6.4 miles, turn left to return to the parking lot and trailhead where the hike began.

FIND THE TRAILHEAD

To reach Grindstone Trailhead, head south on Grindstone Canyon Road for 0.63 miles and turn right on Resort Drive. Travel 0.7 miles and turn right onto Sunrise Court. After 100 feet, turn left onto Hideaway Pk for 1,000 feet to where the road ends in the trailhead parking area.

DOWNSHIFT BREWING COMPANY

Downshift Brewing Company has two locations close to each other in the center of Ruidoso. Downshift Hidden Tap is the location of the brewhouse and a small pub operation, whereas the larger Riverside is a combined taproom, coffeehouse, and event venue with great outdoor space along the Rio Ruidoso. We chose Riverside for the larger food selection and riverside ambiance. The name Ruidoso comes from the Spanish word for noisy, which is a reference to the babbling stream that runs past the brewery and through the village.

Downshift has a real community vibe. Owners Eddie and Shelby Gutierrez both grew up in Ruidoso, moved away to Houston to pursue careers, and then came back home. I met with key man Jamey to get the lowdown over an aptly named Hikin' Beer. Jamey explained that the brewery's name, "Downshift," described what Eddie and Shelby were after when they moved back from the fast-paced city to their mountain hometown in 2021. Eddie had learned the craft as a brewer at Saint Arnold Brewing Company in Houston, a larger brewery. It didn't sound like they downshifted too much, though, as they have continually expanded their business and are stepping up a new production facility nearby.

The Riverside location has a clubhouse feel and offers a little bit of everything: beer, bar, food, coffee, and baked goods. Jamey told me there are frequent events, including live music, open mike nights, and film screenings. They even held a *Rocky Horror Picture Show* event. The place morphs between being tourist-focused during high-volume season to being a comfortable local hangout at quieter times.

In addition to the Hikin' Beer, Downshift offered a big range of draft beers with names like Collective Good Kölsch, B-Side Blonde, Uphill in the Snow (Both Ways IPA), Fresh Hop Snowday (New England IPA), Thirsty People IPA, Camping Vibes Red Ale, Team Lift Wee Heavy (Scotch ale), Lil' Boo Thang Pumpkin Ale, Resignation Porter, Brewer's Brunch French Toast Stout, and Giggle Bush (a sour). The simply named Helles and Munich Dunkel were on offer for the traditional lager drinkers.

Another local craft brewery of note is Lost Hiker Brewing Company, just down the street between the two Downshift locations. It is a smaller, rustic spot with a laid-back vibe and a handful of beers on tap. Check out the Das Hefen Hiker.

CONTACT INFORMATION

Lincoln National Forest
3463 Las Palomas
Alamogordo, NM 88310
+ 1 (575)-434-7200

BREWERY/RESTAURANT

Downshift Brewing Company
2704 Sudderth Drive
Ruidoso, NM 88345
Distance from trailhead: 1 mile

LOBO CANYON

PANORAMIC VIEWS AND NEARBY BREWS ON THE CONTINENTAL DIVIDE

STARTING POINT	OBJECTIVE
CDT LOBO CANYON TRAILHEAD	LOBO CANYON OVERLOOK
BEER	HIKE TYPE
JUNKYARD LAGER	MODERATE
FEES	SEASON
NONE	APRIL TO OCTOBER
MAP REFERENCE	DOG FRIENDLY
POSTED AT TRAILHEAD	YES
DURATION	LENGTH
2 HOURS	4.3 MILES
LOW POINT / HIGH POINT	ELEVATION GAIN
6,863 FEET / 7,828 FEET	961 FEET

ALCOHOL **4.7%** CONTENT

LIGHT LAGER

GOLDEN

FRESH, SLIGHT MALTINESS

WELL-BALANCED, PLEASANT HOP-NOSE

BITTERNESS
IBU: 30

SWEETNESS

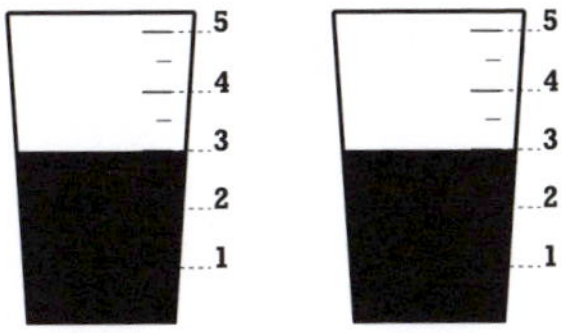

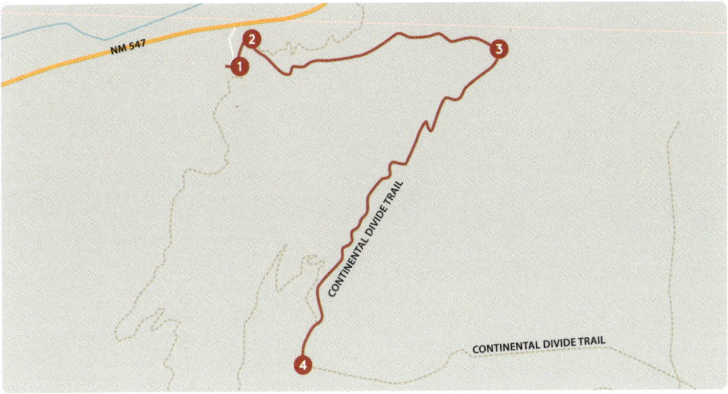

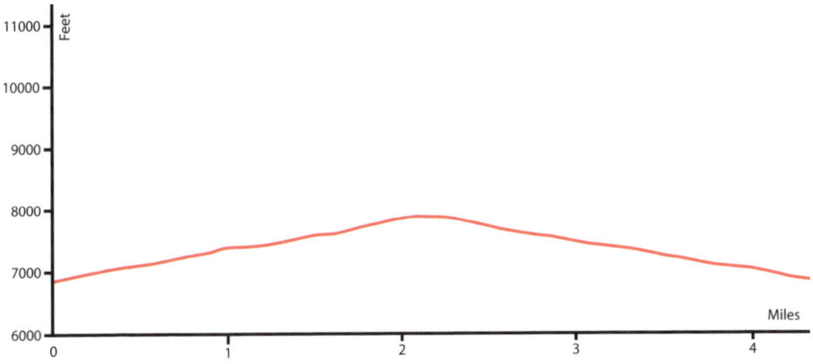

HIKE DESCRIPTION

Hike a segment of the Continental Divide Trail (CDT) in Lobo Canyon and reward yourself with a Junkyard Brew.

This hike on the Continental Divide Trail (CDT) in Lobo Canyon near Grants, NM, offers a unique blend of history, stunning landscapes, and challenging terrain. This portion of the CDT is a historic trail that has been used by Native Americans and early European settlers for centuries.

The CDT is a 3,100-mile-long route that stretches from Canada to Mexico, roughly tracking the Continental Divide. It remains a work in progress, with some segments still using roadway shoulders until offroad connectors are built and designated. The New Mexico section of the CDT is approximately 460 miles long and passes through some of the state's most dramatic scenery, including the Jemez Mountains, the Gila Wilderness, and Mount Taylor near Grants.

This Lobo Canyon hike on the CDT starts at 6,870 feet (2,093 m) altitude and ascends steadily to a large meadow on a flat mesa top. A pause on the mesa's edge offers big views down Lobo Canyon to the community of Grants. The trail climbs a desert landscape through mixed piñon pine and juniper forest and reaches an elevation of 7,828 feet (2,386 m) at the turnaround. There is occasional shade from bigger trees, and cactus is scattered across the terrain at ground level. Along the way, hikers will encounter frequent scenic views up and down the canyon, as well as the prospect of spotting wildlife, including birds, deer, elk, and bighorn sheep.

This segment of the CDT is well-marked, with CDT trail markers along the way. If you want a longer hike, you could go all the way to Canada and back! I was more interested in finding a beer. Further along the trail is the approach toward Mount Taylor, a volcanic peak that rises above all of the surrounding lands to 11,305 feet (3,445 m). The mountain is sacred to the nearby pueblos of Acoma, Laguna, and Zuni. To the Navajo, it is known as Tsoodził, the blue bead mountain (think turquoise stones) that marks the southeast extent of traditional Navajo territory.

The CDT route also travels south through the town of Grants, a place with a logging, agricultural, mining, and railroad past. It is also on the route of historic Route 66, and you can spot occasional remnants of that history as well. El Malpais National Monument is on the southern periphery of Grants, a crazy-looking jumble of lava fields stretching into the distance.

TURN-BY-TURN DIRECTIONS

1. From the trailhead kiosk, follow the dirt trail crossing a small ravine for 200 feet to a signed trail intersection, then turn left on the single-track path.
2. At 0.1 miles, bear right at the junction where the trail splits and proceed upslope.
3. At 0.9 miles, the trail makes a sharp right turn. Follow the trail continuing upslope.
4. At 2.2 miles, reach a viewpoint at the edge of a large meadow. A signpost indicates that the CDT takes a sharp left turn. From this point, retrace your steps back to the trailhead.

The CDT is reasonably well signed with CDT trail markers. The hike can be made longer by following the CDT as far as you want before turning back.

FIND THE TRAILHEAD

From the E Santa Fe Ave interchange with I-40 in Grants, head northeast on E Santa Fe Ave for 1.29 miles, and turn right onto George Hanosh Blvd. Travel 0.9 miles and turn left onto Redondo Rd. Travel 0.8 miles and continue onto Sakelares Blvd. Travel 1 mile and turn right onto NM-547 N/Lobo Canyon Rd. Proceed 3 miles to turn into the large Lobo Canyon Continental Divide Trailhead parking area.

JUNKYARD ON ROUTE 66 BREWERY

Junkyard on Route 66 Brewery on the outskirts of Grants, NM, is housed in an auto salvage yard that has been mostly cleared of cast-off vehicles but still does some salvage sales. A row of interesting junkers still line the frontage of the large property, which is along the old Route 66 on the east side of town. The brewery and taproom are housed in a rustic building that was the old shop for the salvage business.

Henry Lackey, an Air Force veteran who grew up in Grants, told me he bought the salvage business around 2010. The brewery opened in 2016, with Henry as the brewer, barbeque-meister, and all-around driving force. He envisioned the place as a community hub offering a place for entertainment, charity events, and other gatherings, as well as an interesting spot for travelers. The junkyard has hosted concerts and served as a place for drive-in movies.

I ordered up a flagship Junkyard Lager, which turned out to be an easy-drinking thirst quencher. The beer had a golden hue, with a faint citrusy aroma and a hoppy bitterness that balanced perfectly with a subdued malty sweetness. It provided excellent refreshment after the hike, quenching thirst and invigorating senses. This is a small brewery operation with a small range, with Piston Colada Wheat Beer (Belgian white) and El Camino (Mexican lager) as other popular mainstays. Henry told me that he started with no brewing experience but has benefitted greatly from help offered by other New Mexico breweries and brewers.

The taproom and brewery are one-of-a-kind. Recycled auto and truck parts are used for tabletops and seating, and repurposed objects adorn the walls. It's a big, open space with full classic vehicles in various states of restoration here and there. Classic blues on the sound system added to the ambiance. The brewhouse is roped off at one end. The atmosphere is authentic gritty industrial rather than frou-frou in any way. In addition to brewing, Henry is a barbeque guy, and the menu includes items like ribs, pulled pork, and brisket.

Henry told me that he hosts a lot of thru-hikers on the CDT and that the brewery gets great word-of-mouth promotion among the hiker community. Surprisingly for such a small town, there is a second brewery in Grants—Elkins Brewing Company—just in case you need a beer after another hike.

CONTACT INFORMATION

Cibola National Forest
1800 Lobo Canyon Rd.
Grants, NM 87020
+1 (505)-287-8833

BREWERY/RESTAURANT

Junkyard on Route 66 Brewery

1436 E. Highway 66
Grants, NM 87020
Distance from trailhead: 6 miles

PASEO DEL BOSQUE

URBAN OASIS AND PEAK BEER

STARTING POINT	OBJECTIVE
RIO GRANDE NATURE CENTER STATE PARK	RIO GRANDE RIVER, BOSQUE FOREST
BEER	**HIKE TYPE**
ELEVATED IPA	EASY
FEES	**SEASON**
$5 PARKING FEE AT STATE PARK	YEAR ROUND
MAP REFERENCE	**DOG FRIENDLY**
POSTED AT TRAILHEAD; USGS 817233	LEASHED
DURATION	**LENGTH**
1.5 HOURS	3.9 MILES
LOW POINT / HIGH POINT	**ELEVATION GAIN**
4,964 FEET / 4,974 FEET	10 FEET

ALCOHOL 7.2% CONTENT

IPA

DEEP GOLDEN

ORANGE, TOFFEE, HOPS

NICE MOUTHFEEL, PLEASANT BITTERNESS THAT LASTS

BITTERNESS
IBU: 100

SWEETNESS

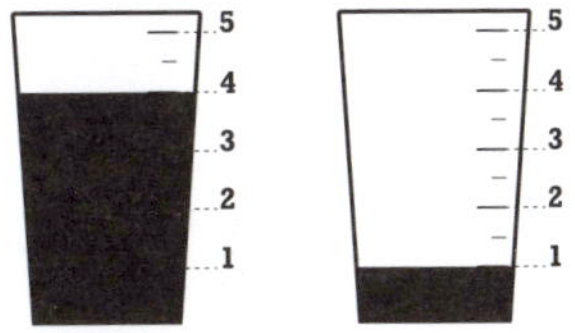

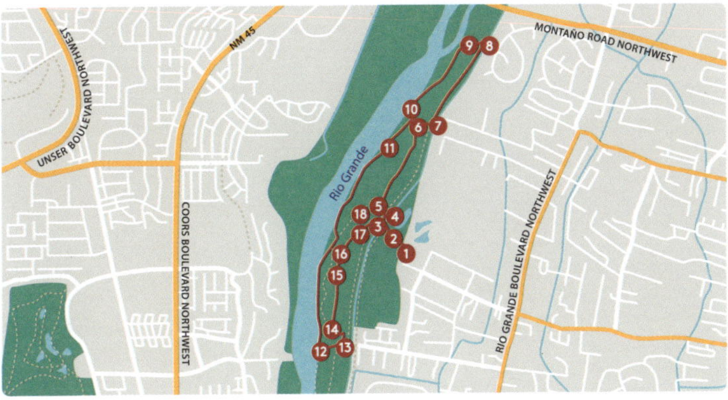

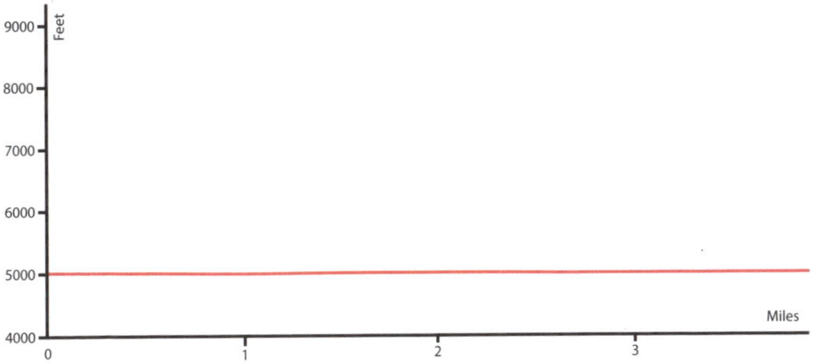

HIKE DESCRIPTION

A riverside journey through Albuquerque's enchanting cottonwood bosque.

The Albuquerque area presents a wealth of options for interesting beer hikes. The Petroglyph National Monument to the West offers high desert hiking amidst ancient rock art. Piedras Marcadas Canyon is home to the densest concentration of petroglyphs in the Monument, with more than 5,000 images. The Sandia Mountains rise majestically all along the eastern flank of the city, and hikes from the foothills rise all the way to the peak of the crest at nearly 11,000 feet (3,350 m) elevation. The Sandia Peak Tramway from the city to nearly the top is the longest single-span tramway in North America (nearly a mile and a half), and it is possible to ride up and hike back.

The Rio Grande River cuts right through Albuquerque from north to south and is lined by bosque. The Paseo del Bosque Loop Hike is in the heart of the Bosque just north of the city center, immersing you in an enchanting riverside ecosystem. The hike starts with a visit through the small but impressive Rio Grande Nature Center State Park (RGNC) and combines portions of the Paseo del Bosque Trail, the Aldo Leopold Trails, and segments of unnamed pathways along the river and through the

forest. The hike starts and ends on paved-surface trails, but most of the route is on dirt and sandy-surfaced single-track paths.

The RGNC itself is a 38-acre urban wildlife preserve with a visitor center and multiple lagoons providing habitat for migrating birds. The parking area and park are gated at night, so check to find out the current hours depending when you plan to end. The hike can also be accessed from parking areas that are always open (such as the Pueblo Montaño Picnic Area and Trailhead). The beginning of the hike goes through the park, and a stop to explore the visitor center is worthwhile, with interesting architecture built right into the earth. A room with glass walls is equipped with soft chairs that look out over the surface of one of the lagoons. The sounds of nature and the birds outside are piped into the room.

The park and the hike are great for birders. More than 250 species of birds and waterfowl, including sandhill cranes, Canada geese, bald eagles, roadrunners, green-winged teals, northern shovelers, cinnamon teals, hooded mergansers, mallards, northern flickers, hairy woodpeckers, downy woodpeckers, white-breasted nuthatches, yellow-rumped warblers, red-winged blackbirds, and wood ducks, can be observed during different times of the year. We spotted porcupines twice, sleeping high up in trees. Coyotes and other mammals also inhabit the area.

The Paseo del Bosque Trail is a paved multi-use trail that runs for about 16 miles paralleling the Rio Grande through most of Albuquerque. At many points along the way, areas of cottonwood bosque open up between the trail and the river, and numerous connected trails snake through these areas. Our route laces through one of these areas and is open to hikers, bicyclists, and equestrians.

A bosque is a riverside forest, and huge cottonwoods line the sandy banks of the Rio Grande in Albuquerque. The forest is thick and impenetrable in some areas and seems like a fruitless orchard in others. Several places along the way give the opportunity to emerge on the bank of the river to check out the views and the abundant birdlife. We saw plenty. As you make your way, it is easy to forget that you are in the middle of a large urban area.

The first part of the hike is on the Aldo Leopold Trail, which winds through shady cottonwood groves and commemorates its namesake's work. Aldo was born in the 1880s and, as a conservationist, was a contemporary of historical figures like John Muir, Gifford Pinchot, and Teddy Roosevelt. His philosophy emphasized the interconnectedness of humans and the environment and asserted a moral responsibility to care for the land. A good deal of his career was spent in New Mexico, and an important part of that in Albuquerque, where he championed the idea of the green belt along the Rio Grande. Elsewhere in New Mexico, he was instrumental in the establishment of the nation's first designated wilderness in the Gila, and he was the supervisor of the Carson National Forest.

TURN-BY-TURN DIRECTIONS

1. From the parking lot, follow the trail into the park.
2. After 400 feet, bear left at the junction. The trail to the right leads into the Visitor Center through a large culvert.
3. At 0.2 miles, after crossing the footbridge, turn right and walk up the ramp (to the left is your return route).
4. After 200 feet at the top of the ramp, cross the Paseo del Bosque multi-purpose trail and continue on the Aldo Leopold Trail leading down the slope into the forest.
5. After 100 feet at the bottom of the slope, bear right and continue to follow the Aldo Leopold Trail.
6. At 0.7 miles, turn right onto an unnamed dirt path.
7. After 400 feet, turn left onto the Paseo del Bosque trail.
8. At 1.2 miles, turn left onto an unnamed dirt path leading downslope into the forest.
9. After 100 feet, turn left onto an unnamed dirt path. Signage along this path occasionally refers to this path as the Aldo Leopold Forest Trail
10. At 1.7 miles, turn right on an unnamed path toward the river.
11. At 1.9 miles, bear right on an unnamed path and continue to follow the river. As you follow the river, continue to bear right at any intersections. The multiple trails to the left will lead back to the Paseo del Bosque Trail.
12. At 2.9 miles, turn left on an unnamed trail.
13. At 3.0 miles, turn left on an unnamed trail.
14. At 3.1 miles, bear right at the intersection onto an unnamed trail.
15. At 3.4 miles, continue straight at the intersection.
16. After 150 feet, continue straight at the intersection.
17. At 3.7 miles, bear right on an unnamed trail up the slope to the Paseo del Bosque Trail.
18. After 100 feet, continue straight across the Paseo del Bosque Trail and down the slope to the footbridge to return to the parking area.

FIND THE TRAILHEAD

Southbound on I-25, take exit 227 onto the frontage road to Candelaria Road NW (2nd stop light). Turn right onto Candelaria Road NW.

Northbound on I-25, take exit 226A onto the frontage road to Candelaria Road NW (4th stoplight). Turn left onto Candelaria Road NW.

Follow Candelaria Road NW for 3.5 miles to the entry road to Rio Grande Nature Center State Park. Turn right and travel 350 feet to the self-serve entry station, parking lot, and trailhead.

LA CUMBRE BREWING

La Cumbre Brewing Company is New Mexico's third largest. Their brewery and taproom is located in a vintage industrial park in central Albuquerque that was once home to four or five craft brewers (only La Cumbre and nearby Canteen Brewhouse remain). La Cumbre has a second taproom located on the west side of Albuquerque that is hikeable from the Paseo del Bosque Loop Hike route. Founder and owner Jeff Erway showed me around the brewery and told me his story.

Jeff and his wife are easterners who relocated to Gallup, New Mexico, to become teachers on the Navajo Reservation. Jeff was a music teacher, and his wife taught kindergarten. They love the outdoors (Jeff is a trail runner) and latched onto the name La Cumbre while exploring peaks in the area (La Cumbre means the peak). Jeff discovered a passion for home brewing in those times and went deep, winning many medals and competitions for his brews and becoming a beer judge. Several times, awards came with the opportunity to collaborate with professional brewers in the area, and that led to Jeff's introduction to the brewing business. As the craft beer scene developed in New Mexico, he noticed what he considered a gap. No one was making what he thought of as a top-flight IPA.

Jeff eventually earned credentials in fermentation science through an American Brewer's Guild program and learned his chops as a professional brewer at Albuquerque's Chama River Brewing and Marble

Brewery. The out-of-the-box vision for La Cumbre was to fill that IPA gap, and that resulted in La Cumbre Elevated IPA, the brewery's flagship beer that accounts for 55% of its sales. Elevated is an intense, hop-forward beer that is a Great American Beer Festival Gold Medal winner. Jeff told me that the success of the beer is 100% dependent on freshness to present its distinctive character. Jeff spoke with obvious pride about his quality and consistency-driven team led by himself and two other key employees he considers equals when it comes to making the beer. Attention to detail and precision brewing processes were evident from a walk through the brewery.

La Cumbre was founded in 2010 at the current brewery location, although they have expanded the facility considerably since that time. The building looks like a warehouse with a small fenced seating area, a curbside food truck, and a grain silo outside. All around are anonymous-looking industrial buildings. Inside, there is a well-worn, dark, funky ambiance, and the place was busy. This is an old-school taproom—no restaurant here. One wall displays an array of Great American Beer Festival and World Beer Cup recognitions.

Although IPA was the brewery's starting point and its bread and butter, Jeff also expressed a love for what he called "beer like grandfather used to drink." "Beer-flavored beer" that is clean and easy drinking is another passion of his. I got the impression that he is deeply respectful of brewing history and tradition but has no fear of innovation. La Cumbre offers seven core beers supplemented by a purposeful complement of seasonals and special brews. Other than Elevated IPA, core beers include A Slice of Hefen, Malpais Stout, Acclimated APA, Project Dank IPA, Blue Corn Mexican Lager, and "Beer" (a flavorful light lager and another GABF Gold Medalist). Seasonals carry names like Wild Story Hazy IPA, Munich Dunkel, Azul Oscura Dark Blue Corn Mexican Lager, Mosaic West Coast IPA, Fudge It! Chocolate Ale, Jet Pilot Pale Ale, and Dortmunder Lager. There are also special releases, including various hazy double IPAs and barrel-aged beers.

There is no shortage of breweries to visit for a post-hike in Albuquerque. Marble Brewery, Bosque Brewing, Boxing Bear Brewing, Ex Novo, Tractor Brewing, Sidetrack, Flock of Moons, Rio Bravo, Ponderosa, and Native American-owned Bow and Arrow Brewing Co. are just a few. We enjoyed dinner and a nice dunkel around the corner from La Cumbre at Canteen Brewhouse.

CONTACT INFORMATION

Rio Grande Nature Center State Park
2901 Candelaria Rd., NW
Albuquerque, NM 87107
+1 (505) 344-7240

BREWERY/RESTAURANT

La Cumbre Brewing
3313 Girard NE
Albuquerque, NM 87107
Distance from trailhead: 4 miles

SANTA FE RIVER

TAPROOM TO TAPROOM HIKING IN OLD SANTA FE

STARTING POINT	OBJECTIVE
TUMBLEROOT BREWERY & DISTILLERY TAPROOM	SANTA FE RIVER, SANTA FE RAILYARD DISTRICT, ADDITIONAL TAPROOMS
BEER	HIKE TYPE
PATIO PALE ALE	EASY, URBAN HIKE
FEES	SEASON
NONE	YEAR ROUND
MAP REFERENCE	DOG FRIENDLY
USGS 818690	YES, LEASHED
DURATION	LENGTH
3 HOURS	7 MILES
LOW POINT / HIGH POINT	ELEVATION GAIN
6,673 FEET / 6,956 FEET	285 FEET

ALCOHOL 5.5% CONTENT

PALE ALE

COPPERY AMBER

HINTS OF CITRUS AND HOPPINESS

CLEAN MALT BACKBONE WITH A TOUCH OF BITTERNESS

BITTERNESS
IBU: 40

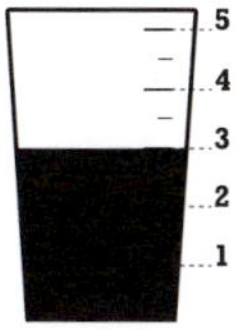

SWEETNESS

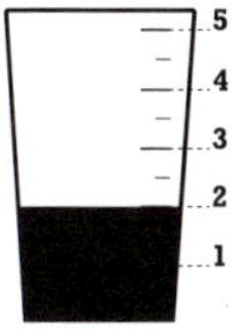

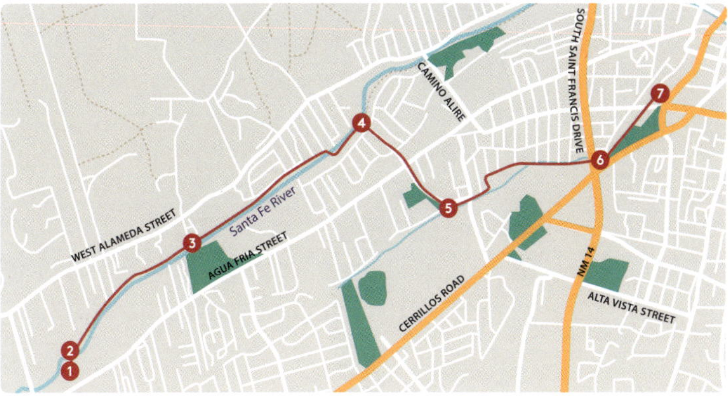

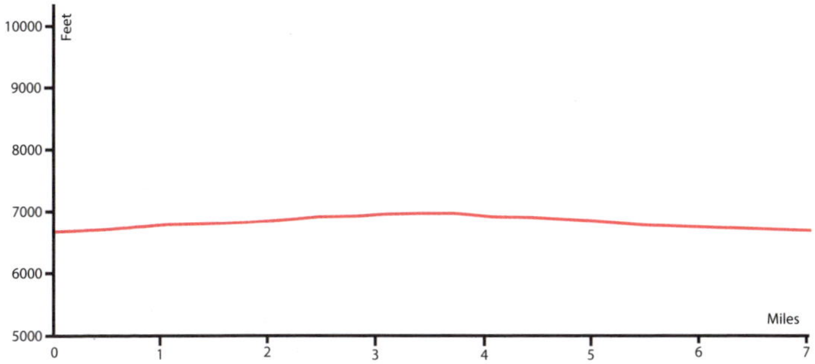

HIKE DESCRIPTION

From Tumbleroot to taprooms: a hike into old Santa Fe

Santa Fe is the oldest capital city in the United States, founded in 1610 by the Spanish. To this day, it is a place where Indigenous Puebloan traditions, Spanish colonization, Mexican rule, and, lately, American influence merge to manifest what many call "the city different." Various aspects of this unique heritage are palpable on a hike from Tumbleroot Brewery's Agua Fria Taproom to the vibrant Santa Fe Railyard District near the old city center. The route follows the last part of the journey travelers walked hundreds of years ago along the Santa Fe River into the city, well before there was a bustling railyard.

The route begins at Tumbleroot Brewery & Distillery's Agua Fria Taproom, a local favorite known for its lively atmosphere, live music, and family-friendly vibe. Before Tumbleroot, this spot was the legendary Club Alegría, a cultural cornerstone for decades. The taproom resides in the historic village of Agua Fria, a community along the Santa Fe River that boasts settlements dating back to 7000 BCE. Tumbleroot, established in 2018, carries on this legacy, serving its beers, spirits, and cocktails with organic, garden-grown, and wild-harvested ingredients, adding another layer to the rich tapestry of this location.

Tumbleroot has created a short, dirt connector pathway from the back of its parking lot to join with the Santa Fe River Trail after crossing the now intermittent stream. Alternately called the Camino Real Trail, it

generally follows part of the historic route that once connected Mexico City to Okay Owinghe Pueblo at the confluence of the Chama and Rio Grande Rivers 30 miles to the north. This ancient route, used by Native Americans for millennia, evokes images of trade, migration, and cultural exchange. The multi-use trail is paved, making for easy walking as the trail meanders through the river landscape, crossing via a pedestrian bridge. The area along the route is home to cottonwoods, elms, native shrubs and grasses, birds, lizards, and other small animals.

The Santa Fe River Trail is part of the Santa Fe River Greenway project, a 15-mile continuous greenway. Flowing from the Sangre de Cristo mountains that tower above Santa Fe, the river was a perennial stream that provided important support for people, agriculture, and wildlife. While its flow was extensively changed in the past, the Greenway project is a joint effort between the city and county that has been working to restore the river with natural materials and native plants, creating a continuous greenway with parks and trails. El Camino Real Park, Romero Park, and Frenchy's Field are parks along the Greenway.

A second part of the route is on the Acequia Trail, another paved path that winds through mid-town Santa Fe toward the center. This 1.4-mile trail, a peaceful interlude through old neighborhoods, follows the Acequia Madre, a historic irrigation ditch that has nourished the landscape for centuries. The use of acequias is an important remnant of a traditional approach to sharing scarce water resources in this arid region for community benefit. The link between the river trail and the Acequia Trail is a short walk along Avenida Cristobal Colon, much of it through Larragoite Park.

The final leg of the route is on the Santa Fe Rail Trail, another paved multiuse pathway along the route of the historic Atchison, Topeka, and Santa Fe Railway as it nears the center of the city. The arrival of the

railroad in 1880 marked a turning point for Santa Fe, transforming its economy and society and replacing travel by horseback and stagecoach. There is still activity on the rails, and as you walk it, a New Mexico Rail Runner train may rumble past. The Rail Runner is a heavy rail commuter train connecting Santa Fe with Albuquerque and other points south. Our route ends in the Railyard District, a bustling commercial area with shops, galleries, a farmers' market, museums, and the historic depot. The Nuckolls Brewery and a taproom of the Second Street Brewery are right on the route, and the Brakeroom, a taproom of the Santa Fe Brewery, is close by. The center of Santa Fe is a short walk away on city streets.

The area surrounding Santa Fe has numerous additional hiking opportunities, from foothills to mountain trails to desert highlands to spectacular desert canyons. Check out the expansive Galisteo Basin Preserve (40 miles of trails), the varied trails of the Dale Ball system (25 miles of trails), the full length of the Santa Fe Rail Trail to Lamy (nearly 17 miles), and excursions into the Pecos Wilderness from the ski basin.

TURN-BY-TURN DIRECTIONS

1. From the trailhead at the back of the Tumbleroot Brewing Company parking lot, pass through the opening in the fence and follow the dirt path that switchbacks down to the river channel. Cross the channel and ascend the incline on the other side to the paved El Camino Real Trail. If the channel is flooded, the hike can be started from nearby Frenchy's Field, a city park with parking and a pedestrian bridge.
2. After 400 feet, turn right onto the paved El Camino Real Trail.
3. At 0.8 miles, continue straight on the El Camino Real Trail at the intersection with the Frenchy's Field pedestrian bridge.
4. At 1.7 miles, leave the trail and turn right onto Avenida Cristobal Colon. Continue straight along this city street for four blocks.
5. At 2.3 miles, turn left onto the paved, multi-purpose Acequia Trail and cross a footbridge over the acequia.
6. At 3.1 miles, pass through the pedestrian tunnel under St. Francis Drive and turn left at the junction with the Santa Fe Rail Trail.
7. At 3.5 miles, reach the Santa Fe Railyards. The Second Street Brewery Taproom and Nuckolls Brewing Company will be on your right. When ready, retrace the route back to Tumbleroot Brewing Company Taproom, where you started.

FIND THE TRAILHEAD

From the Cerillos Road exit on I-25, travel north on Cerillos Road for 4.7 miles, and turn left onto Siler Road. Travel 0.65 miles to Agua Fria Street and turn right. Travel 1,200 feet and turn left into the Tumbleroot Brewery and Distillery Taproom entrance. The trail begins at the back of the Tumbleroot parking lot.

TUMBLEROOT BREWERY AND DISTILLERY

Stepping into Tumbleroot Brewery & Distillery's Agua Fria taproom is like walking into a combined community center, nightclub, and beer venue. Housed in the historic Club Alegría building, the taproom was hosting a silent auction as a benefit for a local when we arrived during happy hour. The large, open space, with a lit-up stage and dance floor, hints at the many events that unfold here, from live music and DJs to artist markets and fundraisers. The decor is part woodsy rustic charm and part modern comfort.

Jason Kirkman, co-owner with his wife Angela, told me he was a homebrewer since the 1990s, he has a background in biochemistry, and he taught elementary school before gravitating into professional brewing gigs. Tumbleroot was founded in 2018 with the concept "of place," firmly underpinning the idea: I gathered that "of place" means that everything fits with the location. The use of organic, garden-grown, and wild-harvested ingredients, the seasonal beer and cocktail menu, and connections to the community and local environment are all part of that ideal.

From the beginning, Tumbleroot has had multiple locations. The brewing and distilling operation is located just south of town in a small industrial park. The original taproom on Agua Fria Street is the rebirth of a locally famous roadhouse called Club Alegría that operated there for decades. Additional taprooms are the Pottery Pub in the old Santa Fe center and at the brewery. At the Pottery Pub, you can combine trying out the beer and spirits in unique ceramic serviceware with fashioning your own clay creations. Food offerings are simple pub fare designed for fast service. Music events at the Agua Fria taproom routinely draw as many as 450 people. Food trucks supplement Tumbleroot's own offerings.

Tumbleroot's 10-barrel brewhouse and distillery operation was created for flexibility and allows them to produce a diverse range of beers and spirits. Everything from lagers, Belgian-styles, American-styles, and dark beers. While their focus is on draft beer, they also release some seasonal, bottle-conditioned brews, including cask-aged sours, and strong ales matured in spirit barrels come and go on the menu. Although small by brewery standards, they are one of the larger distillers in New Mexico, making vodka, rums, whiskies, gins, and agave spirits. Their spirits and cocktails often use organic and wild-harvested ingredients and incorporate herbs and botanicals from Angela and Jason's garden.

Of course, I was there for a beer. The rotating beer menu featured ten beers on tap with names like Sunrise Lager, Sunset Hazy IPA, Helles, Smoked Porter, Golden Bear IPA, Honey Double Imperial IPA, and a Belgian Tripel. A couple of seasonal specials Jason talked about being particularly fond of are Funk Farm (farmhouse ale) and a high-octane Molé Stout.

There are multiple craft breweries and craft beer venues in the Santa Fe area. Nuckolls Brewing, Second Street Brewery, and Santa Fe Brewing Company (New Mexico's oldest and biggest brewery) have locations right along our hike route. Rowley Farmhouse Ales, Beer Creek Brewing Company, and Hidden Mountain Brewing Company are other places to give a try.

CONTACT INFORMATION

Santa Fe County
Open Space Parks and Trails
240 Grant Ave.
Santa Fe, NM 87501-2061
+1 (505) 992-9873

BREWERY/RESTAURANT

Tumbleroot Brewery and Distillery
2791 Agua Fria St.
Santa Fe, NM 87507
Distance from trailhead: 0 miles

LOS ALAMOS MESA

MOUNTAIN HIKE WITH EXPANSIVE VIEWS AND A BREWERY EN ROUTE

STARTING POINT	OBJECTIVE
LOS ALAMOS CANYON RIM TRAIL TRAILHEAD	PUEBLO CANYON
BEER	HIKE TYPE
HOPPENHEIMER IPA	MODERATE
FEES	SEASON
NO	YEAR-ROUND
MAP REFERENCE	DOG FRIENDLY
HELLO.HELVETIQ.COM/BHSR	YES. LEASH REQUIRED
DURATION	LENGTH
2.5 HOURS	6 MILES
LOW POINT / HIGH POINT	ELEVATION GAIN
7,024 FEET / 7,322 FEET	580 FEET

ALCOHOL
7.2%
CONTENT

AMERICAN IPA

CLEAR, RICH, GOLDEN COLOR

HOPPY-NOSE

HOPPY, GRAPEFRUIT

BITTERNESS
IBU: 100

SWEETNESS

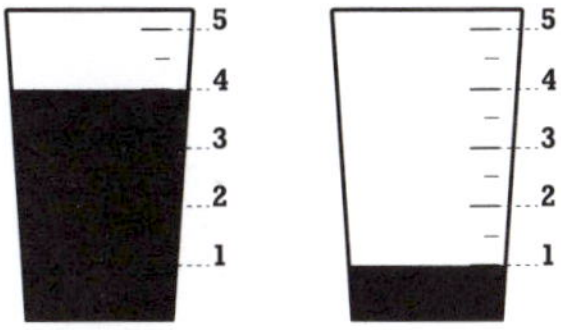

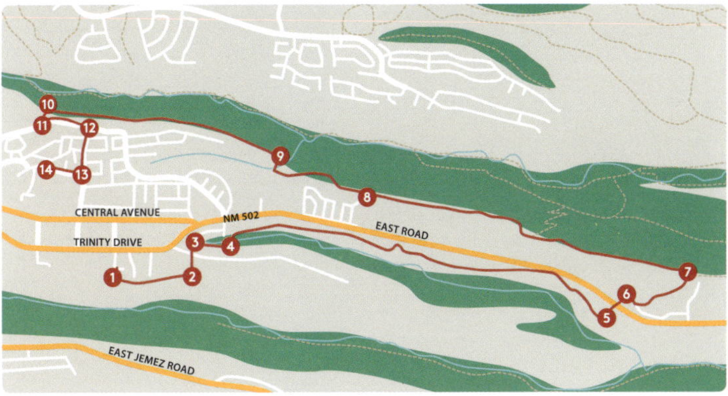

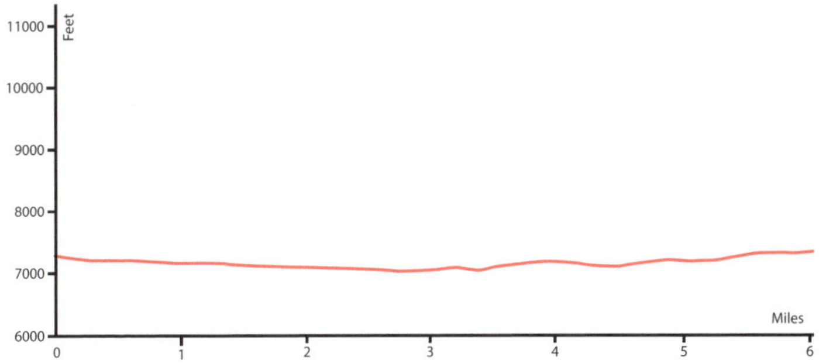

HIKE DESCRIPTION

The Los Alamos Beer Hike route traverses the rim of Los Alamos Mesa on a combination of the Los Alamos Canyon Rim Trail and the Pueblo Canyon Rim Trail. The elevation exceeds 7,000 feet for most of the hike, which ends at Bathtub Row Brewing in downtown Los Alamos, which is one of the few craft breweries in the US organized as a co-op.

Steep drops into the adjacent canyons are close by nearly every step of the way along the route. The Los Alamos Canyon Rim Trail is a paved segment through piñon, juniper, and ponderosa pine woodlands. Two large pedestrian bridges punctuate this trail. There are big views to the Sangre de Cristo Mountains to the east, the Jemez Mountains behind, and the Los Alamos National Laboratory's Linear Accelerator facility across the canyon.

After 2.2 miles, the trail turns sharply, passes through a pedestrian tunnel underneath NM Highway 502, and emerges at the Los Alamos Co-op grocery— an excellent drink/snack/deli opportunity. From this point, the route proceeds on the dirt, single-track Pueblo Canyon Rim Trail curling around the end of the airport runway. The Los Alamos Airport is a lightly used general aviation airport. For the next 1.25 miles through piñon/juniper woodlands, the route follows the airport fenceline affording expansive views into Pueblo Canyon and the sheer cliffs on the other side.

Just past the airport, the route drops into a forested area climaxing at the views at Graduation Point, overlooking Pueblo Canyon and Sangre de Cristo peaks to the east. This is a great spot to sit and ponder birds soaring below you over the forested canyon. Pueblo Canyon Trail continues into denser ponderosa pine forest that offers glimpses of the Guaje Ridge ahead. After a mile, a single-track spur trail leads back up into the downtown and the brewery.

As the home of the Manhattan Project during World War II, Los Alamos is a place of world-changing history that continues to be the home of a massive scientific laboratory. You can learn about other historical periods in the downtown, including Puebloan Indian culture, the homesteader era, and the days of the Los Alamos Ranch School. Los Alamos is a gateway to three National Parks: Bandelier National Monument, the Valles Caldera National Preserve, and the Manhattan Project National Historic Park. The trail system includes hundreds of miles of federal, state, and county lands.

Bathtub Row is just one of several craft beer venues in downtown Los Alamos. Others include the Boese Brothers Taproom (Albuquerque-based craft brewery and distillery), the Pajarito Brew Pub (local pub and eatery with a large beer selection), and even the Atomic taproom embedded within the liquor department of the Smith's Marketplace supermarket. A short walk (0.4 miles) through downtown Los Alamos gets you back to your vehicle, where you started the hike.

TURN-BY-TURN DIRECTIONS

1. Park near the trail access in the Smith's Marketplace parking lot. The paved trail runs all along the south edge of the parking area.
2. At 0.3 miles, the trail makes a sharp bend to the left.
3. At 0.5 miles, the trail makes a sharp bend to the right.
4. At 0.6 miles, the trail makes a sharp turn to the left and crosses a pedestrian bridge over DP Canyon.
5. At 2.2 miles, turn left and pass through a pedestrian tunnel beneath NM Highway 502.
6. At 2.4 miles, turn right and walk 350 feet on Entrada Drive to a small parking area and trailhead on the left (north) side of the road. A sign identifies this as the start of the Pueblo Canyon Rim Trail, a dirt single-track.
7. At 2.7 miles, continue straight onto the Pueblo Canyon Rim Trail as it curls around the end of the fenced Los Alamos Airport. The trail follows the fence line.
8. At 4.0 miles, bear right on an unpaved pathway that dips into a wooded area just past the airport terminal and parking.
9. At 4.5 miles, you reach Graduation Point, a spectacular scenic overview of Pueblo Canyon. Continue straight on Pueblo Canyon Rim Trail (this section is also called the Jim Billen Memorial Trail).
10. At 5.4 miles, turn left and ascend a spur trail with a sign pointing to Canyon Road.
11. After 400 feet, turn left (east)at the T junction and walk to the crosswalk at Canyon Road and 15th Street.
12. Cross Canyon Road heading south on 15th Street for three blocks to Nectar Street.
13. Turn right (west) on Nectar and proceed one block. Bathtub Row Brewery will be right in front of you.
14. At 6.0 miles, arrive at Bathtub Row Brewery. The walk from the brewery back to the Smith's Marketplace parking lot is about 0.4 miles through downtown streets and walkways.

FIND THE TRAILHEAD

Turn south onto Knecht Street from Trinity Drive in downtown Los Alamos. The street curves sharply to the left into the Smith's Supermarket parking area at the beginning of the Los Alamos Canyon Trail. Hiker parking is allowed in this area.

BATHTUB ROW BREWING CO-OP

Bathtub Row Brewing Co-op is one of just a few cooperative breweries in the USA. Bathtub Row Brewing is a non-profit organization founded in 2008 by local homebrewers and beer lovers who wanted to create a social place in the community to enjoy good beer. The name is a nod to the brewery's location adjacent to a historic area called "Bathtub Row." At the time of the Manhattan Project, there were only a few bathtubs in the community. There were plenty of showers, but to luxuriate in one of the few bathtubs required a visit to a house on "Bathtub Row."

The professionally staffed brewery has grown steadily since its founding and now has over 500 members. Bathtub Row brews a core set of flagship beers as well as an interesting line-up of seasonals and specials including ales, IPAs, stouts, lagers, and sours.

In addition to its solid beer line-up, Bathtub Row is a popular spot for socializing. The brewery's dog-friendly taproom and beer garden have become a true community hub. The setting under big trees, communal seating options, and the policy allowing your own food and snacks are true to the ideals of classic beer gardens, making it one of the best beer gardens I can think of in the US.

CONTACT INFORMATION

Los Alamos County
1000 Central Avenue
Los Alamos, NM 87544
(505) 662-8333

BREWERY/RESTAURANT

Bathtub Row Brewing Co-op
163 Central Park Square
Los Alamos, NM 87544
Distance from trailhead: 0.4 miles

ANIMAS RIVER

STROLL THROUGH A BOSQUE TO WHERE TWO RIVERS MEET

STARTING POINT	OBJECTIVE
BERG PARK EAST PARKING & TRAILHEAD	CONFLUENCE OF THE ANIMAS AND SAN JUAN RIVERS
BEER	**HIKE TYPE**
PIÑON HILLS PILS	EASY
FEES	**SEASON**
NO	YEAR-ROUND
MAP REFERENCE	**DOG FRIENDLY**
FARMINGTON RIVER WALK TRAIL NM	YES
DURATION	**LENGTH**
2.5 HOURS	7.5 MILES
LOW POINT / HIGH POINT	**ELEVATION GAIN**
5,244 FEET / 5,329 FEET	141 FEET

ALCOHOL 4.5% CONTENT

PILSENER

PALE, GOLDEN

SLIGHT HOP AROMA

NICELY BALANCED MALT AND HOPS. CLEAN, CRISP

BITTERNESS

IBU: 20

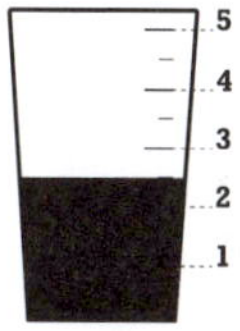

SWEETNESS

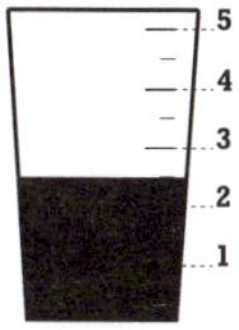

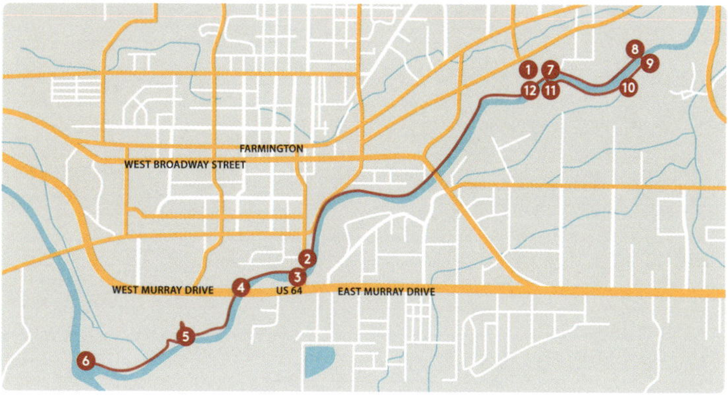

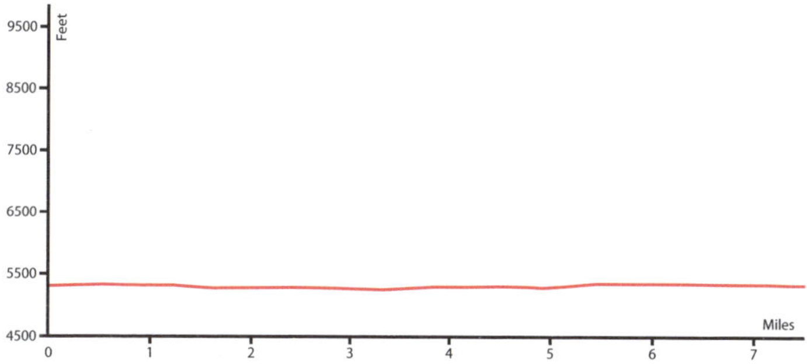

HIKE DESCRIPTION

Animas River Trail is a popular exercise and recreation route for nature lovers, winding through several miles of riverside bosque near the Three Rivers Brewery in downtown Farmington, New Mexico.

Nestled amidst several miles of riverside bosque (an oasis of forest in arid regions), the Animas River Trail offers a captivating blend of exercise, recreation, and exploration. The trail takes you along the picturesque Animas River, where ancient cottonwood trees create a canopy of shade, providing respite from the warm New Mexican sun.

As you embark on this hike, you'll be immersed in the beauty of the bosque, which is a Spanish word for forest. The Animas River Trail is a mosaic of diverse plant life, vibrant bird species, and wildlife that thrive along the riverbanks. Keep your eyes peeled for majestic bald eagles soaring overhead, herons standing tall and proud, and busy beavers working in the water.

The trail surface alternates between paved and packed earth, making it accessible to hikers of all abilities. As you meander alongside the river, you'll encounter historic landmarks like the All Veterans Memorial in Berg Park, featuring a floating stone globe suspended over water. Rotating it reveals stars signifying the United States' involvement in conflicts worldwide. It is a solemn, optional stop along the way.

These are the last few miles of the Animas River, which, in addition to providing some pleasant hiking, is a place for fishing, rafting, and kayaking and is a vital source of water for agriculture in the region. A turnaround place along the hike is where the waters of the Animas dump into the San Juan River. Both rivers flow into New Mexico from their origins in the San Juan Mountains in nearby Colorado. The San Juan eventually joins the Colorado River further west.

Along the hike, you'll come across a historic hydroelectric plant, a testament to a vision of using the river's power for human purposes. The water still forms a big cascade as it empties back into the river, but the turbine building has seen better days. It is unclear whether it is still operational or just an artifact of human activity in the bosque.

Another highlight of the Animas River Trail is the Riverside Nature Center, a hidden gem for nature enthusiasts who want to dive deeper into understanding this bosque ecosystem. Eagles, herons, and over 135 other species of birds live along the river here. During open hours, knowledgeable staff and volunteers are on hand to provide insights into local flora and fauna.

You can walk the whole route up and back, or you can park at the brewery and fashion a loop route by cutting across to the river along a half mile of city streets. You can also shorten the hike by turning around at any point. Whether seeking a leisurely stroll, an invigorating workout, a profound connection with the natural world, or just to work up a substantial thirst, the Animas River Trail has something for everyone. Embrace the beauty of Farmington's natural landscape and create lasting memories on this enchanting trail.

TURN-BY-TURN DIRECTIONS

1. Park in the Berg Park parking area and follow signs to the trailhead.
2. Travel west on the trail 0.7 miles to an underpass under US Highway 64 Business Route.
3. Continue on the trail 1 mile to Boyd Park and an underpass under South Miller Avenue.
4. Travel 0.3 miles to another underpass under US Highway 64.
5. Travel 0.5 miles to the base of a stairway and switchback leading up a small bluff. A kiosk at the top of the bluff marks Lehmer's Lookout.
6. Travel 0.7 miles to reach a point on the river where the Animas joins the San Juan River flowing from the east.
7. Retrace the route for 3.2 miles to Berg Park where you joined the trail near the parking lot.
8. Travel 0.4 miles east on the trail to a pedestrian bridge crossing the Animas River.
9. Turn right and cross the bridge to the trail intersection immediately on the far side of the bridge.
10. Turn right again and travel east along the river for 0.1 miles to a pedestrian bridge crossing a drainage channel.
11. Cross the bridge and travel straight for 0.4 miles to another pedestrian bridge crossing the Animas River
12. Cross the bridge back over the Animas River, take a left on the trail, and follow the short spur 0.1 miles back to the parking area.

FIND THE TRAILHEAD

From San Juan Boulevard, turn south on South Tucker Road and travel 700 feet to River Road. Turn right on River Road and follow it 0.3 miles to where it ends at the trailhead parking lot.

THREE RIVERS BREWERY

Three Rivers Brewery reuses a 100+-year-old former pharmacy and soda fountain building on a prominent corner in the center of Farmington while retaining plenty of historic charm. Founder and owner John Silva started with a brewery restaurant in 1997. Over the years, the operation expanded down the block to add a "Brewstillery" lounge, a pizzeria, and a tap and game room space with an outdoor patio. They added a distillery in 2017. The enterprises each have their separate entries and operating practices but leverage the core brewery operation. They all share an interest in history, with artifacts throughout, including a huge collection of vintage beer mats and labels on display. One-of-a-kind vintage photographs, posters, and framed documents adorn the walls.

The third river referenced in the brewery's name—the La Plata—also joins the San Juan further downstream from where the Animas joins.

One server recommended their biggest seller: the Three Rivers Piñon Hills Pils. It is a crisp, clean lager perfect for post-hike refreshment. There was a welcoming atmosphere, and the crowd was mostly locals. Families were enjoying lunch, friends were catching up, and several cyclists celebrated a successful ride.

Three Rivers takes pride in using high-quality ingredients, many sourced regionally in New Mexico and Colorado. They focus on crafting approachable and sessionable beers, meaning they're easy to drink and suitable for any occasion. Their regular range of beers are branded with names like Animas Amber, Mesa Verde Porter, Arroyo Amber, and Sky High IPA. Red Apple Flyer Cider is a semi-sweet, light, and crisp cider made with real apples that pays homage to Farmington's history as a place of apple orchards. They also experiment with seasonal offerings, ensuring there's always something new to discover. These may include a hoppy India pale ale (IPA) in the summer, a pumpkin spice ale in the fall, or a strong Belgian-style holiday beer. Three Rivers does not do large-scale canning but does offer crowlers for takeaway.

Nearby Lauter Haus Brewing Company is another Farmington brewery in a former industrial building, and Rambler Taproom is a strip center outlet connected to Albuquerque's Bow and Arrow Brewery.

CONTACT INFORMATION

City of Farmington
800 N Municipal Dr
Farmington, NM 87401
(505) 599 1100

BREWERY/RESTAURANT

Three Rivers Brewery
101 E. Main Street
Farmington, NM 87401
Distance from trailhead: 0.5 miles

EL SALTO DEL AGUA CAÑONCITO

FOREST ADVENTURING WITH STREAM CROSSINGS AND MAJESTIC VIEWS

STARTING POINT	OBJECTIVE
EL SALTO DEL AGUA CAÑONCITO	THE THRONE
BEER	HIKE TYPE
KOLSCH 45	MODERATE
FEES	SEASON
$10 DAY USE PERMIT	MAY-OCT
MAP REFERENCE	DOG FRIENDLY
POSTED AT TRAILHEAD	YES - PETS ARE REQUIRED TO BE LEASHED
DURATION	LENGTH
3 HOURS	5.2 MILES OUT-AND-BACK
LOW POINT / HIGH POINT	ELEVATION GAIN
8,149 FEET / 9,516 FEET	1,378 FEET

ALCOHOL 5.5% CONTENT

KOLSCH

PALE STRAW COLOR, CLEAR

BALANCED, MILD GRAININESS

BALANCED TASTE, AN EASY DRINKER

BITTERNESS

IBU: 25

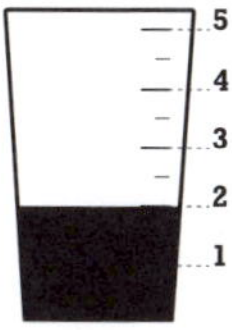

SWEETNESS

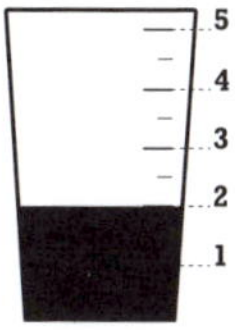

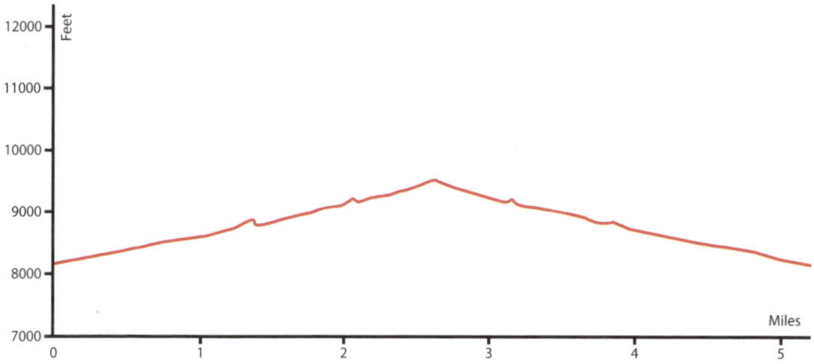

HIKE DESCRIPTION

The El Salto del Agua Cañoncito Hike is a trek through history and nature with a cold beer waiting for the finish at the nearby Taos Mesa Brewing Mothership.

The El Salto del Agua Cañoncito Trail follows a year-round stream called Arroyo Seco into a narrow canyon below the high peaks that dominate the Taos landscape. It is an out-and-back hike, so the distance can be varied by the decision of where to turn around. The ownership and land management for this trail is private, although well-behaved hikers are welcome.

The canyon is located in a wilderness area on the El Salto del Agua Land Grant, which has a rich history dating back to the 18th century. The owner and land steward is the El Salto del Agua Association, a non-profit organization formed in 1947 by descendants of Antonio Martinez, the original recipient of the Spanish land grant in 1716–1717. The vision of the association is to preserve the cultural and natural legacy of the original land grant. A kiosk at the trailhead lays out the rules of the trail, one of which is that hikers complete a liability waiver and purchase a day pass. All of this can be done using envelopes provided at the kiosk or a smartphone with PayPal or Venmo. Nearby residents purchase annual passes.

El Salto means waterfall, and *Cañoncito* means small canyon in this context, but those words seem to refer to the owner and steward of the land rather than what you will encounter on the trail. There is a well-known waterfall and cave nearby that can be reached by a short drive and a different trail. And the canyon containing Arroyo Seco isn't really small, depending on what you compare it to. There is plenty to experience, though.

The trailhead is at 8,150 feet altitude (2,484 m), and the first half of the hike is a steady ascent following the Arroyo Seco. The canyon walls climb steeply on either side of the trail and are heavily forested with fir and aspen. Expect a beautiful hike, though, as you crisscross back and forth over the stream. Don't expect bridges or anything formal like that. More like well-placed step stones and logs. We hiked in September and didn't get our boots wet even though we lost track of how many stream crossings there were.

Along the way, the forest occasionally gives way to views of dramatic outcroppings. At one point, the stream and the trail curl around a massive stone cliff before continuing to ascend. The turnaround place for the hike described in this chapter is called "the throne." Along the route, we stopped to chat with a local who told us that this was a common turnaround point. The throne is a place where someone assembled an array of flat rocks into a hard-surfaced lounge chair in a tranquil setting with a great view. A fine place for a snack before the descent back down the canyon to head to the Taos Mesa Brewing Mothership.

TURN-BY-TURN DIRECTIONS

1. From the trailhead kiosk, follow the path upstream. The path is well-worn and easy to follow. There are no intersecting trails along the route, although there are occasional diversions where people have tried to find better stream crossings. There is no signage along the route. Follow the well-beaten path and resist ad hoc cut-throughs the best you can. If you are heading upstream, you are on course.
2. Pick a turnaround point that suits you. The turnaround point at "the throne" is reached at 2.6 miles. Follow the trail back to the trailhead.

FIND THE TRAILHEAD

From Taos, take Highway 64 north 4 miles to the intersection with NM Highways 522 and 150. Take a right onto Highway 150 toward Taos Ski Valley and continue 4.8 miles to the village of Arroyo Seco. In the village of Arroyo Seco, turn right onto El Salto Road and continue 1.7 miles to the Cañoncito Trailhead. Obey all signs indicating appropriate parking.

TAOS MESA BREWING MOTHERSHIP

The Taos Mesa Brewing Mothership is located along US Highway 64 on what locals refer to as "the mesa." The Mothership is the original location where brewing operations take place. The brewery also has a taproom pub near the center of Taos a block or so walk from the Taos Plaza.

The Mothership opened in 2012 in a repurposed hangar-type building with creative metalwork features that reflect the artsy nature of the town. Both food and beer are offered. Bar bites, burgers, sandwiches, and salads are offered. The brewery suffered through a fire a few years ago, when the interior was reimagined and rebuilt into a modern-feeling space—it had been Taos-funky previously. The pleasant and shady outdoor space has big views across the mesa to the high peaks. In summer, both local and national acts perform at the amphitheater outside.

The TMB beer list features a rotating selection of 16 taps. Typically, 12 are pouring in-house brews, and the others are guest taps. Like most breweries these days, tasters are available either individually or in a flight. Featured beers include names like Amarillo Rojo (a red ale), Koenig Lager (Helles), Black Widow Porter, Great Scot Scottish Ale, Mesa IPA, and Green Chili Kolsch. I settled on a Kolsch 45 as a thirst quencher, and it did not disappoint.

A must-see if you've never been is the nearby Rio Grande Gorge Bridge. At 650 feet (200 m) above the river, it is the second-highest bridge on the U.S. Highway System and the fifth-highest bridge in the United States.

CONTACT INFORMATION

El Salto del Agua Association, Inc.
Po Box 2987
Taos, NM 87571
(505) 398 0090

BREWERY/RESTAURANT

Taos Mesa Brewing Mothership
20 ABC Mesa Road
El Prado, NM 87529
Distance from trailhead: 10 miles

TOLBY CANYON

STUNNING VIEWS AND HANDCRAFTED BEERS ON A HISTORIC RANCH

STARTING POINT	OBJECTIVE
TOLBY TRAILHEAD	TOLBY CREEK
BEER	HIKE TYPE
HOMESTEAD AMBER	MODERATE
FEES	SEASON
NM STATE PARK DAY USE FEE (CURRENTLY $5 PER VEHICLE)	MAY–OCTOBER
MAP REFERENCE	DOG FRIENDLY
TRAILS ILLUSTRATED 730: TAOS, WHEELER PEAK	YES
DURATION	LENGTH
3 HOURS	8 MILES
LOW POINT / HIGH POINT	ELEVATION GAIN
8,061 FEET / 9,359 FEET	1,480 FEET

ALCOHOL 4.7% CONTENT

AMBER ALTBIER

DEEP AMBER

MALTY WITH FLORAL NOTES

MALTY WITH A SUBTLE HOP FLAVOR AND A FLORAL FINISH

BITTERNESS IBU:25

SWEETNESS

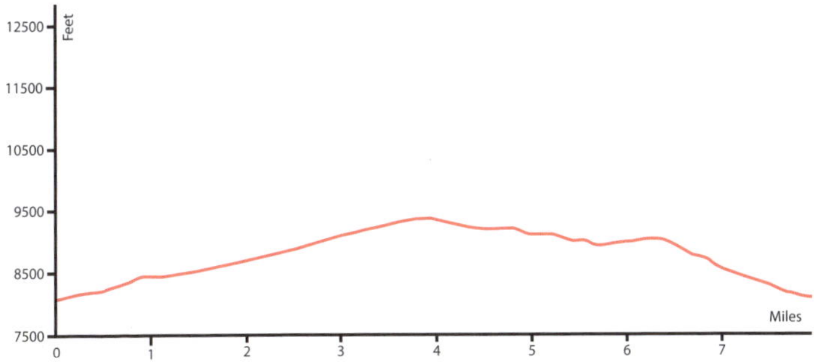

HIKE DESCRIPTION

The Tolby Canyon Loop mixes hiking in a riparian canyon with a hike ridge with views opening to the highest New Mexico peaks.

The lower trail is a single track following the creek and is largely shaded. The upper trail is a closed forest road with sun exposure but great views.

The canyon is fenced and gated at the trailhead and there is an informal parking area spread out among the trees. A permanent corral structure inside the gate suggests this may be a popular place to ride horses, although we didn't encounter any. The trailhead sits at an elevation of 8,000 feet (2,438 m) just off U.S. Highway 64. Tolby Creek, a year-round stream, flows into the Cimarron River near the trailhead at a point just below the dam that forms Eagle Nest Lake.

Proceeding up the canyon along the stream, the trail passes through stretches of thick, jungly undergrowth, fir and aspen forest, and occasional open meadows. There are multiple stream crossings, usually at places where a small culvert passes under the trail. The altitude gain is mostly gentle but steady as the trail ascends the narrow canyon floor. There is a strong scent of pine needles and damp earth. Filtered sunlight dapples the trail, painting shifting patterns on the forest floor.

The path is well-worn and easy to follow. Tolby Creek gurgles melodically as it tumbles over moss-covered rocks. Plentiful bird calls and occasional bear scat are reminders of the wildlife in the canyon. The connector to Upper Tolby Road and the loop back to the trailhead is a large side canyon with an intermittent stream. Another single-track path ascends to the road.

The Upper Tolby Road follows a high contour that enables fantastic westward views into the Moreno Valley. Mount Wheeler and other high peaks near Taos rise in the distance. There are glimpses of Eagle Nest Lake, a popular destination for fishing and boating. Eventually, the route begins to descend, winding its way back down towards the canyon floor. The descent is steep in places, providing a good challenge to the "brake muscles" in the legs. As the route rejoins Lower Tolby Trail near the end of the loop, you'll be greeted by the familiar sound of Tolby Creek. Once you reach the water, you'll cross a small wooden bridge and rejoin the main trail, completing your loop.

On the short way back to the trailhead, I was already anticipating a well-deserved reward—a cold, refreshing beer at the nearby Comanche Creek Brewing Company.

TURN-BY-TURN DIRECTIONS

1. From the trailhead gate, follow the path upstream.
2. At 0.2 miles, you reach the junction with Upper Tolby Road to the left. Continue straight on the single-track pathway following the creek.
3. At 2.8 miles, you reach a large side canyon branching to the left. Turn left on a single-track path proceeding into the side canyon.
4. At 3.4 miles, the path intersects with Upper Tolby Road, a closed dirt-surfaced forest road. Turn left and proceed.
5. At 7.8 miles, you return to the junction with the Tolby Creek Trail and turn right to return to the trailhead.

FIND THE TRAILHEAD

From Eagle Nest, New Mexico, drive east on U.S. Highway 64 for 2.6 miles. The entry to the parking area at Tolby Trailhead is on the right side of the road and is marked with a sign.

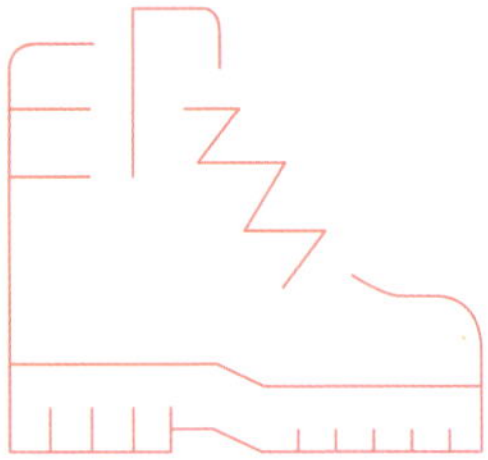

COMANCHE CREEK BREWING COMPANY

Comanche Creek Brewing Company is a small family-owned brewery nestled in the heart of the breathtaking landscape of the Moreno Valley. It is located along NM Highway 38, about 1.9 miles north of the village of Eagle Nest. When I first visited this brewery it was housed in a log cabin way back on a dirt road. The cabin was a structure built long ago by the owners' ancestors. The brewery was jammed into the structure, but the owners made and served tasty beer in an unforgettable setting. Since then, the brewery has been relocated to a larger log structure right off the highway. There are spectacular panoramas in every direction.

Inside, the atmosphere is comfortable and friendly. When I was there, locals came and went, striking up conversations with the beertender and with each other. The taproom features eight handles with names like Homestead Amber, Creekside Blond, Touch-Me-Not IPA (named for a mountain overlooking the brewery), and Ol' Smokey (a brown ale with a hint of smoke). Comanche Creek is primarily an ale brewery, but the owner told me he does brew an occasional lager. A sunny terrace complements the space when the weather is good.

The Homestead Amber Ale is the flagship brew. The style is a German altbier, and is very well executed. It is a full-bodied beer that the brewer, Kody Mutz, describes as having "sweet maltiness with a subtle hop flavor and a floral finish."

Comanche Creek Brewing Company was established in 2010 on Kody's family's 1880s-era ranch. The family heritage is German, which led to interest in German brewing traditions and visits to Germany. The move to the new facility was made in 2019. The brewhouse is a three-barrel

system, and the brewery makes about 100 gallons of beer in a typical week. Most of the sales are on-site, although they do distribute to a restaurant in Eagle Nest from time to time.

CONTACT INFORMATION

Cimarron Canyon State Park (Colin Neblett Wildlife Area)
28869 Highway 64
Eagle Nest, NM 87718
+ 1 (575)-377-6271

BREWERY/RESTAURANT

Comanche Creek Brewing Company
5 Comanche Creek Road
Eagle Nest, NM 87718
Distance from trailhead: 5 miles

DOUBLE DRAW

FOREST LOOP TO THE HIGHEST-ALTITUDE BREWERY IN NEW MEXICO

STARTING POINT	OBJECTIVE
RED RIVER BREWING COMPANY	RED RIVER
BEER	HIKE TYPE
CATSKINNER IPA	MODERATE
FEES	SEASON
NONE	JUNE–OCTOBER
MAP REFERENCE	DOG FRIENDLY
TRAILS ILLUSTRATED 730: TAOS, WHEELER PEAK	YES (LEASH ADVISABLE)
DURATION	LENGTH
2.5 HOURS	3.6 MILES (LOOP)
LOW POINT / HIGH POINT	ELEVATION GAIN
8,642 FEET / 9,118 FEET	650 FEET

ALCOHOL 7.8% CONTENT

AMERICAN IPA

LIGHT BROWN

FRUITY NOTES

HOPPY WEST COAST IPA MADE WITH MOSAIC HOPS

BITTERNESS
IBU: 70

SWEETNESS

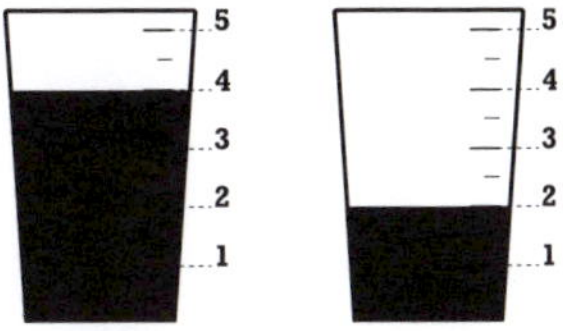

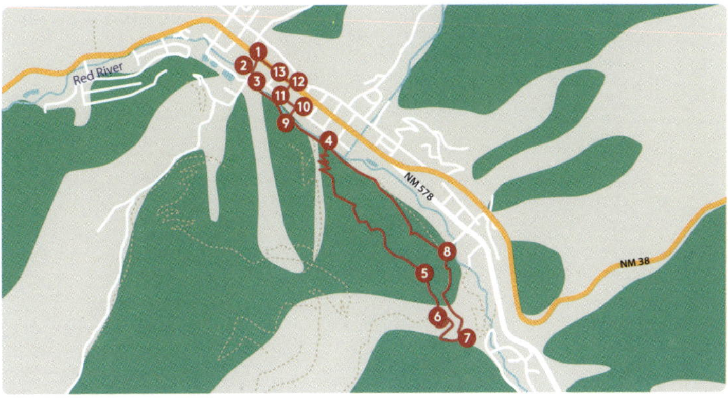

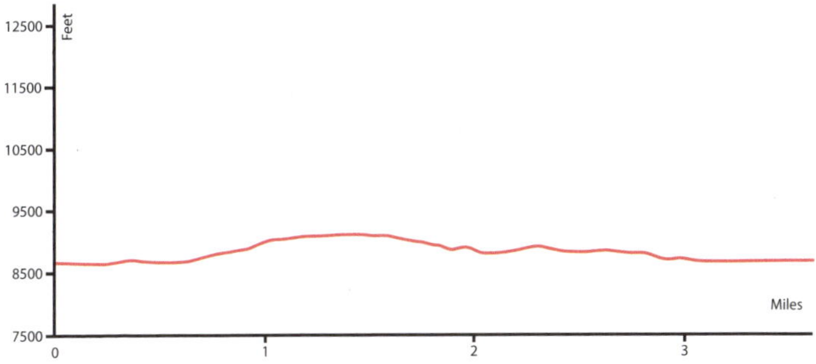

HIKE DESCRIPTION

Escape to the enchanting mountain village of Red River, New Mexico, where outdoor adventures and small-town charm await, and reward yourself with a refreshing craft beer after a scenic hike.

Red River is a picturesque mountain village (pop. 520) in a narrow valley of the Sangre de Cristo Mountains of northern New Mexico. It offers a nice blend of outdoor activity and small-town charm. In the winter, there is skiing and snowboarding at the Red River Ski Area. During the other seasons, hiking, mountain biking, fishing, and camping are popular activities. Red River is a tourist town with more than 550,000 visitors per year, many coming from western Oklahoma and Texas flatlands. Events and festivals are a year-round feature as well.

The Double Draw Beer Hike is a 3.6-mile (5.8-km) loop route starting and ending at Red River Brewing Company near the center of Red River, New Mexico. It's a moderately challenging route that starts at 8,650 feet (2,635 m) altitude and gains 650 feet (200 m) to reach the highest point. The trails that make up this route are popular with hikers, birders, and dog walkers. We didn't encounter many other people along the way, but we weren't there during Red River's busiest time (summer and ski season).

The start of the route follows the Red River Nature Trail along the river at the base of the ski area. After a short distance, the nature trail intersects with the Double Draw Loop Trail. This is a forest trail climbing through pine, fir, and aspen forest before looping back down the mountainside into town. As we ascended, we were greeted by occasional fall wildflowers. The flowers would be plentiful in summer. Occasional openings in the forest offer rewarding views of the Red River valley and the surrounding mountains.

A connecting trail to Goose Lake Road leads to the loop back on a segment of the Fence-line Trail. There are multiple options for shorter and longer variations of the hiking route. The Red River Brewing Company owner, a cartographer by trade, offers an excellent map of area trails at the brewery.

TURN-BY-TURN DIRECTIONS

1. From the brewery entry, walk west on Main Street for two blocks and turn left onto Pioneer Trail.
2. Proceed one block to the corner of Pioneer Trail and River Street. Turn left onto River Street.
3. After 50 feet, you will see a marker for the beginning of the Nature Trail on the right side of the street. Turn onto the Nature Trail.
4. At 0.6 miles, turn right and proceed upslope on the Double Draw Loop Trail on a series of switchbacks.
5. At 1.5 miles, there is a signed intersection showing the Double Draw Loop Trail taking a left. Proceed to the right on a spur leading to Goose Lake Road.
6. At 1.7 miles, turn left downslope onto Goose Lake Road.
7. At 2.0 miles, take a sharp left onto a single-track trail heading west.
8. At 2.5 miles, bear left at an unsigned intersection to rejoin the Double Draw Loop Trail.
9. At 3.3 miles, turn right and cross the covered pedestrian bridge over the Red River back into town.
10. At 3.4 miles, turn left onto River Street.
11. Walk one block and turn right onto Jumping Jack Trail.
12. Proceed two blocks and turn left onto Main Street.
13. Walk one block to the brewery entry.

FIND THE TRAILHEAD

The hike starts and ends at Red River Brewing Company near the center of Red River.

RED RIVER BREWING COMPANY AND DISTILLERY

Completing the Double Draw Loop sets the stage for a well-deserved reward at the Red River Brewing Company. Established in 2018, this family-run establishment is the first and only brewery and distillery in Red River (the distillery tasting room is just up the street). The owners, Mike and Sharon Calhoun, have strong roots in the community, Mike having grown up here. Mike's family goes back three generations. His grandfather Glenn started and ran a grocery in the 1960s and also started a real estate business that Mike's father, Ted, ran for many years. Mike's mother, Linda, was also involved in the real estate business and became a multi-term mayor of Red River. Mike's brother Brian is an architect who designed the 9,000-square-foot brewery and restaurant on a prime family property in the town center. Mike and Sharon's son Chris, a bio-engineer, became the first head brewer. Their other son Steven, an industrial designer and artist, designed the brewery's logo, tap

handles, and artistic features. The whole idea for Red River Brewing was conceived at a family gathering over a beer at (no surprise) a brewery.

Red River Brewing claims to be one of the highest-altitude breweries in the world, as well as the third-highest-altitude distillery in the world—this may be hard to prove, but it's among the highest I have ever visited! There are comfortable indoor and outdoor spaces with great views of the surrounding mountains. The atmosphere is "mountain casual." The 350-seat restaurant serves lunch and dinner in addition to beer and spirits. The menu of pub snacks, soups, salads, sandwiches, brewery tacos, and other comfort food offers something to please everyone.

A wide range of beers, from classic lagers and ales to more experimental brews, is offered from 18 taps. The flagship beer and best seller is Catskinner IPA, an American IPA. Other beers on tap when I visited included Lazy Bear Blonde (for converting West Texans to craft beer drinkers), Angry Bear Blonde, Pumpkin Pistachio Porter, Butter Pecan ESB, Greenie Peak Witbier, Swingtown Pineapple Milkshake IPA, Copper Chair Amber Ale, Imperial Cream Ale, Cranberry Sour, Freedom 65 Pale Ale, and Sweet Potato Casserole Stout.

LAND MANAGER

Carson National Forest
208 Cruz Alta Road
Taos, NM 87571
+1 (575) 758-6200

BREWERY/RESTAURANT

Red River Brewing Company and Distillery
217 W Main St
Red River, NM 87558
Distance from trailhead: 0 miles

COLORADO

CORTEZ

A PEACEFUL DESERT TOUR THROUGH CANYON OF THE ANCIENTS

STARTING POINT	OBJECTIVE
SAND CANYON TRAILHEAD	ASSORTED RUINS
BEER	HIKE TYPE
SCHNORZENBOOMER AMBER DOPPELBOCK	EASY-MODERATE
FEES	SEASON
NO	MARCH TO NOVEMBER
MAP REFERENCE	DOG FRIENDLY
CANYONS OF THE ANCIENTS ON BLM.GOV	YES (LEASH REQUIRED)
DURATION	LENGTH
2-3 HOURS	5.5 MILES
LOW POINT / HIGH POINT	ELEVATION GAIN
5,456 FEET / 5,909 FEET	550 FEET

ALCOHOL 8.5% CONTENT

AMBER DOPPELBOCK

DARK AMBER

BUTTERSCOTCH

MALT, CHERRIES

BITTERNESS
IBU: UNLISTED

SWEETNESS

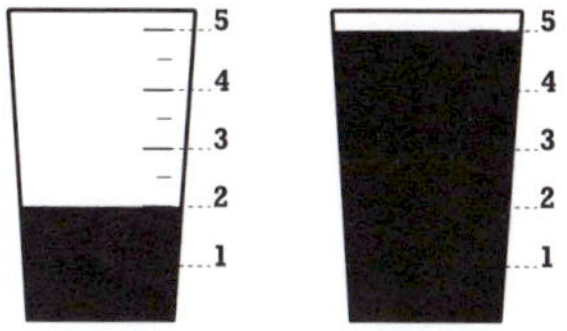

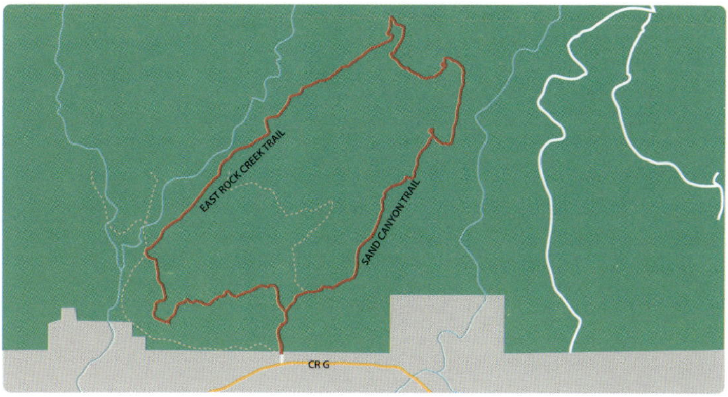

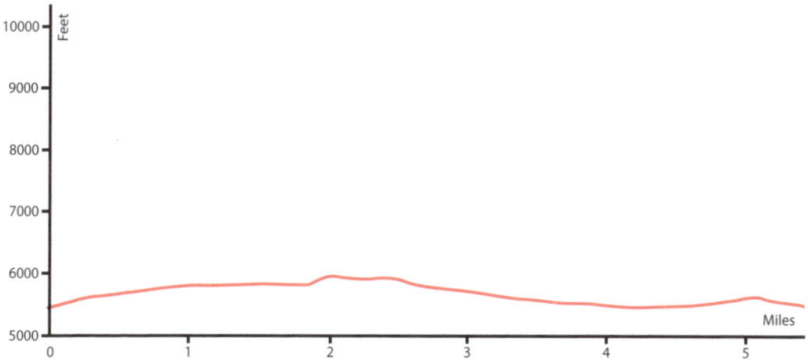

HIKE DESCRIPTION

Take a peaceful desert tour through this outdoor museum of ancient ruins before stopping in nearby Cortez for a "mesa cerveza."

Situated on the southern flank of the massive Canyons of the Ancients National Monument, this scenic loop is peppered with ancient cliff dwellings, Puebloan ruins, caves, sandstone bluffs, and sprawling canyons. It's the closest you can get to the otherworldly landscapes of Utah's famous national parks (think Bryce, Zion, and Arches) without actually crossing the state border. The Monument itself contains more than 6,000 archaeological sites and artifacts dating back a millennium to the ancient Anasazi and Puebloan people, many of whom once farmed in the valley.

The Sand Canyon trailhead is a bit of a haul from downtown Cortez, but don't let this discourage you. It's an easy, quick paved road out to the trailhead at a small slickrock parking area.

Start up the slickrock, following the orange diamonds and large cairn to a more obvious trail. You'll pass through trees on a trail with both footprints and bike tracks. (Mountain biking and horseback riding are also permitted in the Monument, so do keep an eye out.) Stay left, following the wooden posts over the slickrock.

Along the way, you'll pass small trail spurs marked with white diamonds. These frequently lead to ruins or artifacts, so be on the lookout for these and don't skip the opportunities for short, worthwhile detours before rejoining the main trail. One of the first you'll come to is the Castle Rock Pueblo.

Endless trail options exist here. If you carry a map, which you can pick up at the Anasazi Heritage Center in nearby Dolores, you can shorten or extend this loop as desired. (Major trail intersections along the loop have "You Are Here" signs with maps, too.) Carry plenty of water with you, and don't forget your hat, sunscreen, and sunglasses. Avoid this trail at the height of summer, for temperatures can be scorching and there is virtually no shade.

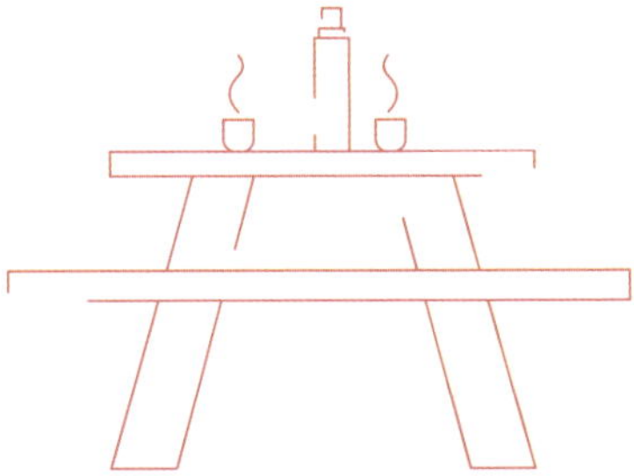

TURN BY TURN DIRECTIONS:

1. Follow the orange diamonds. White diamonds often lead to short trail spurs to ruins.
2. At 1.8 miles, go left at the junction.
3. At 2.5, go left to take the East Rock Creek Trail.
4. At 3.5, stay right; at 4.1, go left, following the blue blaze.
5. At 4.5, follow wooden posts over the slickrock.
6. At 5.25, go right to complete your loop.

FIND THE TRAILHEAD

Head south of Cortez on Highway 491 for 2.5 miles. Make a right on County Road G (signs for Hovenweep National Monument), drive 12.5 miles and find the small Sand Canyon trailhead on your right. Park on the slickrock.

MAIN STREET BREWERY

Cleverly dubbing their brews "Mesa Cerveza," the Main Street Brewery in downtown Cortez offers up an extensive line of in-house beers. Many are European-style brews, ranging from German pilsners and doppelbocks to Scottish ales and Irish stouts. For a truly one-of-a-kind experience, order one of their signature blends. These two-beer combinations are mixed at the tap, such as the "Boomerang"—a super-sweet blend of the Schnorzenboomer and their Honey Raspberry Wheat.

CONTACT INFORMATION

Canyons of the Ancients and Anasazi Heritage Center,
27501 Highway 184,
Dolores, CO 81323;
970-882-5600

BREWERY/RESTAURANT

Main Street Brewery
21 E Main Street,
Cortez, CO 81321
Miles from trailhead: 16

DURANGO

A SHORT, STEEP LOLLIPOP-LOOP HIKE AND RIDGE SCRAMBLE

STARTING POINT	OBJECTIVE
WEST END OF LEYDEN STREET	HOGSBACK
BEER	HIKE TYPE
COLORADO KÖLSCH	STRENUOUS
FEES	SEASON
NONE	MARCH TO NOVEMBER
MAP REFERENCE	DOG FRIENDLY
OVEREND MOUNTAIN PARK MAP ON DURANGOGOV.ORG	YES
DURATION	LENGTH
1.5–2 HOURS	2.5 MILES
LOW POINT / HIGH POINT	ELEVATION GAIN
6,686 FEET / 7,493 FEET	780 FEET

ALCOHOL 4.8% CONTENT

KÖLSCH

PALE STRAW

BISCUITY; HINTS OF PEAR

CRISP, DRY, FIZZY

BITTERNESS

IBU: 16

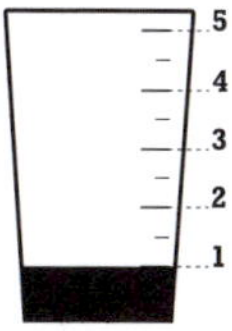

SWEETNESS

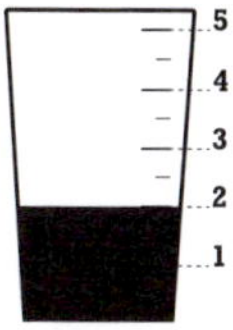

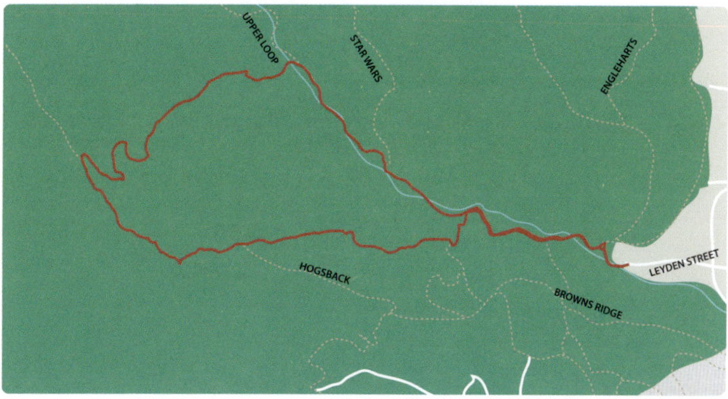

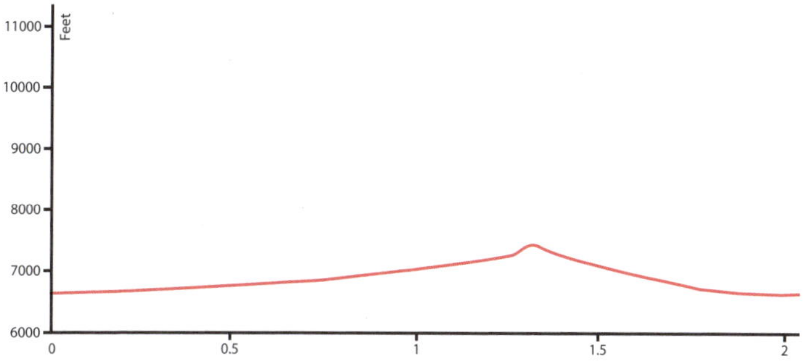

HIKE DESCRIPTION

A short, steep lollipop-loop hike and ridge scramble, rewarded with a crisp Colorado Kölsch to quench your thirst.

Hogsback Ridge looms over downtown Durango like a sleeping giant. Snaking up the spine of Hogsback is a narrow, steep trail visible from just about anywhere in town. The foothills along its flanks comprise Overend Mountain Park, a city-owned treasure of singletrack for hiking, mountain biking, and trail running. Though hiking opportunities abound in all directions, standing atop the iconic Hogsback is a veritable rite of passage for locals.

Numerous trailheads exist for Overend Mountain Park, but the easiest starting point for a short jaunt on Hogsback is the trailhead tucked into a residential neighborhood at the west end of Leyden Street. From here, trail maps are posted on signs at nearly every intersection, so it's easy to navigate as you go.

This loop option takes you up the backside of Hogsback first, following the popular Perins Gulch trail. (Watch out for mountain bikers, as the lower trails in Overend are a popular haunt for a variety of trail users.) Follow the main Perins Gulch trail through ponderosa and pinyon pines, sandy washes, and scrubby vegetation.

At 0.6 miles, you'll turn left to get on the Hogsback trail, which switchbacks gently up out of the woods, eventually popping out on the backside ridgeline of Hogsback. Enjoy the up-close view of another Durango icon, nearby Perins Peak. On the other side, you'll have a terrific view of bustling downtown Durango and the Animas River.

If you have a fear of heights or are wearing shoes that lack good traction, this is a good place to turn around and go back the way you came. The trail that lies ahead is never cliffy, but it is narrow and drops off dramatically on both sides. After veering left, you'll begin the absurdly steep hike (or scramble, in some places) to follow the spine and attain the summit. You'll know you're there when you reach the large, flat boulder affording 360-degree views.

If you know what you're looking for, you can glimpse the back deck of the Steamworks Brewing Co. from here, where a crisp, refreshing Kölsch awaits you. Facing Durango, the trail down is to the left of the boulder. This trail can feel like you're plummeting down a roller coaster, stomach drops and all. Hold it together and pick your way down the steepest parts carefully until you hit the intersection with 8 Bells. Bear left to hook back in with the Perins Gulch trail and complete your lollipop loop.

TURN BY TURN DIRECTIONS:

1. From the end of Leyden Street, follow Perins Gulch Trail.
2. At 0.4 miles, veer left to stay on Perins Gulch.
3. At 0.6, make another left onto the Hogsback trail and cross a footbridge.
4. At 1.1, pop up on the ridgeline. Go left until you reach the summit at 1.3 miles.
5. Descend steeply on the frontside Hogsback trail.
6. When you reach 8 Bells Trail, make a left to hook back in to Perins Gulch Trail and return to the trailhead.

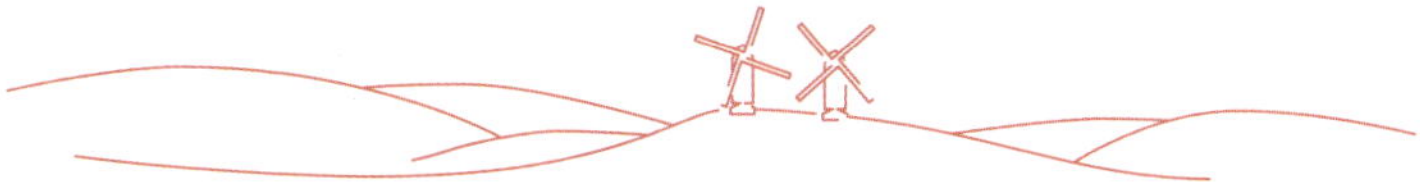

FIND THE TRAILHEAD

From downtown Durango, drive west on 9th Street. Turn right on Roosa Avenue, left on El Paso Street, right on Forest Avenue, then left on Leyden Street. The trailhead is at the end of this street. Park on the street.

STEAMWORKS BREWING COMPANY

Durango is affectionately called the "Napa Valley of Beer," as many of its breweries are among the oldest in the state. Brewing since 1996, Steamworks sports a warehouse-like atmosphere and sizable outdoor deck with a straight-shot view of Hogsback. As you quench the thirst you worked up hiking, you can enjoy gazing at exactly what you accomplished with a crisp, German-style Kölsch in hand, a perennial award winner at beer festivals around the world.

CONTACT INFORMATION

City of Durango Parks and Recreation,
970-375-7321

BREWERY/RESTAURANT

Steamworks Brewing Company
801 E 2nd Avenue,
Durango, CO 81301
970-259-9200
Miles from trailhead: 1.4

PAGOSA SPRINGS

VENTURE INTO AN OUTDOOR CATHEDRAL OF WATERFALLS

STARTING POINT	OBJECTIVE
FOURMILE FALLS TRAILHEAD	FOURMILE FALLS
BEER	HIKE TYPE
EL DUENDE VERDE CHILE ALE	EASY/MODERATE
FEES	SEASON
NONE	MAY TO SEPTEMBER
MAP REFERENCE	DOG FRIENDLY
TRAILS ILLUSTRATED 145: PAGOSA SPRINGS, BAYFIELD	YES
DURATION	LENGTH
3-4 HOURS	6.2 MILES
LOW POINT / HIGH POINT	ELEVATION GAIN
8,996 FEET / 9,895 FEET	1,080 FEET

ALCOHOL 7.3% CONTENT

PALE ALE

DARK GOLDEN, SLIGHTLY HAZY

GREEN CHILE PEPPERS, BREAD

LIGHT, DRY; SLIGHT KICK

BITTERNESS IBU: 30

SWEETNESS

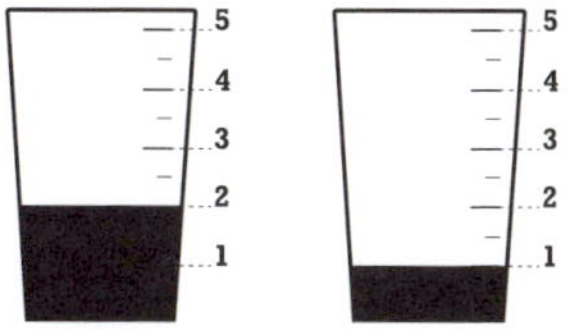

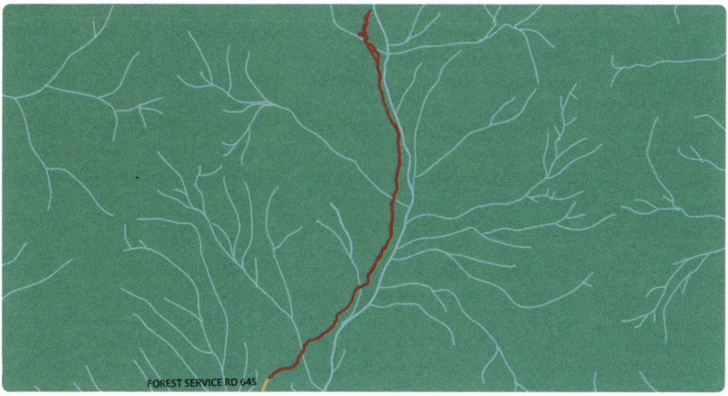

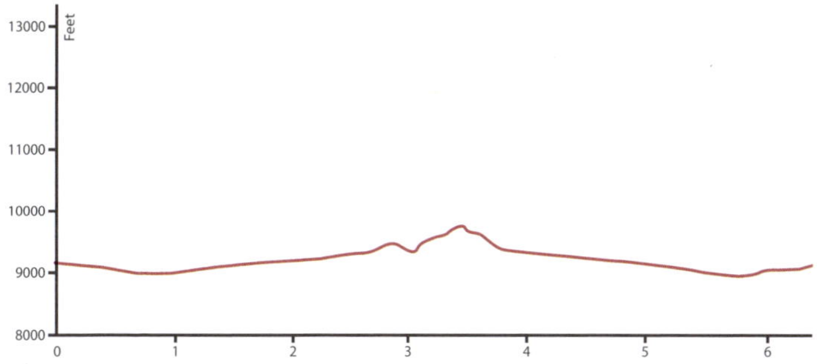

HIKE DESCRIPTION

Spice up your day with waterfalls and a green-chile-spiked pale ale in this off-the-beaten-path gem of a mountain town.

Surrounded by three million acres of wilderness areas and national forests, Pagosa Springs is the perfect base camp for adventure. It boasts multiple breweries for tasting connoisseurs, and is jam packed with mineral hot springs pools to soak weary muscles after a long day on the trail. In the winter, it's also a hit with powder hounds, thanks to its proximity (24 miles) to Wolf Creek Ski Area, which frequently receives more snow annually than any other ski area in the state of Colorado.

Nestled in the Weminuche Wilderness Area, this classic Pagosa hike is a little ways outside of town—but it's well worth the drive to the trailhead. The hike's namesake falls sit in the belly of a steep valley, flanked on all sides with prominent rocky bluffs and hoodoo-like outcroppings. You'll feel as though you're venturing into an immense outdoor cathedral.

The rocky trail begins slightly downhill, crossing some small creeks (larger in the spring). After a half-mile, you'll pass the Weminuche Wilderness Area boundary and catch your first glimpses of the looming peaks surrounding you.

Unfortunately, this area has been hit hard in recent years by beetle kill, so the pine trees are not what they used to be. Nevertheless, wildflowers abound in the summer, and prolific copses of aspen light up the valley at the height of fall.

The trail is easy to follow. Before you reach Fourmile Falls, you'll first come to the stream at the foot of the almost equally impressive Falls Creek Falls. They spill from a tall cliff to your left, with peak runoff in the late spring as Colorado's snowpack melts out of the high alpine. You'll have to crane your neck to get a good view here!

After you've had your fill, cross the creek and continue on to Fourmile Falls. You'll get an excellent view of them from the trail around 3 miles in, at which point you'll have just a couple more minutes to clamber your way up the trail to the top of them. A peaceful lunch spot awaits you next to the rushing river above the falls.

TURN BY TURN DIRECTIONS:

1. Follow the main trail; the sign says Fourmile Stock Drive Tr. 569.
2. At 0.5 miles, enter Weminuche Wilderness Area.
3. At 2.7, the trail appears to fork. Go left/up to reach creek at the bottom of Falls Creek Falls.
4. After crossing the creek, come to an intersection. Go left to get closer to the falls or go right to stay on the main trail to Fourmile Falls at 3.1 miles.

FIND THE TRAILHEAD

From downtown Pagosa Springs, head west on Pagosa Street. Turn right onto Lewis Street, then left onto N 5th Street and continue on Four Mile Road (County Road 400) for 7.5 miles. Make a right at the fork and continue another 4.5 miles on Four Mile Road, which becomes Forest Service Road #645, to reach the trailhead.

RIFF RAFF BREWING COMPANY

Don't miss "hoppy hour" at this friendly neighborhood joint on the main drag through historic downtown Pagosa. (Or visit their more recently opened second location, The Rio by Riff Raff Brewing Co, on the east end of town, for riverfront dining and drinks.) They pour their own flagships brews, guest beers, and seasonal picks such as a black cherry porter, plum wheat, and "spruce juice," brewed with locally harvested spruce tips. An environmentally forward-thinking brewery focused on "keeping the earth hoppy," Riff Raff is heated by geothermal heat from the world's deepest hot spring.

CONTACT INFORMATION
U.S. Forest Service,
Pagosa Ranger District,
180 Pagosa Street,
Pagosa Springs, CO 81147;
970-264-2268

BREWERY/RESTAURANT
Riff Raff Brewing Company
274 Pagosa Street,
Pagosa Springs, CO 81147
970-264-4677
Miles from trailhead: 13.6

SILVERTON

A STUNNING, HIGH-ALTITUDE LOOP THROUGH ALPINE TUNDRA

STARTING POINT	OBJECTIVE
CUNNINGHAM GULCH	HIGHLAND MARY LAKES
BEER	HIKE TYPE
PRIDE OF THE WEST PORTER	MODERATE-STRENUOUS
FEES	SEASON
NONE	JULY TO SEPTEMBER
MAP REFERENCE	DOG FRIENDLY
LATITUDE 40° MAPS TELLURIDE-SILVERTON-OURAY	YES (LEASH REQUIRED)
DURATION	LENGTH
5-7 HOURS	7.7 MILES
LOW POINT / HIGH POINT	ELEVATION GAIN
10,820 FEET / 12,612 FEET	1,900 FEET

ALCOHOL 5.2% CONTENT

PORTER

DARK BROWN; CARAMEL HUE

COFFEE, TOFFEE

CHOCOLATE, ROASTED MALT

BITTERNESS
IBU: 15

SWEETNESS

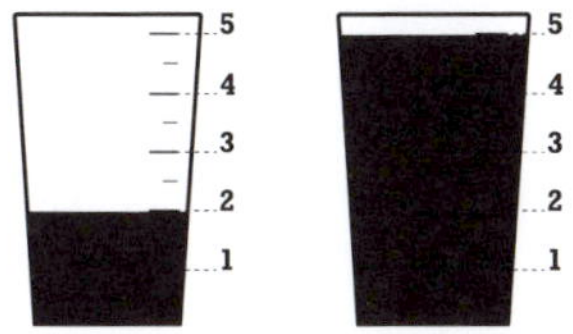

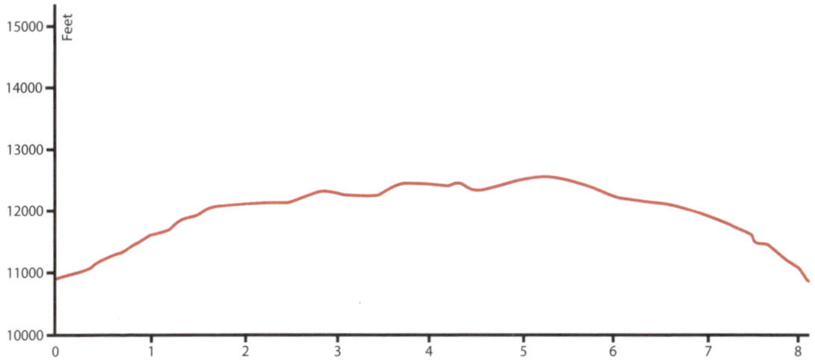

HIKE DESCRIPTION

Celebrate this stunning, high-altitude loop through alpine tundra with a rich porter in Silverton's historic district.

"Pride of the West" is a term to describe many things—a now-defunct dive bar in the historically rowdy miners' town of Silverton, the sweet porter that awaits you at the end of this hike at Avalanche Brewing Company, or the San Juan Mountains themselves—arguably one of the most impressive mountain ranges in the country.

The trailhead for Highland Mary Lakes takes a little more work than others to reach, which is perhaps why this unbelievable, high-alpine loop hike remains less crowded than other hikes in the San Juans. Along your hike, though, you'll pass everything from pristine waterfalls to meadows blanketed in wildflowers to a number of shimmering lakes.

The steepest part occurs right off the bat as you make your way up the gulch along a cascading creek on your way to the Weminuche Wilderness Area boundary. Shortly after, there are some confusing social trails. Stay on the main route by going right up over some big rocks, then left through the woods and across another a creek.

At 1 mile, a simple wooden "Trail" sign offers an ambiguous arrow. Make a hard right here across the creek. Follow cairns. In another half-mile, the trail forks. Either way will do, as they'll rejoin shortly. The left way along the creek is easiest. The right way through the talus garden is more circuitous and scrambly. Either way, soon you'll arrive at the first of the three Highland Mary Lakes.

Past the third lake, follow the wooden posts up to the ridgeline saddle. From here, you'll be able to glimpse the iconic jagged teeth of the Grenadier range's Arrow and Vestal peaks ahead of you, and Verde Lakes down to your right—a short, optional out-and-back addition. Whether or not you take this side trip, your loop hike continues by veering left (when facing the Grenadiers) at the saddle, following the wooden posts farther up the ridge.

After the Continental Divide Trail (CDT) feeds in to the trail from your right, you may see some CDT or Colorado Trail thru-hikers; your route shares a short stretch with these celebrated long-distance trails. In a little over a mile, though, you'll stay straight/left at the CDT turn-off sign to make your way back to your trailhead. In another half-mile at the signed trail fork, stay straight/right to take a different path down to the Continental Divide Trailhead, just a scoot down the road from the trailhead where you started your day.

A few final words of advice: start early in the day and do not attempt this loop if thunderstorms are forecasted, as it lies almost entirely above tree line. Also, many intersections are unmarked, so bring a topo map.

TURN BY TURN DIRECTIONS:

1. At the well-signed intersection at 0.25 miles, stay right on the main trail.
2. At 1.5, the trail forks. Stay left for the easier, more direct route.
3. Stay right around first small lake. Stay left around second, larger lake. Stay right around third. Follow wooden posts up to the saddle.
4. When you reach the saddle, either make a quick (0.5-mile) out-and-back trip to Verde Lakes to your right, or veer left to continue on the loop, following wooden posts.
5. At 5.7 (or 6.2 if you went to Verde Lakes), stay straight/left, passing the CDT sign.
6. At 6.9 (or 7.4 if you went to Verde Lakes), stay straight/right for new scenery that still loops you back to your starting point.

FIND THE TRAILHEAD

Drive northwest out of Silverton on County Road 2, which turns to gravel in 2 miles. In 2 more miles, make a right on County Road 4 and follow it to the trailhead in 5 more miles. The final mile to the trailhead is rough, so 2WD vehicles should park lower down (near the confluence of Cunningham Creek and Royal Tiger Creek) and add 2 miles to their roundtrip hike mileage.

AVALANCHE BREWING COMPANY

Avalanche Brewing Company is situated on the only paved road in all of Silverton, a true Colorado mountain town that's retained much of its quaint old Western character since its mining heyday. Soak in big mountain views from the outdoor seating in front and enjoy artisan pizza alongside an "elevated ale" or two.

CONTACT INFORMATION
U.S. Forest Service,
Silverton Field Station,
1468 Greene Street,
Silverton, CO 81433;
970-387-5530

BREWERY/RESTAURANT
Avalanche Brewing Company
1151 Greene Street,
Silverton, CO 81433
970-387-5282
Miles from trailhead: 9.2

OURAY

LITTLE SWITZERLAND'S PEAK-BAGGING BUTT-KICKER OF A HIKE

STARTING POINT	OBJECTIVE
OLD TWIN PEAKS TRAILHEAD	TWIN PEAKS
BEER	HIKE TYPE
BOX CANYON BROWN ALE	VERY STRENUOUS
FEES	SEASON
NONE	JUNE TO OCTOBER
MAP REFERENCE	DOG FRIENDLY
OURAY TRAIL GROUP HIKING TRAILS, OURAYTRAILS.ORG	YES (LEASH REQUIRED)
DURATION	LENGTH
4-6 HOURS	5.5 MILES
LOW POINT / HIGH POINT	ELEVATION GAIN
7,861 FEET / 10,801 FEET	2,900 FEET

ALCOHOL 5.6% CONTENT

BROWN ALE

DARK BROWN

CHOCOLATE, BUTTERSCOTCH

EARTHY; SWEET MALTS

BITTERNESS
IBU: 29

SWEETNESS

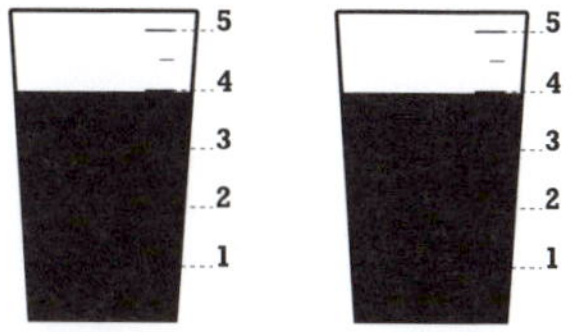

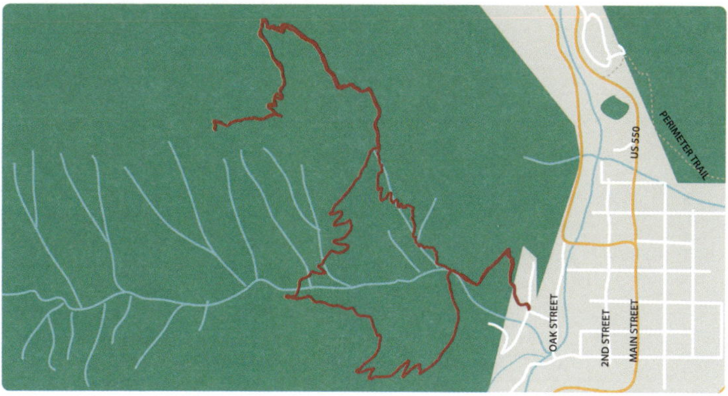

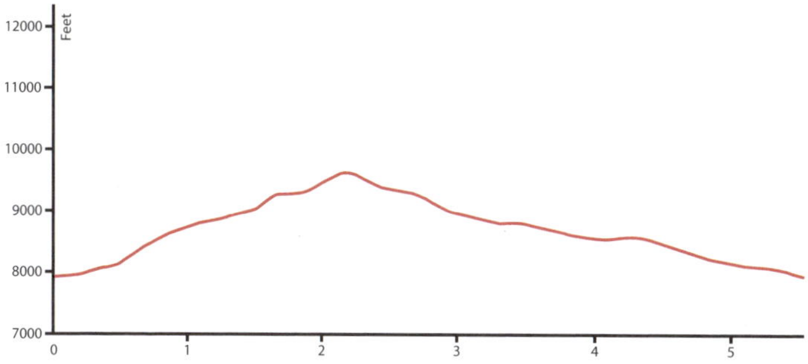

HIKE DESCRIPTION

This peakbagging butt-kicker of a hike offers a challenging, respectable preamble to your Box Canyon Brown Ale on the Ouray Brewery's sunny rooftop deck.

Nicknamed "Little Switzerland" for good reason, Ouray is an old mining town surrounded by steep cliffs, peaks, canyons, and waterfalls. In the winter, a picturesque gorge on the edge of town offers some 200 of the world's best ice and mixed climbing routes. In the summer, buttery singletrack snaking up into the surrounding mountains and canyons beckons hikers.

The rocky summits of Twin Peaks are visible from just about anywhere in town, including the sun-drenched rooftop deck of the Ouray Brewery—a can't-miss stop for locals and tourists alike on Ouray's main drag.

From the Old Twin Peaks trailhead, start up the gravel road before joining the singletrack that rapidly steepens, switchbacking up through woods, talus, and pink-tinged rock cliffs. Within a quarter mile, you'll have great views of the town below, the ice park canyon walls and, across the valley, Ouray's infamous natural "Amphitheater."

After you pass the fenced-off Henns' Overlook, the trail wraps right and you'll begin to hear the rushing rapids of Oak Creek. Look up and you'll see Twin Peaks towering above in the sky. Soon, just shy of the large bridge over Oak Creek, look to your right for two signs nailed to a tree—one that says "Old Twin Peaks Trail," one that reads (forebodingly, but accurately), "Caution: steep and difficult trail." Veer off the well-established Perimeter Trail here and up onto the narrow, rocky Old Twin Peaks trail.

From here, the trail is a butt-kicker—literally a staircase of logs and cribbing in places, passing avalanche chutes, mining ruins, lush forest, and aspen stands. At just shy of 2 miles, you'll pop out on the ridgeline with expansive views of the Camp Bird valley and the highway up to Red Mountain Pass. To your left is a scenic overlook at Sister Peak. To your right, the trail continues—a steep, loose calf-burner—up to the scrambly Twin Peaks summit. Enjoy soaring views of the Sneffels and Cimarron mountain ranges, and—if you know where to look—the rooftop deck of the Ouray Brewery where you'll soon be resting your weary legs and enjoying a cold one.

You can either return the same way you came up or, for a change of scenery and a longer but slightly more forgivingly graded descent, take the Oak Creek Trail on your way down. To do so, hang a right at the signed junction at 3.3 miles, following signs for Oak Creek. At 4 miles, cross the creek, then go left and down at the signed trail junction shortly after. (Note: at peak spring runoff in May or early June, this creek may not be passable.) At 5 miles, hang a left on the Perimeter Trail to cross the bridge over Oak Creek and return to town on the same trail you first came up.

TURN BY TURN DIRECTIONS:

1. Start up the gravel road before quickly getting on singletrack.
2. At 0.4 miles, about 50 feet shy of the bridge, veer off of the Perimeter Trail and up onto the narrow, rocky Old Twin Peaks trail on your right.
3. At 1 mile, make a left, then a right at the well-signed trail junction, following signs for Twin Peaks.
4. At 2.2, reach the summit.
5. Complete a loop by following signs for Oak Creek on your way down, then making a left on the Perimeter Trail.

FIND THE TRAILHEAD

From downtown Ouray, walk or drive west on 7th Avenue to cross the Uncompahgre River. Go right on Oak Street, then left on Queen Street until it meets Pinecrest Drive. A few parking spots exist at the trailhead.

OURAY BREWERY

With a rooftop terrace surrounded on all sides by steep canyons and dramatic mountains—including the visible dual summits of Twin Peaks—the Ouray Brewery is *the* spot to be on sunny afternoon in the San Juan Mountains. Its old-timey saloon vibe is complemented by the comfiest swinging barstools you've ever sat on and a diverse lineup of beers—many named for old local mining roads, trails, and other relics of a bygone era.

CONTACT INFORMATION

U.S. Forest Service,
Ouray Ranger District,
2505 S. Townsend,
Montrose, CO 81401;
970-240-5300

BREWERY/RESTAURANT

Ouray Brewery
607 Main Street,
Ouray, CO 81427
970-325-7388
Miles from trailhead: 0.5

RIDGWAY

SUMMIT THE *GUNSMOKE*-THEMED LOCAL FOOTHILL

STARTING POINT	OBJECTIVE
NORTH END OF RAILROAD ST.	BOOT HILL SUMMIT
BEER	HIKE TYPE
IRISH RED ALE	EASY-MODERATE
FEES	SEASON
NONE	APRIL TO OCTOBER
MAP REFERENCE	DOG FRIENDLY
DENNISWEAVERPARK.COM	YES
DURATION	LENGTH
1.5-2 HOURS	3.75 MILES
LOW POINT / HIGH POINT	ELEVATION GAIN
6,952 FEET / 7,172 FEET	220 FEET

ALCOHOL
6%
CONTENT

RED ALE

CLEAR RED/AMBER

CARAMEL

MALTY, EARTHY

BITTERNESS
IBU: 25

SWEETNESS

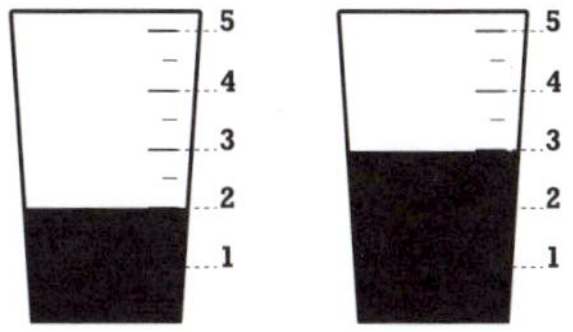

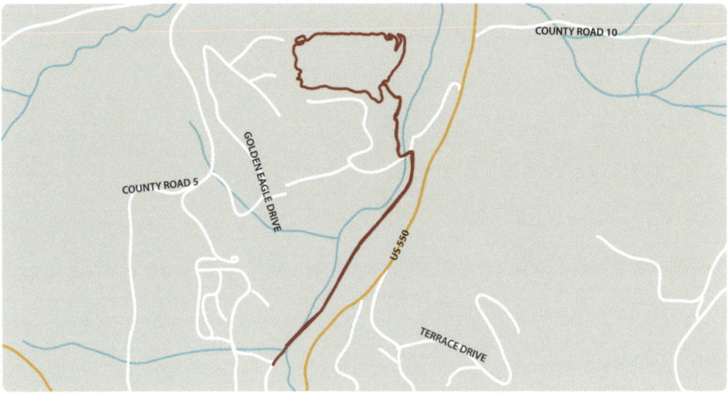

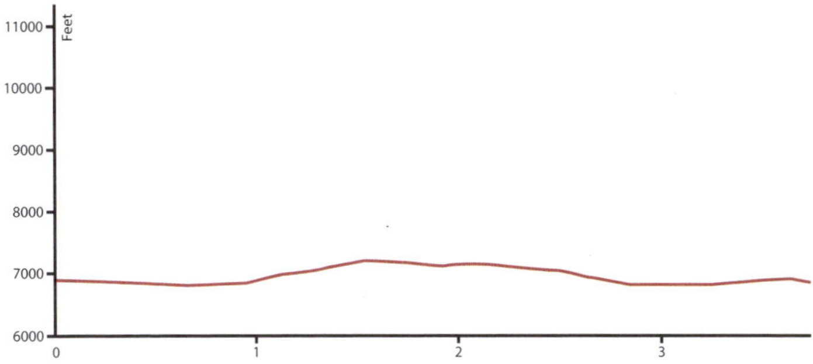

HIKE DESCRIPTION

Get a taste for the Wild West with this hike through a wildlife reserve and to the summit of Gunsmoke-themed local foothill.

The tiny town of Ridgway carries an immense amount of history, having once served as home of the Ute Indians, then in the 1890s as the railroad gateway to the nearby mining districts of Ouray, Telluride, Rico, and Durango. In the 1960s, the Hollywood movies *How the West was Won* and *True Grit* were both filmed here, and to this date, the town retains its moniker of "Gateway to the San Juans"—the majestic, craggy peaks that loom over Ridgway's southern horizon.

For some 14 years, Dennis Weaver, a longtime environmentalist and famous actor who played Chester Goode in the old TV western, *Gunsmoke*, called Ridgway home before passing away in 2006. Today, a beautiful, 60-acre park and permanent wildlife reserve dedicated in his memory exist on the northern flanks of Ridgway, sandwiched between downtown and the expansive Ridgway State Park (where further trails abound).

A paved bike-path corridor lets you walk or cycle from the edges of town to the park's central trailhead, which is otherwise accessible by car from Highway 550. Start by crossing the historic railroad bridge. From here, the bike path parallels the beautiful Uncompahgre River, where it's not uncommon to catch glimpses of wildlife ranging from deer and foxes to bald eagles and blue herons. Once you reach the Dennis Weaver Memorial Park trailhead, follow the turn-by-turn directions to hike up through fields of fragrant sagebrush toward the summit of Boot Hill. There, Dennis Weaver's son, Rick, constructed a humorous "boot hill cemetery" to pay homage to his father and several characters on *Gunsmoke*. At the summit, take time to scope out the various cowboy-boot faux tombstones and Gunsmoke-themed epitaphs, as well as the awe-inspiring views of the Cimarron mountain range to the east and the Sneffels range (including its prominent and eponymous crown jewel, the 14,157-foot Mount Sneffels) to the south.

After you complete the loop in the park and reach the Boot Hill trailhead again, take time to relax for a while on the banks of the river. There's a 2,800-pound bronze eagle sculpture to admire and an astronomically aligned medicine wheel surrounding it, decorated with cairns, prayer stones, and poetry. From here, it's not far to stroll back to town, where bar stools, picnic tables, and a host of friendly locals at the Colorado Boy brewpub will help you feel right at home.

TURN BY TURN DIRECTIONS:

1. Head north on the bike path to cross the bridge over the river.
2. Follow the bike path for 0.8 miles, then go left over the bridge and make a right onto the Dennis Weaver Park Stagecoach Trail.
3. At 1.06, go left at the signed junction, following signs for Boot Hill Summit.
4. At 1.14, go right.
5. At 1.5, reach Boot Hill summit. Continue down over the backside onto the River Sage Scenic Loop Trail. Stay right to stay on the singletrack.
6. At 2.5, stay straight, then make a right at 2.6 to finish the lollipop loop.

FIND THE TRAILHEAD

This hike incorporates a walk on a bike path from the edge of town to the official Boot Hill trailhead in Dennis Weaver Memorial Park, so start by making your way to the north end of Railroad Street. There is a small gravel parking lot next to the bike path you'll take.

COLORADO BOY PUB AND BREWERY

Pull up a stool at this "wee humble pub," located in a historic 1915 brick building in the old section of downtown Ridgway. The seating area indoors is small, but seats at the oak bar provide glimpses of the brewing equipment. (On nice days, picnic tables let crowds spill out onto the town sidewalks.) The brewpub relies on wind-powered electricity and hot water from solar collectors on the roof to make its craft ales and artisan pizza. Growlers and 32-oz. "cowboy cans" are available to go.

CONTACT INFORMATION

Town of Ridgway,
201 N. Railroad St.,
Ridgway, CO 81432;
970-626-5738

BREWERY/RESTAURANT

Colorado Boy Pub and Brewery
602 Clinton Street,
Ridgway, CO 81432
970-626-5333
Miles from trailhead: 0.5

TELLURIDE

HIKE ALONGSIDE THE TUMBLING RAPIDS OF THE SAN MIGUEL RIVER

STARTING POINT	OBJECTIVE
TRAILHEAD ON SAN MIGUEL RIVER ROAD	KEYSTONE GORGE
BEER	**HIKE TYPE**
FACE DOWN BROWN ALE	MODERATE
FEES	**SEASON**
NONE	APRIL TO OCTOBER
MAP REFERENCE	**DOG FRIENDLY**
KEYSTONE GORGE LOOP TRAIL ON SANMIGUELCOUNTYCO.GOV	NO
DURATION	**LENGTH**
1-1.5 HOURS	2.5 MILES
LOW POINT / HIGH POINT	**ELEVATION GAIN**
8,182 FEET / 8,710 FEET	528 FEET

ALCOHOL
5.7%
CONTENT

BROWN ALE

DARK BROWN

MALTY; CHESTNUTS, TOFFEE

SMOOTH;
ROASTED COFFEE BEANS

BITTERNESS
IBU: 37

SWEETNESS

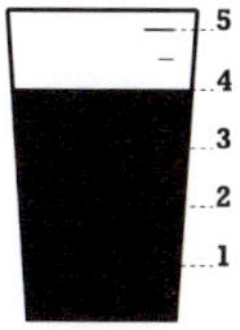

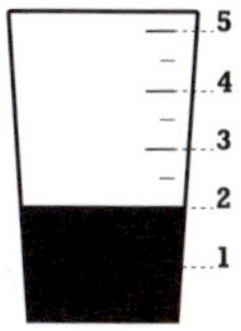

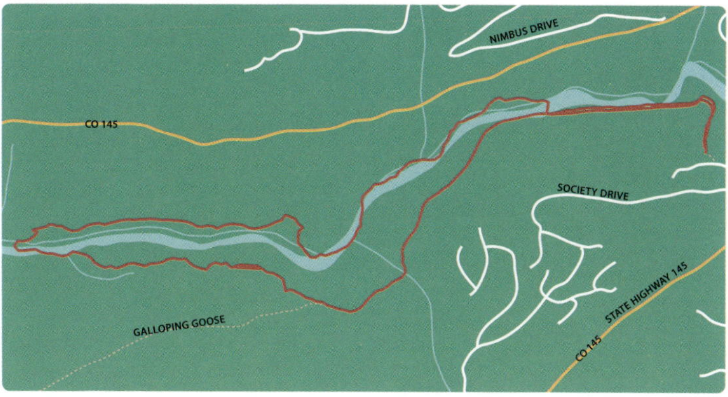

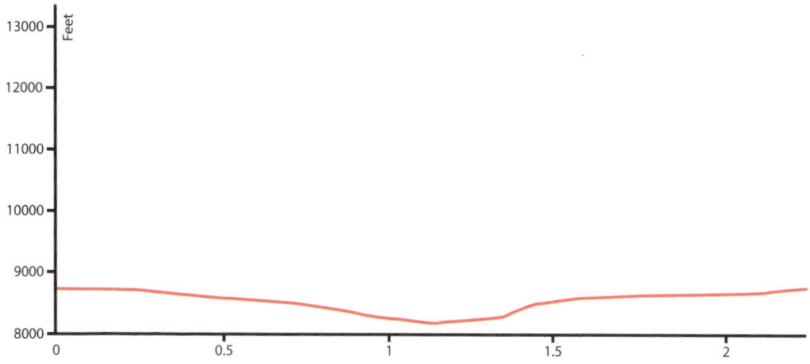

HIKE DESCRIPTION

Hike along the tumbling rapids of the San Miguel River before sampling an award-winning brown ale made from the same snow melt that fuels the river.

The picturesque mountain town of Telluride sits tucked away into the back of a jaw-dropping box canyon. It's known as much for its epic ski runs as its summer festivals, including favorites like the Telluride Bluegrass Festival and, for the beer aficionados, Telluride Blues & Brews. Beer culture comes baked in to most ski towns anyway, but not every ski town boasts a brewery that regularly earns the kind of international accolades that Telluride Brewing Company reels in.

One of the highest microbreweries in the world at 8,750 feet, Telluride Brewing Company sits three miles west of downtown Telluride in a satellite community called Lawson Hill. It's on the west end of the Valley Floor, a large tract of land acquired in 2007 by the town of Telluride to be preserved for the public and undeveloped.

While tourists often flock to the iconic day hikes accessible from town itself—Bear Creek and the Jud Wiebe—the Keystone Gorge loop offers a quiet respite from such crowds. This lovely lollipop loop dips down into a river gorge, rather than climbing in elevation, which makes it a great early- or late-season hike when other trails are snowed in. It crams in a lot in a few short miles, including relics from the town's mining days—scattered artifacts and ruins, as well as several abandoned mine entrances.

Shortly after crossing the first footbridge over the river, you'll catch a fleeting glimpse of Wilson Peak, which should look familiar if you've ever looked at a can of Coors beer. As the singletrack winds down along the river, you'll toe the edges of high bluffs before dropping down next to the river. Watch your footing, as the trail grows narrow and loose in places. The trail hugs the river's edges, so enjoy the clamor of the rapids by your side as they gush over boulders and spill toward the neighboring Ilium Valley. The woods here are lush and cool.

At the lower suspension bridge, there's a picnic table and some rock beaches for relaxing in the glow of the afternoon sun. On the south side of the loop, you'll pass through more conifer forest before popping out into stands of aspen that look aflame come late September or early October. Pop out on the railroad-grade Galloping Goose Trail (named for the motorized railcars that once ran here, when the Rio Grande Southern Railroad still existed in the 1950s), which will take you back to your starting point where the brewery awaits.

TURN BY TURN DIRECTIONS:

1. Go down the gravel hill and stay left to parallel the river on doubletrack going west.
2. At 0.25 miles, go right over the bridge, then left to follow Keystone Gorge loop.
3. At 1.1, cross the lower bridge and hang a left.
4. At 1.6, go left onto the Galloping Goose Trail.
5. At 2, pass the original junction with the upper bridge; stay straight to finish the lollipop loop.

FIND THE TRAILHEAD

From the town of Telluride, drive west for 3 miles, make a left at the roundabout onto Highway 145, then a right onto Society Drive. After passing the brewery, turn right onto San Miguel River Road. The trailhead, signed for the Galloping Goose and Keystone Gorge, is just behind the Lawson Hill bus circle on your right-hand side. It's also possible to take the free Galloping Goose bus here, or walk or bike from town via the paved bike path or singletrack trails across the Valley Floor.

TELLURIDE BREWING COMPANY

Formed by best friends, adventure buddies, and longtime beer enthusiasts Chris Fish and Tommy Thacher, Telluride Brewing Company opened its doors in 2012. Its popular Face Down Brown has taken home the gold three times at GABF (Great American Beer Festival) and the World Beer Cup. Though TBC has greatly expanded its production and distribution all across Colorado and more recently Arizona, their beers are not currently available outside of the Southern Rockies region.

CONTACT INFORMATION

San Miguel County Parks & Open Space,
333 W Colorado Avenue,
3rd Floor, Telluride, CO 81435;
970-369-5469

BREWERY/RESTAURANT

Telluride Brewing Company
156 Society Drive,
Telluride, CO 81435
970-728-5094
Miles from trailhead: 0.2

PALISADE

A CLIFF-EDGE TOUR OF ANCIENT PETROGLYPHS AND ROCK FORMATIONS

STARTING POINT	OBJECTIVE
RAPID CREEK TRAILHEAD	PALISADE RIM
BEER	HIKE TYPE
DIRTY HIPPIE DARK AMERICAN WHEAT	STRENUOUS
FEES	SEASON
NONE	FEBRUARY TO NOVEMBER
MAP REFERENCE	DOG FRIENDLY
PALISADE RIM TRAIL ON COPMOBA.ORG	YES
DURATION	LENGTH
2-3 HOURS	5.2 MILES
LOW POINT / HIGH POINT	ELEVATION GAIN
4,724 FEET / 5,617 FEET	850 FEET

ALCOHOL 5.3% CONTENT

AMERICAN WHEAT

MEDIUM-DARK BROWN

FAINT CARAMEL

LIGHT, MALTY, CHOCOLATE

BITTERNESS

IBU: 17

SWEETNESS

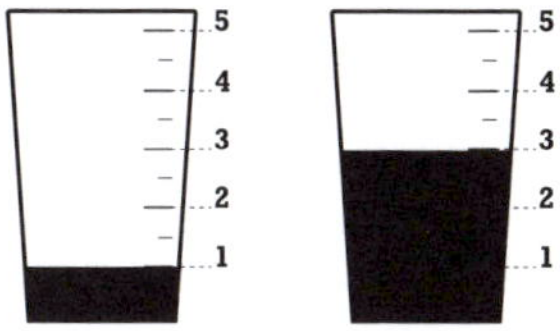

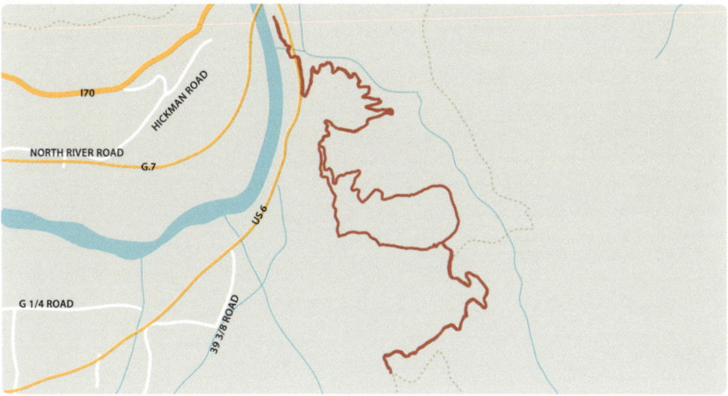

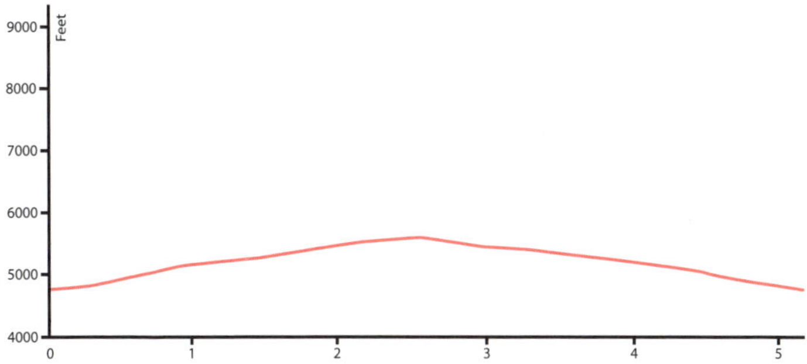

HIKE DESCRIPTION

Hike high above the vineyards and orchards of Grand Valley on a cliff-edge tour of ancient petroglyphs and rock formations.

There may be no better part of Colorado to work up your appetite and thirst than the town of Palisade. Thanks to its relatively low elevation, sunny climate, and six-month-long growing season, it's well situated for the many farms, ranches, vineyards, orchards and roadside fruit stands that call Palisade home. From July to September, local orchards harvest countless tons of giant, juicy Palisade peaches that are famous and highly sought all over the American West.

This cliff-side jaunt offers the best bird's-eye views of Palisade's patchwork farms and vineyards and the Colorado River below. Utilizing trails built only recently (read: not yet on many people's radar screens) after the granting of a land easement for public recreational use, this loop provides near-constant panoramic views of the Grand Valley below. It also passes by a series of ancient petroglyphs carved into rock faces.

The hike begins with a brief, flat section paralleling the river. Duck under the giant cottonwood tree next to the trailhead sign to find your route, and enjoy the easy terrain while it lasts before crossing the highway on your left. Pick up the signed singletrack that begins winding up the canyon. From here, you'll have a steep climb up through gnarled, twisty junipers into an impressive amphitheater of high rock canyons and bluffs. About three quarters of a mile in, keep an eye out for the improbably balanced boulder in the gully below you. Once you reach the higher plateau, the trail mellows to an easier grade while winding along cliff edges. Some areas of extreme exposure do exist, so do not attempt if you have a fear of heights. Otherwise, it's hard to overstate the magnificence of the views from the steep slopes the trail traverses.

Around mile 1.5, look for small social trails that detour off the main route over to the petroglyphs—well worth a side trip to check out.

Several options exist: you can complete just the Lower Loop Trail for a 4-mile lollipop loop, the Upper Loop Trail for a 9.3-mile double lollipop loop (including longer sections of exposed, cliff-edge hiking), or the hybrid compromise outlined here that includes the Lower Loop plus an out-and-back on the connector trail.

As with many hikes in the desert environs of western Colorado, this trail was largely developed by and for mountain bikers. Though hiking and equestrian use is permitted, do take extra care to remain aware of your surroundings and be respectful of other trail users. Wear a hat and sunscreen, carry ample water, and avoid this trail after heavy rains or during the height of the day in extreme summer heat.

TURN BY TURN DIRECTIONS:

1. Start hiking along the river from the southeast corner of the parking area.
2. At 0.1 miles, cross the highway on your left and pick up the signed singletrack.
3. At 1.1, go right at the junction to initiate a counterclockwise loop.
4. At 1.7, go right, following signs for Upper Rim Trail.
5. At 2.45, you have an option to extend your hike by 4 miles by doing the upper loop. Otherwise, turn around and head back.
6. At mile 4 (or 8 if you've done the upper loop), go right to complete your lollipop loop.

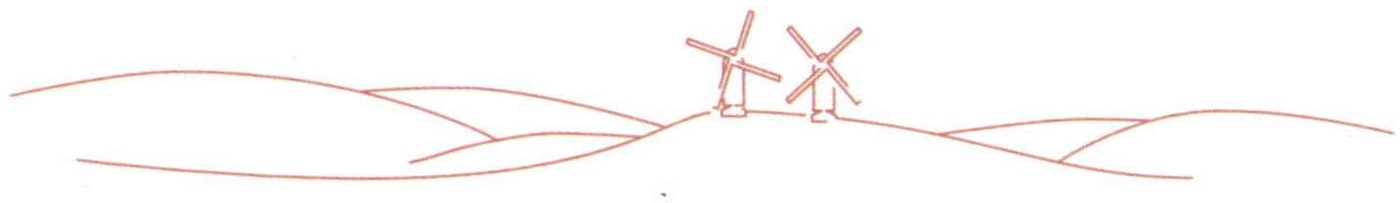

FIND THE TRAILHEAD

From Palisade, drive northeast out of town on North River Road. In about 2 miles, make a right onto Highway 6, then make an immediate right into the Rapid Creek parking area on the left, next to the visitor information structure by the river.

PALISADE BREWING COMPANY

Palisade is a place primarily known for its fruit (peaches especially) and wine. But, as Palisade Brewing Company's owners love to ask, "Who says you can't make beer in wine country?" With a focus on American-style ales and barbecue, this brewery and its sun-drenched outdoor beer garden are a perfect place to relax, refuel, and enjoy views of the surrounding foothills and rock formations. Enjoy this sessionable Dirty Hippie Dark American Wheat with a slice of orange.

CONTACT INFORMATION

BLM, Grand Junction Field Office,
2815 H Road,
Grand Junction, CO 81506; 970-244-3000

BREWERY/RESTAURANT

Palisade Brewing Company
200 Peach Ave,
Palisade, CO 81526
970-464-1462
Miles from trailhead: 2.7

GLENWOOD SPRINGS

A CLASSIC, HISTORIC LOOP HIKE FROM DOWNTOWN

STARTING POINT	OBJECTIVE
SCOUT TRAILHEAD	LOOKOUT MOUNTAIN; DOC HOLLIDAY'S GRAVE
BEER	HIKE TYPE
BURNING LOTUS HAZY IPA	STRENUOUS
FEES	SEASON
NO FEES	MARCH TO NOVEMBER
MAP REFERENCE	DOG FRIENDLY
TRAILS ILLUSTRATED 151: FLAT TOPS SOUTH	(LEASH REQUIRED)
DURATION	LENGTH
4-5 HOURS	7.5 MILES
LOW POINT / HIGH POINT	ELEVATION GAIN
5,912 FEET / 8,074 FEET	2,090 FEET

ALCOHOL
7.6%
CONTENT

HAZY IPA

CLOUDY YELLOW-ORANGE

CITRUS, MANGO, VANILLA

ORANGE CREAMSICLE, BREAD

BITTERNESS
IBU: 42

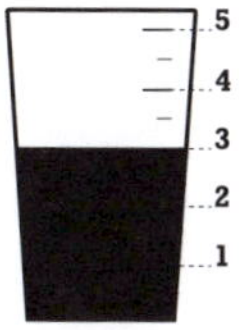

SWEETNESS

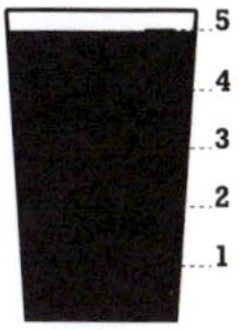

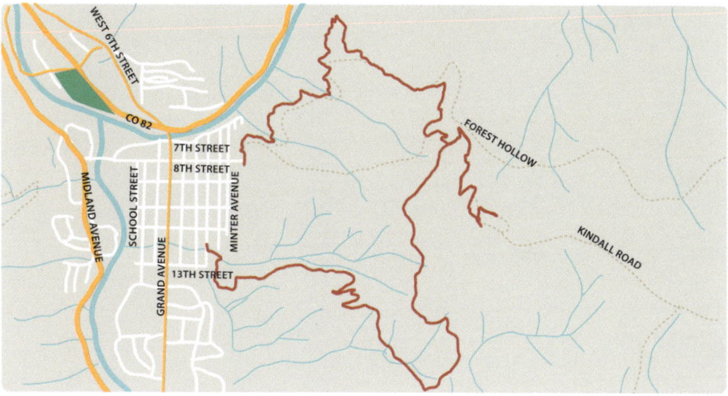

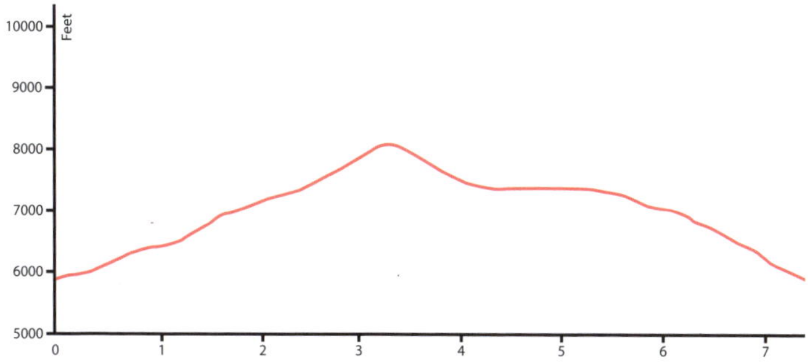

HIKE DESCRIPTION

This loop hike is well loved by locals for its easy accessibility from downtown, beautiful views and historic landmarks.

The Scout Trail—or "Boy Scout Trail," as it's called by locals—is a classic Glenwood hike that sits just a few blocks away from the Glenwood Canyon Brewpub, one of Colorado's original breweries. The Scout Trail is a historic path that the Ute Indians once used to access the area's natural hot springs. The springs' 124-degree mineral waters are what first put Glenwood on the map and now also supply the town's popular, often raucous (albeit family-friendly) Hot Springs Pool and Spa.

As an out-and-back, the Scout Trail is just under 5 miles (or 6.5 if you go all the way to Lookout Mountain Park). But, for a few extra smooth, relatively easy miles, it's possible to turn this hike into a loop that concludes near another iconic Glenwood landmark: the grave of infamous gambler and gunfighter "Doc" Holliday.

Holliday traveled to Glenwood in his final days, hoping (in vain, ultimately) that the hot springs could help treat his tuberculosis. The Pioneer Cemetery trailhead near his tombstone is just a few blocks away from the Scout trailhead where you started, as well as the Glenwood Canyon Brewpub, where you'll finish.

After a steep initial climb through pinyon and juniper, you'll emerge in a high meadow of sagebrush and scrub oak. Along the way, enjoy great views of the iconic Horseshoe Bend in the Colorado River and the steep cliffs of Glenwood Canyon. Don't be alarmed if you hear screams either; they likely belong to the hearty-souled riders of the Giant Canyon Swing at Glenwood Caverns Adventure Park, perched high atop the bluffs across the valley, and visible from much of the Scout Trail.

From the top of Lookout Mountain Park, scope out local mountains like Capitol Peak, Mount Sopris, Chair Mountain, and Glenwood's own Sunlight Ski Area. Don't neglect to pop your head inside the historic outhouse just below the radio tower. More than 80 years old and no longer functional, but preserved by the BLM as a cultural resource, it's certain to be one of the more spectacularly positioned commodes you've ever come across!

Many splintering trails exist on the patch of BLM land that these trails use, so it is wise to carry a map. Also, stay alert for mountain bikers.

TURN BY TURN DIRECTIONS:

1. At mile 2.4, go left at the signed intersection, then make a right shortly thereafter (not straight onto Forest Hollow) to climb up to Lookout Mountain.
2. At 3.1, reach a fire ring and unmarked trail intersections. Go straight through to visit the historic outhouse, or hang a left to climb up to the radio towers and the best views.
3. Return down the way you came until you again reach the junction with Forest Hollow. Go left (also the way you came) here, then either right (the way you came) for an out-and-back, or straight (new trail) to initiate a longer loop over to Doc Holliday's grave.
4. If taking the longer loop, follow the main route by going right at 5.4, right (through a fence opening) at 5.6, right at 6.1, right again at 6.2, then left and steep down at 6.8 until you reach the cemetery, four blocks south of the Scout trailhead.

FIND THE TRAILHEAD

From downtown Glenwood Springs, travel east on 8th Street for several blocks until it dead-ends at the Scout trailhead.

GLENWOOD CANYON BREWPUB

Founded in 1996, Glenwood Canyon Brewpub was built in the historic Hotel Denver, located just across the Colorado River from Glenwood's infamous hot springs pool. It boasts tasty pub fare (try the beer-battered onion rings or beer cheese soup made with their Vapor Cave IPA) and numerous award-winning beers—many named after local trails, mountains, river rapids or other locals' favorite outdoor haunts.

CONTACT INFORMATION

BLM,
Colorado River Valley Field Office,
2300 River Frontage Road,
Silt, CO 81652;
970-876-9000

BREWERY/RESTAURANT

Glenwood Canyon Brewpub
402 7th Street,
Glenwood Springs, CO 81601
970-945-1276
Miles from trailhead: 0.3

CARBONDALE

GET UP HIGH ABOVE TOWN ON RED HILL'S MOST PROMINENT LOOKOUT

STARTING POINT	OBJECTIVE
RED HILL TRAILHEAD	MUSHROOM ROCK
BEER	HIKE TYPE
VALLEY GIRL BLONDE	STRENUOUS
FEES	SEASON
NONE	MARCH TO NOVEMBER
MAP REFERENCE	DOG FRIENDLY
RED HILL TRAIL MAP AT ASPENTRAILFINDER.COM	YES
DURATION	LENGTH
1–1.5 HOURS	2 MILES
LOW POINT / HIGH POINT	ELEVATION GAIN
6,138 FEET / 6,978 FEET	875 FEET

ALCOHOL 5.2% CONTENT

BLONDE ALE

GOLDEN, CLEAR

MILD HOPS

CRISP, LIGHT

BITTERNESS
IBU: 12.5

SWEETNESS

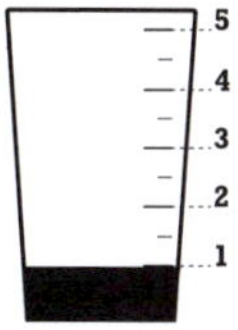

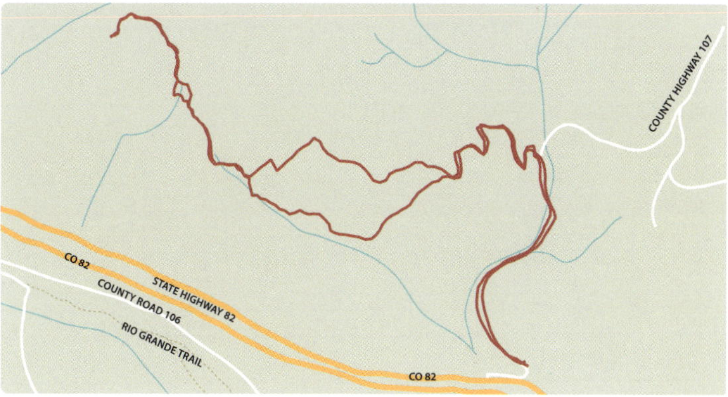

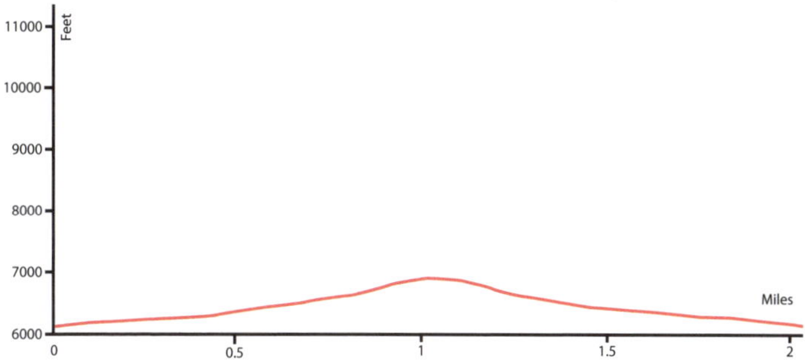

HIKE DESCRIPTION

Get up high above town on this lung-searing gut buster of a hike and enjoy a front-row seat to admire one of Colorado's most prominent peaks.

The aptly named Red Hill Special Recreation Management Area sits north of downtown Carbondale, a quaint, artsy mountain town nestled in ranching country at the foot of Colorado's Elk Mountains. The area's red rocks, sagebrush meadows, and juniper trees are home to some 19 miles of singletrack, as well as herds of deer and elk.

From the trails that wend steeply up Red Hill's southern-facing walls, you'll enjoy many views—the town of Carbondale itself, the convergence of the mighty Roaring Fork and Crystal rivers, and poised in stunning prominence to the south, the frequently snow-capped Mount Sopris. With its twin summits clocking in at 12,965 feet, Sopris does not reach as high as many of its more famous neighboring 13er and 14er peaks, but its near 7,000 feet of relative prominence (the total elevation change from a peak's base to its summit) make it one of the largest mountains in the contiguous United States. And there's no better place from which to ogle the looming giant than Mushroom Rock, a beautiful red-rock formation you can clamber your way steeply up to on the southern flanks of Red Hill.

The trail gets a bit splintered in places toward the top, but do your best to prevent further soil erosion by staying on the main route. It's a calf burner, to be sure, but well worth it for the views you'll enjoy along the way, not to mention the sense of accomplishment you'll feel splayed out atop the fiery red Mushroom Rock.

If you'd like to extend your hike, many options exist up top, once you've gotten the initial climb over with; carry a trail map, or snap a photo of the one at the trailhead to use for reference. Tacking on Skeeters Ridge and a loop of the Faerie and Bogus trails, followed by a descent back to the trailhead on Three Gulch, offers a great way to extend your hike along the cliffs and through the woods and sagebrush. Otherwise, it's a quad burner of a descent back down to the bottom, where fresh, seasonal brews at Carbondale Beer Works will be calling your name.

TURN BY TURN DIRECTIONS:

1. Walk up the dirt road a quarter-mile and look for the Red Hill trailhead sign on your left.
2. Stay left to follow the Three Poles Trail.
3. Stay left at the junctions at 0.5 and 0.75 miles in, following signs for Mushroom Rock.
4. At 1 mile, reach Mushroom Rock. Return the way you came, or for a slight change of scenery, go left at 1.3 miles, then right at 1.4, before returning on the trail you came up.

FIND THE TRAILHEAD

From downtown Carbondale, go north on Highway 133. The Red Hill trailhead can be found on the north side of the intersection of Highway 82 and Highway 133. Park in the large dirt lot.

CARBONDALE BEER WORKS

After spending just 36 hours in Carbondale in 2016, Patrice Fuller and Chachi Rodriguez became owners of Carbondale Beer Works. They credit their impulsive decision-making to the inspiration of the local mountains and laid-back and welcoming local Carbondale community. The brewpub honors their whirlwind business start-up with its On a Whim IPA, a Pacific Northwest-style India pale ale. Their bar serves locally produced small-batch liquors instead of those that are widely available and their restaurant, which has been referred to as "Carbondale's living room," has a mostly Colorado-sourced menu. Carbondale Beer Works is an ideal way to refuel and rehydrate after a day on the trails.

CONTACT INFORMATION
BLM,
Colorado River Valley Field Office,
2300 River Frontage Road,
Silt, CO 81652;
970-876-9000

BREWERY/RESTAURANT
Carbondale Beer Works
647 Main St.
Carbondale, CO 81623
carbondalebeerworks.com
970-704-1216
Miles from trailhead: 1.5

ASPEN

WOODS, ABANDONED MINE SHAFTS, AND EPIC VIEWS

STARTING POINT	OBJECTIVE
HUNTER CREEK TRAILHEAD	SMUGGLER MOUNTAIN
BEER	HIKE TYPE
ITALIAN PILS	MODERATE
FEES	SEASON
NONE	APRIL TO OCTOBER
MAP REFERENCE	DOG FRIENDLY
WWW.PITKINOUTSIDE.ORG	YES (LEASH REQUIRED)
DURATION	LENGTH
2–3 HOURS	4.1 MILES
LOW POINT / HIGH POINT	ELEVATION GAIN
7,933 FEET / 9,029 FEET	1,050 FEET

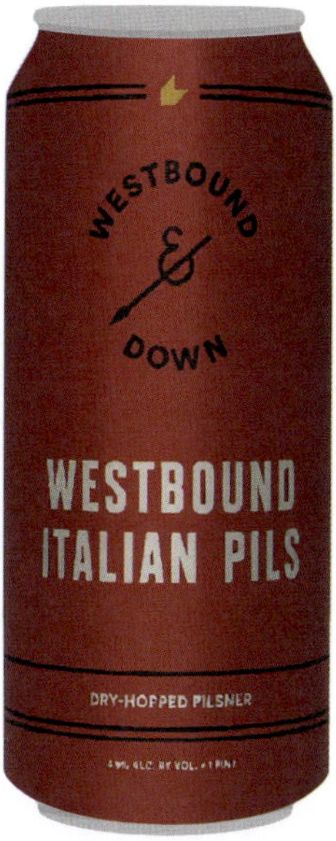

ALCOHOL 4.9% CONTENT

PILSNER

CLEAR STRAW, FOAMY

FLORAL, GRASS

CLEAN, CRISP; DRY FINISH

BITTERNESS
IBU: N/A

SWEETNESS

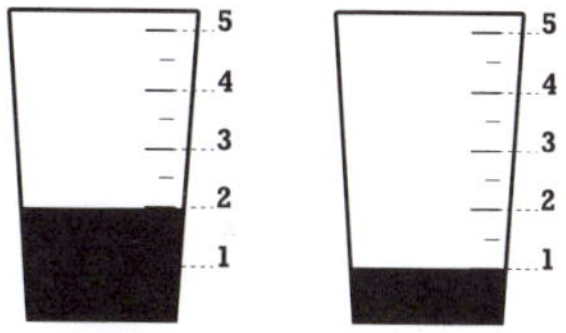

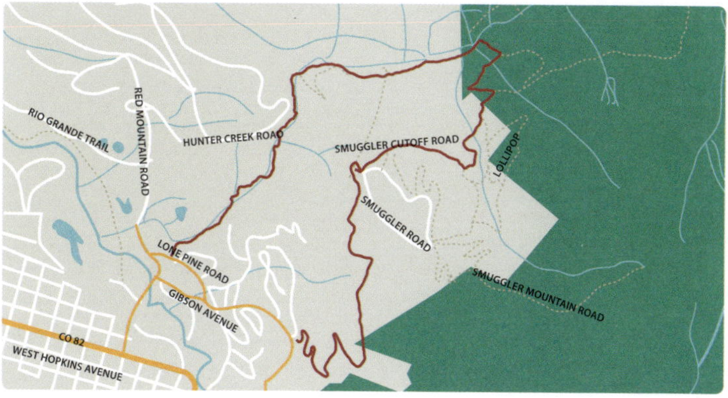

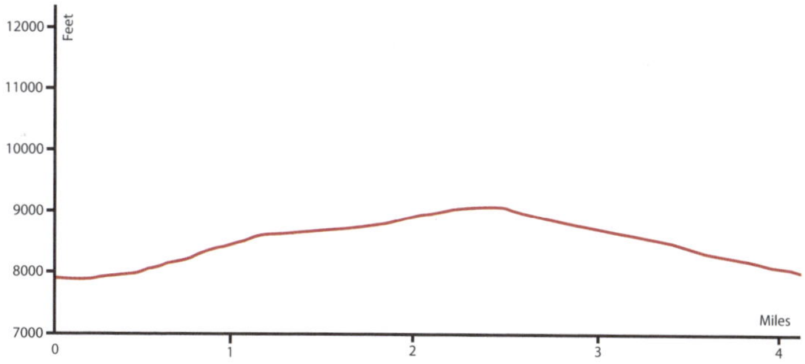

HIKE DESCRIPTION

Take a "hiking tour de Aspen" through the woods, past an abandoned mine shaft, up to the notorious Smuggler Mountain observation deck, and back down to town for a crisp pilsner.

It's easy to get overwhelmed by the multitude of trails that radiate out of Aspen like a massive spider web. Before venturing too far into the beckoning high-altitude backcountry, get acclimated and oriented with this popular hike right out of town.

This loop combines hiking up the Hunter Creek and Hunter Creek Cutoff trails with a descent down the popular Smuggler Mountain Road, which overlooks all of Aspen, the ski area, and many of the surrounding peaks.

You'll begin on a very well-shaded trail through lush, mixed forest and along Hunter Creek. Watch your footing over the rocks and roots on the fun, twisting singletrack. At times, you'll also be on wooden boardwalks, rock staircases, or crossing bridges back and forth over the creek. After venturing onto the quieter Cutoff trail, enjoy passing through open meadows and dazzling aspen trees. Watch out for mountain bikers here.

After turning off toward Smuggler Mountain, you'll pass the long-abandoned Iowa Shaft Mine, complete with informational signs and a map of the historical site. Shortly after, check out the Smuggler observation deck—a lovely wooden platform that proffers a terrific view of tiny Aspen below. From here, it's an easy walk down the dirt Smuggler Mountain Road back to town. Enjoy the people-watching-dog walkers, mountain bikers, yoga-pants-clad locals, winded tourists, fellow hikers, and more.

When you get down to the Smuggler Mountain trailhead, it's just half a mile back to the Hunter Creek trailhead (if you drove and left a car there), or less than a mile to meander into town and grab yourself a barstool at Westy's Tap & Tavern, where you can sample a variety of brews from Colorado-based Westbound & Down Brewing as well as the original Aspen Brewing Company.

TURN BY TURN DIRECTIONS:

1. Cross five bridges in the first mile.
2. At mile 0.85, go right to cross the fifth bridge (Benedict Bridge) and stay on the main trail up.
3. At 1.5, turn right onto the well-signed Hunter Creek Cutoff trail. Keep following signs for Hunter Creek Cutoff.
4. At 2.2, make a right, following signs for the observation deck and Smuggler Mountain Road.
5. At 2.6, go straight across the trail intersection to check out the observation deck before returning to the intersection and walking 1.5 miles down the wide, dirt Smuggler Road.

FIND THE TRAILHEAD

No car necessary, though there is a small parking area at the Hunter Creek trailhead. Either take the free Hunter Creek shuttle or walk north out of town on Mill St (which turns into Red Mountain Rd) and make a right on Lone Pine Rd; the well-marked Hunter Creek trailhead will be on your left shortly.

WESTBOUND & DOWN BREWING COMPANY

At the end of 2023, the Idaho-Springs-based brewery, Westbound & Down, acquired Aspen Brewing Company (as well as Capitol Creek Brewing Company from down the road in Basalt) and took over the old ABC taproom in the heart of downtown Aspen—just a few blocks away from both the starting and finishing trailheads of your hiking tour. Their taps now offer brews from all three brewing companies, along with scrumptious tavern-style pizza—and the cozy space itself itself continues to be a lively watering hole for locals and visitors alike. If this crisp, crushable pilsner isn't up your alley, they've got loads of IPAs, wines, cocktails, and non-alcoholic options on the menu, too.

CONTACT INFORMATION

U.S. Forest Service,
Aspen-Sopris Ranger District,
806 W Hallam Street,
Aspen, CO 81611;
970-963-2266

BREWERY/RESTAURANT

Westy's Tap & Tavern
121 S. Galena Street
Aspen, CO 81611
970-710-2461
Miles from trailhead: 0.6

CRESTED BUTTE

A SECLUDED BASIN WITH WILDLIFE, WATERFALLS, AND WILDFLOWERS

STARTING POINT	OBJECTIVE
COPPER CREEK TRAILHEAD	JUDD FALLS, COPPER LAKE, OR EAST MAROON PASS
BEER	HIKE TYPE
OATMEAL STOUT	MODERATE-STRENUOUS
FEES	SEASON
NONE	JULY TO OCTOBER
MAP REFERENCE	DOG FRIENDLY
TRAILS ILLUSTRATED 131: CRESTED BUTTE, PEARL PASS	YES (LEASH REQUIRED)
DURATION	LENGTH
5-8 HOURS	10.5-12.4 MILES
LOW POINT / HIGH POINT	ELEVATION GAIN
9,603 FEET / 11,437-11,864 FEET	2,100-2,410 FEET

ALCOHOL 6.2% CONTENT

OATMEAL STOUT

BLACK,
CREAMY

ROASTED
CHOCOLATE

SILKY SMOOTH,
MALTY

BITTERNESS
IBU: 34

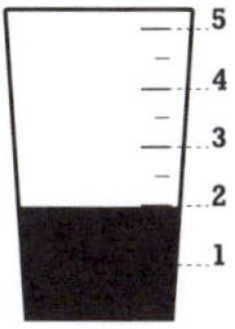

SWEETNESS

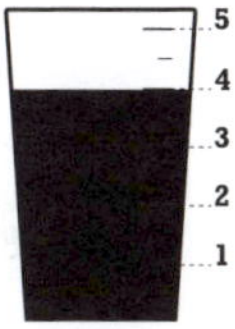

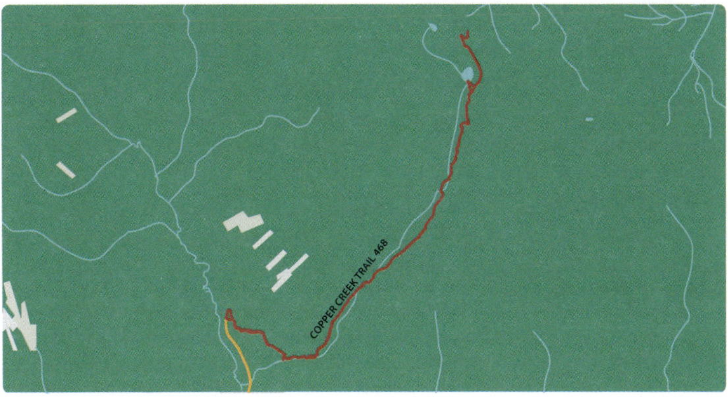

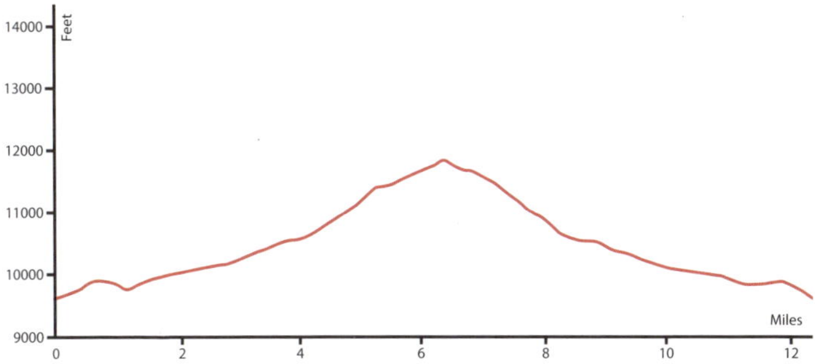

HIKE DESCRIPTION

This secluded basin has it all, from wildlife to waterfalls to wildflowers—and when you're done, grab a decadent oatmeal stout back in town.

On a dirt road just north of Crested Butte lies the tiny mountain hamlet of Gothic—an abandoned mining town turned high-altitude field station for biological scientists and researchers. Behind Gothic lies a massive basin teeming with trails and craggy peaks. The area is renowned for its incredible wildflowers in the summer (which typically peak in July into early August) and fiery-hued leaves in the autumn.

The Copper Creek Trail is a highlights reel of some of the best scenery the basin has to offer, from waterfalls to lakes to wildflowers.

Many people make the stroll through the aspen copse and across the hillside for a glimpse of Judd Falls. The waterfall overlook, complete with a bench, is clearly marked with a sign and is just a few steps off the main trail. If you're not up for a long day hike, this makes a great destination and turnaround spot for a quick, scenic jaunt.

After the falls overlook, though, the crowds thin to a trickle. Continue on the Copper Creek Trail. Some tempting social trails exist, so be diligent about staying on the main trail. The route is exceptionally clear and well marked at all intersections. You'll pass through conifer forest, open meadows, avalanche chutes, and across a number of creeks and streams. Steep, rocky cliffs, and ridges hover over either side of the valley as you make your way toward the jagged massifs at the back.

The "island" at the near edge of Copper Lake makes a great lunch spot. Enjoy gazing up at the immense cirque above and admiring the wildflowers around you. From here, you can see the trail up to East Maroon Pass cutting through the talus slope to your right at a forgiving grade. This part is optional; it tacks on an extra 500 feet of climbing and one mile (two roundtrip) to tag the top of East Maroon Pass, but this bonus stretch is well worth your time and effort if you're up for it. The views and wildflowers will blow your mind.

TURN BY TURN DIRECTIONS:

1. From the lower 2WD trailhead, walk up the road half a mile to reach the official Copper Creek trailhead (far right end of 4WD parking area).
2. At 1.1 miles, reach scenic Judd Falls overlook.
3. At 1.3, pass a large sign for Copper Creek Trail. Continue straight (left of the sign) on the main route.
4. There are sizable creek crossings at miles 2.5 and 4. Your feet will probably get wet.
5. At mile 5.25, stay left to go to Copper Lake. This is a good turnaround spot, or you can continue up to East Maroon Pass.
6. If continuing, follow trail signs to the large rock pile atop East Maroon Pass at 6.35 miles, before returning the way you came.

FIND THE TRAILHEAD

In the summer, you can take the Gothic Bus Shuttle (www.mtnexp.org) from town. Otherwise, drive 8 miles north of Crested Butte on Gothic Road (County Road 371). Park at the first obvious parking area (complete with outhouse) after Gothic, or if you have a high-clearance vehicle, hang a right and proceed another half-mile up the 4WD road to the Copper Creek trailhead. (Subtract 0.5 mile from the trail mileages in the turn-by-turn directions if you do this.)

IRWIN BREWING COMPANY

Irwin Brewing Company opened its door in January 2017 with a 15-barrel brewing system to fill a brewery void in the Gunnison Valley. They launched with a lineup of six year-round beers ranging from a light pilsner to this dark, full-bodied oatmeal stout. Named after the nearby Lake Irwin, the production brewery has canned beer, kegs and growler fills available; however, you'll have to head over to the Public House (same ownership) or other assorted restaurants in town to consume a fresh pint on site.

CONTACT INFORMATION
U.S. Forest Service,
Gunnison Ranger District,
216 N. Colorado Street,
Gunnison, CO 81230;
970-641-0471

VTBREWERY/RESTAURANT
Irwin Brewing Company
326 Belleview Avenue,
Crested Butte, CO 81224
970-275-7578
Miles from trailhead: 8.8

PONCHA SPRINGS

BAG A CLASSIC COLORADO 14ER—OR TWO

STARTING POINT	OBJECTIVE
BLANK GULCH TRAILHEAD	**MOUNT SHAVANO**
BEER	HIKE TYPE
APIS IV BELGIAN QUADRUPEL	**VERY STRENUOUS**
FEES	SEASON
NONE	**JULY TO SEPTEMBER**
MAP REFERENCE	DOG FRIENDLY
TRAILS ILLUSTRATED 130: SALIDA, ST. ELMO, MOUNT SHAVANO	**YES**
DURATION	LENGTH
6-8 HOURS	**8.6 MILES**
LOW POINT / HIGH POINT	ELEVATION GAIN
9,780 FEET / 14,229 FEET	**4,461 FEET**

ALCOHOL
10.9%
CONTENT

BELGIAN QUAD

REDDISH BLACK

BOOZY, EARTHY, MOLASSES

PLUMS, FIGS, HONEY, FLORAL

BITTERNESS
IBU: 41

SWEETNESS

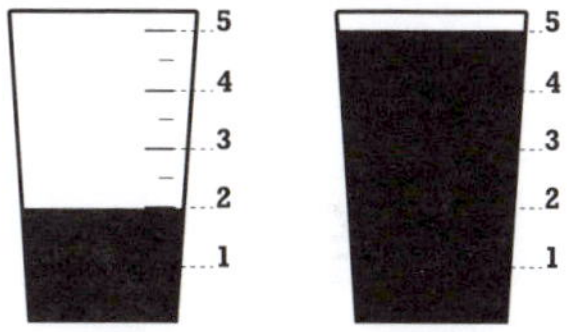

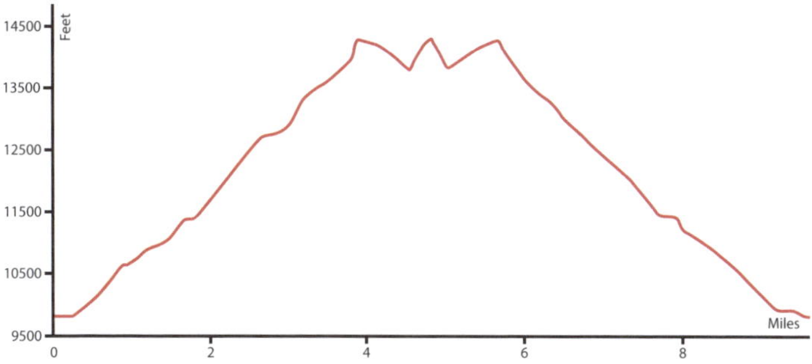

HIKE DESCRIPTION

The most intense hike in this book deserves to be paired with the most intense beer—a classic Colorado 14er, followed by a boozy Dark Belgian-Style Ale.

The state of Colorado is home to 53 "14ers"—that is, peaks whose summits reach at least 14,000 feet above sea level, and which rise at least 300 feet in prominence above saddles connecting it to any neighboring 14ers. It seems that no Colorado hiking guidebook would be complete without at least one 14er hike in it; there is no doubt something magical about standing atop a peak that soars so close to the sky.

Many of the 14ers receive high foot traffic due to their peakbagging bragging rights. However, Shavano, and its neighboring 14er, Tabeguache, are far enough away from metropolitan Denver—and the hike to their summits just challenging enough—that they see far fewer crowds than more popular 14ers in Colorado's Front Range.

Starting at the Blank Gulch Trailhead, this hike begins on a brief stretch of the Colorado Trail, a 486-mile long-distance trail that traverses the state from Denver to Durango. You'll be on it less than a half-mile, though, before veering off onto the Shavano Trail. From here, it's a steady schlep up the mountain, winding up through beautiful, thick forests of pine and aspen trees before popping out above tree line. Here, keep an eye out for marmots, pikas, elk, and other wildlife that love to frequent the alpine tundra. Enjoy the far-reaching views of the valley below and neighboring peaks.

After you reach the saddle at mile 3.7, follow the trail to the right to scramble (Class 2) up to the rocky summit of Shavano in another half-mile or so. Enjoy the sense of accomplishment when you reach the summit. Rest and turn back here or, if you're feeling up to it and the weather is permitting, you can also tack on a second 14er summit by hiking over to nearby Tabeguache Peak (for 10.6 miles roundtrip, with 5,300 feet of total elevation gain). It is the massive rock pile to the northwest. Follow the stony ridge over to it, reaching the low saddle in a half-mile, followed by a short, Class 2 scramble to the true summit. The only way to return is to go back the same way you came, including back up and over Shavano; don't try to skirt around it, as you'll get yourself into trouble.

Even without adding Tabeguache, this hike is long and extremely strenuous, especially as the air thins as you ascend. It's best to do some altitude acclimating before attempting any 14er.

And, as with any hike that goes above tree line, this should not be attempted if lightning is present or imminent. Thunderstorms often roll through in the early afternoon, so start very early in the day and be willing to turn back shy of the summit if storms develop before you make it up there.

TURN BY TURN DIRECTIONS:

1. Start on the Colorado Trail. At 0.15 miles, turn right onto the Shavano Trail, then left at 0.4 miles.
2. At 3.7 miles, reach the saddle. Follow trail to the right to scramble up to the rocky summit.
3. At 4.3, reach the Shavano summit. Turn around here, or tack on the Tabeguache summit by following the stony ridge toward the massive rockpile to the northwest for 1 more mile.

FIND THE TRAILHEAD

From Poncha Springs, drive west on Highway 50 for about 2 miles. Make a right onto County Road 250. In 5 miles, stay straight/left to follow County Road 252 for another 3.2 miles to the Blank Gulch trailhead for Mt. Shavano/Tabeguache Peak.

ELEVATION BEER COMPANY

Elevation Beer Company is an absolute must-visit for any self-respecting beer enthusiast traipsing across Colorado. Its cozy tasting room sits in the shadows of the giants of the Sawatch Range of the Rockies, and its beers are categorized broadly from Light & Crispy (think lagers) to Bold & Hoppy (IPA enthusiasts, get your fix) to Fruit & More, Barrel-Aged Brews, and finally, Dark & Malty, which includes this decadent, boozy, knock-you-on-your-ass Belgian quad.

CONTACT INFORMATION

U.S. Forest Service,
Salida Ranger District,
5575 Cleora Road,
Salida, CO 81201;
719-539-3591

BREWERY/RESTAURANT

Elevation Beer Company
115 Pahlone Parkway,
Poncha Springs, CO 81242
719-539-5258
Miles from trailhead: 10.8

BUENA VISTA

A FUN RAMBLE THROUGH THE DRY, SCRUB-DESERT ENVIRONS

STARTING POINT	OBJECTIVE
EDDYLINE BREWERY	BROKEN BOYFRIEND TRAIL
BEER	HIKE TYPE
JOLLY ROGER BLACK LAGER	EASY-MODERATE
FEES	SEASON
NONE	APRIL TO NOVEMBER
MAP REFERENCE	DOG FRIENDLY
WHIPPLE TRAIL OPTIONS ON BLM.GOV	YES (LEASH REQUIRED)
DURATION	LENGTH
1.5-2 HOURS	4 MILES
LOW POINT / HIGH POINT	ELEVATION GAIN
7,923 FEET / 8,392 FEET	400 FEET

ALCOHOL 5% CONTENT

LAGER

BLACK

EARTHY, SMOKY

CRISP, MALTY; TOFFEE UNDERTONES

BITTERNESS
IBU: 20

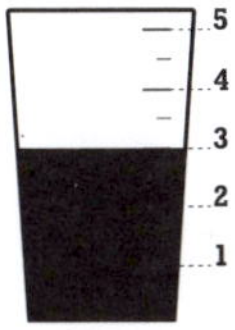

SWEETNESS

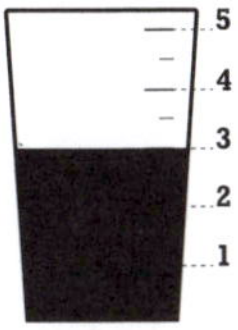

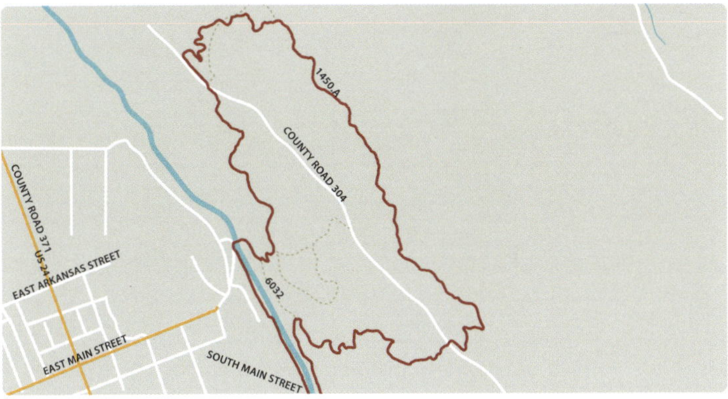

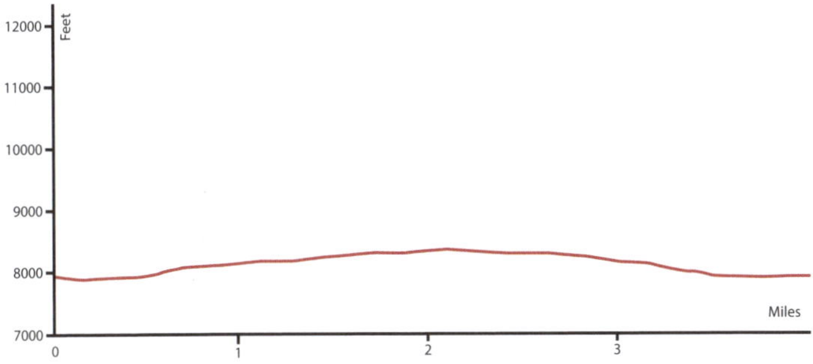

HIKE DESCRIPTION

A fun ramble into the dry, scrub-desert environs above the outdoor enthusiasts' playground that is Buena Vista.

For an in-your-face introduction to the adventurous spirit that permeates Buena Vista, look no further than the Barbara Whipple Trail system that lords over the east side of town. These trails are neither overly crowded, nor deeply secluded. Rather, they're immersed in the heartbeat of Buena Vista's outdoors-loving community, and offer a quick way to gain elevation above town and enjoy panoramic views of the surrounding Collegiate Peaks.

Most of the trails were designed with mountain bikers in mind (so always keep an eye out for bikes on this loop), but they're a favorite haunt of hikers as well. New trails are being created each year. You can access them directly from the Eddyline Brewery by hopping on Riverside Trail, a crushed-gravel route that parallels the Arkansas River. Along your way upstream, enjoy listening to the roar of the rapids and watching for kayakers testing their mettle in the whitewater playholes.

After crossing the Whipple Bridge (also accessible directly from downtown Buena Vista, at the end of East Main Street), start climbing in earnest up the winding singletrack on sandy, hard-packed soil. You'll pass through boulder gardens, scrubby pine trees, rock outcroppings, patches of cacti, and other flowering shrubs. At 0.6 miles, take a breather on the bench to enjoy panoramic views across the valley of the Collegiate Peaks range—some of Colorado's highest "14ers" (14,000+ foot mountains). Directly below, you'll have a clear view of town.

Continue on your ramble through the foothills until you come back down to the river. Here, relatively new singletrack takes you south along the water to a different bridge than the one you first crossed. This one is on private property, but remains open to respectful public foot traffic. Cross the bridge and complete your loop by arriving back at the doorstep of Eddyline—no doubt parched and ready for imbibing.

TURN BY TURN DIRECTIONS:

1. Start by going north (upstream), following the crushed-gravel trail along the river until you reach the bridge at 0.4 miles. Cross it and continue up the singletrack.
2. At 0.5 miles, stay left at an unsigned junction.
3. At 1.1, reach a dirt road. Go left for a short stretch, then hang a right at the T6032A sign (Broken Boyfriend Trail).
4. At 2.6, turn right. Soon, you'll cross the dirt road again. Continue on the trail.
5. At the structure at 3.4, make a left onto the trail dipping into the woods.
6. At 3.8, cross the bridge across the river, then hang a right back onto the River Trail.

FIND THE TRAILHEAD

From the front step of the Eddyline Brewery, cross South Main Street and walk toward the river until you hit the Riverside Trail. Head north along the Riverside Trail for about a half mile to the Whipple Bridge.

EDDYLINE BREWERY

Established in 2009, Eddyline's aim has always been to quench the thirst of the outdoor adventure community. Emblazoned on the bartenders' shirts is their motto: "Beer for every adventure!" And the bright, playful aesthetic of the brewpub fits; bicycles, kayaks, paddles, and mountain-inspired art adorn its walls and vaulted ceiling. A perennial award winner, the rich Jolly Roger looks like a stout, but drinks smooth and easy as a lager.

CONTACT INFORMATION

BLM Colorado,
Royal Gorge Field Office,
3028 East Main Street,
Cañon City, CO 81212;
719-269-8500

BREWERY/RESTAURANT

Eddyline Brewery
926 S Main Buena Vista, CO 81211
719-966-6018
Miles from trailhead: 0.5 miles

LEADVILLE

A SECLUDED LAKE MORE THAN TWO MILES ABOVE SEA LEVEL

STARTING POINT	OBJECTIVE
WEST END OF TURQUOISE LAKE	TIMBERLINE LAKE
BEER	HIKE TYPE
CAMP HALE PALE ALE	MODERATE
FEES	SEASON
NONE	MARCH TO OCTOBER
MAP REFERENCE	DOG FRIENDLY
TRAILS ILLUSTRATED 110: LEADVILLE/FAIRPLAY	YES (LEASH REQUIRED)
DURATION	LENGTH
2-3 HOURS	5-6 MILES
LOW POINT / HIGH POINT	ELEVATION GAIN
10,056 FEET / 10,984 FEET	1,050 FEET

ALCOHOL 5% CONTENT

CAMP HALE PALE ALE

CARAMEL

CALYPSO, CENTENNIAL AND BREWERS GOLD HOPS.

FRUITY, MALT, CARAMEL

BITTERNESS IBU: 40

SWEETNESS

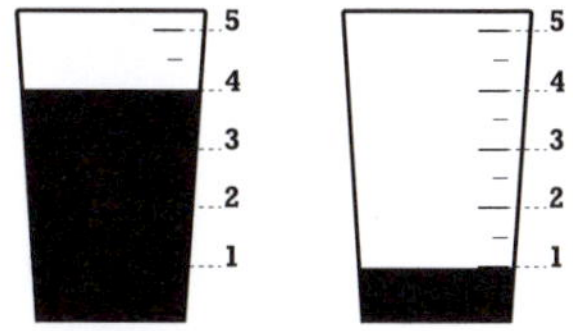

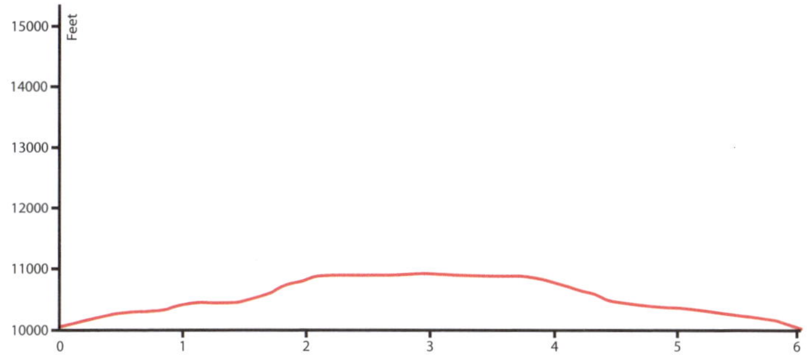

HIKE DESCRIPTION

A relaxing hike through lush forest in the Holy Cross Wilderness area to a secluded lake more than two miles above sea level.

The highest incorporated city in North America at 10,152 feet, Leadville is known for its numerous lakes. Several of them, including Turquoise Lake and Twin Lakes, adorn the routes of Leadville's celebrated endurance races, the Leadville Trail 100 (running) and the Leadville Trail 100 MTB (mountain biking). However, beyond these well-known and much-loved landmarks lie a number of quieter, less visited lakes. One of the most pristine is Timberline Lake, nestled away in the Holy Cross Wilderness, beckoning you to escape the summer jeeping, cycling, and racing crowds. You can even camp along its shores, as a number of secluded backcountry campsites dot the water's edge.

By Colorado standards, the hike is a mellow one, meandering at a gentle grade through lush woods before emerging at the lake. The trail is rocky in places, with a number of creek crossings that will almost certainly soak your feet.

From the trailhead, this hike shares its route for the first tenth of a mile with the illustrious Colorado Trail, a 486-mile route connecting Denver to Durango. Shortly after crossing a bridge over Lake Fork Creek, you'll see your trail to Timberline Lake turn away from the Colorado Trail. Pass the two large railroad-tie Xs and, within a few minutes, enter the Holy Cross Wilderness Area. From here, the trail is easy to follow, passing through woods, marshes, rocky washes, and the occasional meadow. Through the trees you'll glimpse the surrounding high ridges, many of which stay laced with snow through the summer.

Fishing in Timberline Lake is permitted, but catch-and-release, fly-and-lure only. Take a breather or enjoy a picnic at its shores, or meander as long as you like by following an increasingly faint trail around the west side of the lake to a marshy meadow beneath an eye-popping cirque. When you're ready, turn around and head back down the way you came up.

TURN BY TURN DIRECTIONS:

1. At the immediate "fork" in the trail, stay right on the main trail to cross a bridge over the creek.
2. At 0.1 miles, stay right and follow sign for Timberline Lake.
3. At 0.3, enter the Holy Cross Wilderness Area.
4. At 2.15, reach the edge of the lake. You can follow an increasingly faint trail around the west side of the lake as long as you like.
5. Head back down the way you came up.

FIND THE TRAILHEAD

The drive to the trailhead along either the north or south sides of Turquoise Lake packs in a great deal of scenery before you even start hiking. From downtown Leadville, take County Road 4 west for 7 miles. Turn right onto Turquoise Lake Road, then find the trailhead in 2 miles at the sharp bend in the road.

TWO MILE BREWING COMPANY

Initially, homebrewing was just a hobby for Sean Terrill, who went to school in nuclear engineering. After working a 9-to-5 engineering job in rural Tennessee, he moved to Silverton, Colorado, where he learned the commercial brewing trade at Silverton Brewery, Durango Brewery and Ska Brewing. When Terrill moved to Leadville in 2014, he bought an old gas station along the main drag in America's highest incorporated city, which happens to be situated nearly two miles above sea level. After six years of honing his craft and rounding up investors, he finally staged a soft opening in March of 2020 only to have it made softer by the Covid-19 shutdown. However, by the time he re-opened in earnest, Leadville's only other craft brewery was about to shut down for good, leaving Two Mile Brewing Company as the only brewpub in town.

CONTACT INFORMATION

U.S. Forest Service,
Leadville Ranger District,
810 Front Street,
Leadville, CO 80461;
719-486-0749

BREWERY/RESTAURANT

Two Mile Brewing Company
101 Harrison Ave,
Leadville, CO 80461
twomilebrewing.com
719-293-2766
Miles from trailhead: 10.3

FAIRPLAY

VISIT AN OTHERWORLDLY GROVE OF ANCIENT TREES

STARTING POINT	OBJECTIVE
FOURMILE CAMPGROUND	LIMBER GROVE
BEER	HIKE TYPE
ROOKIE GUIDE PALE ALE	EASY
FEES	SEASON
NONE	JUNE TO SEPTEMBER
MAP REFERENCE	DOG FRIENDLY
LIMBER GROVE BROCHURE ON MRHI.ORG	YES (LEASH REQUIRED)
DURATION	LENGTH
1.5–2 HOURS	3 MILES
LOW POINT / HIGH POINT	ELEVATION GAIN
10,518 FEET / 10,938 FEET	370 FEET

ALCOHOL 5.3% CONTENT

HAZY PALE ALE

CLOUDY PALE ORANGE

HERBAL, LEMON, LIME

CITRUSY; CLEAN FINISH

BITTERNESS IBU: 50

SWEETNESS

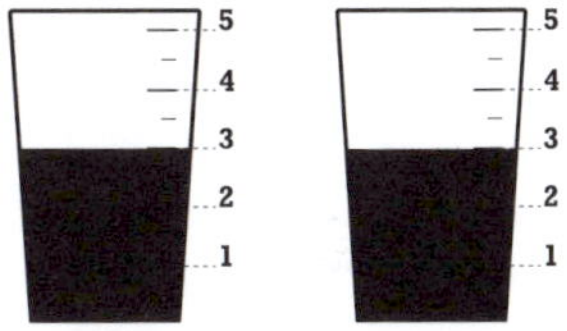

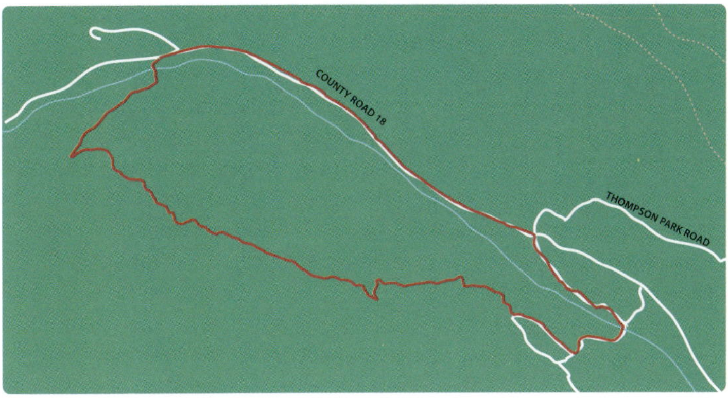

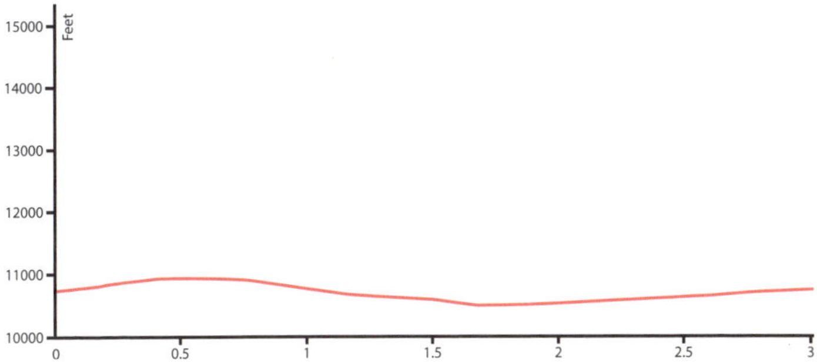

HIKE DESCRIPTION

Visit an otherworldly grove of ancient trees, then indulge in a juicy, hazy New England-style pale ale.

The limber pine is a fascinating tree. Remarkably adapted to growing in arid, rocky environs where most other tree species cannot survive, this rare tree often grows improbably on cliff edges or in the middle of high-altitude talus slopes. This ancient limber grove just outside of Fairplay, nestled into a wind-swept pocket of talus just below 11,000 feet, is no exception.

A short hike through dense forest leads to a more open, rocky slope. A bit of careful footing across the rocks will take you to the edge of the limber grove—an outdoor museum of gnarled, twisted trees, many more than 1,000 years old.

True to their name, the limber pine's branches are flexible enough to withstand the high winds in the areas in which they thrive—so flexible, in fact, that their smaller branches can often be tied in knots without breaking. (Don't be tempted, though; this practice is discouraged by Leave No Trace principles.) It's also important not to leave the trail through the limber grove, as doing so can wear away the soil and protective bark around the limber pine's roots, eventually weakening and killing the tree.

The grove really is the highlight of this trail, so if you're just in the mood for a short hike, you can turn around here and return to the trailhead near the Fourmile Campground. If you'd like to complete a loop, though, it's also possible to continue on the trail through the woods for another mile to Horseshoe Campground. From here, you can wander through the campground out to the dirt road you drove in on and walk back up along the creek.

In early to mid-fall, especially, this makes a nice loop because the road is a corridor of fiery aspens in places, with clear views of many brilliantly bright aspen stands on the shoulders of surrounding peaks otherwise bathed in evergreens. From the road, you'll also enjoy a nice view of the 14,035-foot Mount Sherman, a lesser-known 14er—a nice option in this area if you're interested in a longer day hike.

TURN BY TURN DIRECTIONS:

1. Cross the log bridge over the creek and follow the clear singletrack.
2. At 0.5 miles, enter the limber grove.
3. At 1.5, reach Horseshoe Campground. Stay left on the road.
4. At 1.8, make a left onto the doubletrack trail, which will soon rejoin the road.
5. Go left for one more mile on the road to return to your car.

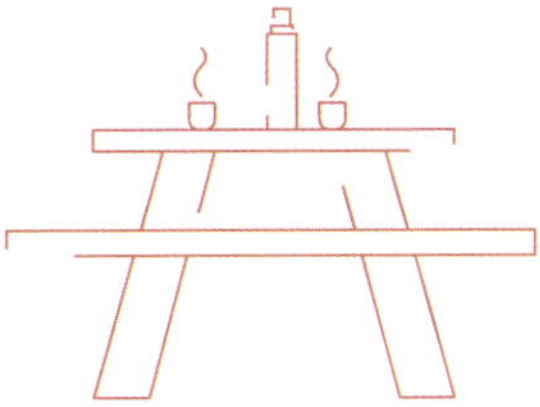

FIND THE TRAILHEAD

Head south on U.S. Route 285 for 1 mile. Turn right onto Fourmile Creek Road and drive 8 miles. Just past the turnoff for Fourmile Campground, look for the Limber Grove trailhead on your left.

HIGHSIDE BREWING

Originating 30 miles north in nearby Frisco, Highside Brewing now operates several taprooms, including their Fairplay location—a lively, 16-tap tasting room where you can watch sports, play billiards and even order beer to go. Or head outdoors to their spacious patio for sprawling views, lawn games and food-truck barbecue.

CONTACT INFORMATION

U.S. Forest Service,
South Park Ranger District,
320 Highway 285,
Fairplay, CO 80440;
719-836-2031

BREWERY/RESTAURANT

Highside Brewing
411 US Hwy 285
Fairplay, CO 80440
970-668-2337
Miles from trailhead: 9.2

BRECKENRIDGE

WOODS, WATERFALLS, LAKES, MINING RUINS, AND MORE

STARTING POINT	OBJECTIVE
MOHAWK LAKES 2WD TRAILHEAD	MOHAWK LAKES
BEER	HIKE TYPE
COCONUT PORTER	MODERATE-STRENUOUS
FEES	SEASON
NONE	JULY TO OCTOBER
MAP REFERENCE	DOG FRIENDLY
TRAILS ILLUSTRATED 109: BRECKENRIDGE, TENNESSEE PASS	YES
DURATION	LENGTH
4-6 HOURS	7 MILES
LOW POINT / HIGH POINT	ELEVATION GAIN
10,407 FEET / 12,136 FEET	1,720 FEET

ALCOHOL 5.6% CONTENT

PORTER

DARK BROWN

HEAVY COCONUT AND SMOKY CARAMEL WITH A FOAMY HEAD

TOASTED COCONUT

BITTERNESS
IBU: 28

SWEETNESS

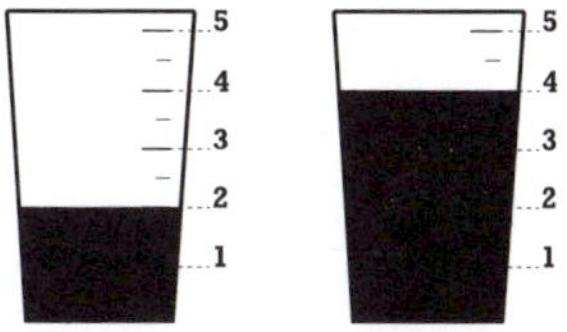

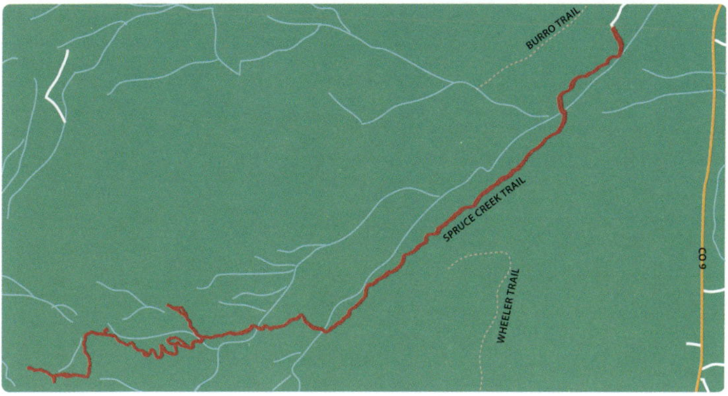

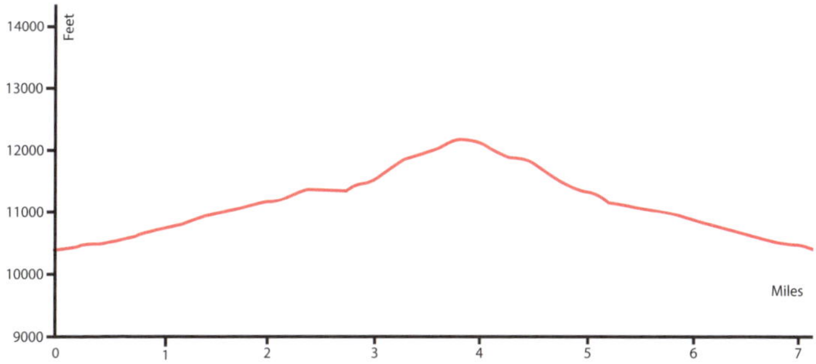

HIKE DESCRIPTION

This hike has woods, waterfalls, wildflowers, glittering alpine lakes, historic mining ruins, postcard views, and a mix of easy ambling and gut-busting climbs.

A secluded trail this is not—but it's popular for good reason. Over the course of just a few miles, it packs in a wallop of astonishing sights and views. And basking in the sun by the shimmering water's edge of Mohawk Lakes will have you jonesin' for the rich, tropical-inspired coconut porter that awaits you in Breckenridge at the end of your hike.

Start early in the day to avoid the crowds. Almost immediately after beginning your hike at the lower trailhead, bear right at what appears to be a fork in the trail. Continue following the rocky doubletrack on its gentle climb up through the woods; be mindful of your footing, as a number of exposed roots will trip you up if you don't watch where you're going. If you start your hike early in the day, the trail is largely shaded and stays quite cool.

Shortly after reaching the upper trailhead, you'll have the option to take a short spur over to Mayflower Lake. This quiet, unassuming pond sits at the bottom of a large talus slope, and is a nice spot for a snack break. Rejoin the main trail to Mohawk Lakes and you'll quickly arrive at a large rock garden and some mining ruins, including an old log cabin.

The trail braids quite a bit here into several different social trails, most of which wind up in the same place, but if in doubt, follow cairns and/or other hikers. Bear right of the rock garden to check out the waterfall before doubling back to the main trail. A trail sign just above the log cabin will point you in the correct direction to continue on your way to Mohawk Lakes.

From here, the trail grows considerably steeper and more challenging, in a few spots you may need to use your hands for light scrambling. Pay attention to cairns again to stay on the main trail. You'll pass more historic mining elements before arriving at Lower Mohawk, a picturesque lake flanked by snow-covered cliffs, cascading streams, more old mining structures and, to the right, the looming 13,176-foot Mount Helen.

Stay left to follow the main trail to the upper Mohawk Lake after a short, steep climb with huge payoff—a cerulean lake, abundant wildflowers, high granite ridges, and commanding views of the valley behind you. Bring a jacket, as it tends to get windy up here.

TURN BY TURN DIRECTIONS:

1. From the lower 2WD trailhead, start by following the blue-diamond blazes.
2. At mile 1.5, cross the well-signed Wheeler Trail.
3. At mile 2, reach the upper 4WD trailhead. Walk to the end of the parking lot and find the Mayflower Lake trailhead sign to the right of the Spruce Creek Diversion.
4. At 2.3, you have the option to take the short spur (0.3 mile out-and-back) to Mayflower Lake.
5. Cross a log bridge over the creek and bear right on the main trail. At the rock garden, take the short spur out to the waterfall before rejoining the main trail up to Mohawk Lakes.
6. At 3.4, arrive at Lower Mohawk Lake.
7. At 3.7, arrive at Mohawk Lake.

FIND THE TRAILHEAD

Drive 3.0 miles south of downtown Breckenridge on Highway 9 and making a right on Spruce Creek Road. Follow the "Lakes & Trails" wooden signs to the lower Spruce Creek trailhead. If you have a high-clearance 4WD vehicle, you can continue up the road to an upper trailhead that shortens the entire hike substantially, but the turn by turn directions are written from the 2WD lot.

BROKEN COMPASS BREWING

Broken Compass Brewing opened its doors in 2014, quickly establishing itself as a favorite haunt of locals and visitors alike. Paying homage to Breckenridge's reputation as an epic mountain town, the tasting room is decked out with ski-lift benches and gorgeous beetle-kill wood tables and bar tops. The brew flavors range from more traditional ales to creative, visionary combinations—zingy chili pepper pale ale, peppery ginger pale ale, and this perennial favorite, the coconut porter.

CONTACT INFORMATION

U.S. Forest Service,
Dillon Ranger District,
680 Blue River Parkway,
Silverthorne, CO 80498;
970-468-5400

BREWERY/RESTAURANT

Broken Compass Brewing
68 Continental Court, Unit B12,
Breckenridge, CO 80424
970-368-2772
Miles from trailhead: 6.5

SILVERTHORNE

PART HIKE, PART SCRAMBLE IN THE EAGLES NEST WILDERNESS

STARTING POINT	OBJECTIVE
BUFFALO MOUNTAIN TRAILHEAD	BUFFALO MOUNTAIN SUMMIT
BEER	HIKE TYPE
ALPEN WEISSE	VERY STRENUOUS
FEES	SEASON
NONE	JULY TO SEPTEMBER
MAP REFERENCE	DOG FRIENDLY
TRAILS ILLUSTRATED 108: VAIL, FRISCO, DILLON	YES (LEASH REQUIRED)
DURATION	LENGTH
5-7 HOURS	5.3 MILES
LOW POINT / HIGH POINT	ELEVATION GAIN
9,790 FEET / 12,777 FEET	3,000 FEET

ALCOHOL
5.3%
CONTENT

HEFEWEIZEN

CLOUDY GOLD

BANANA, CLOVES

YEASTY MALT

BITTERNESS
IBU: 14

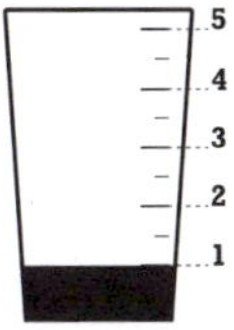

SWEETNESS

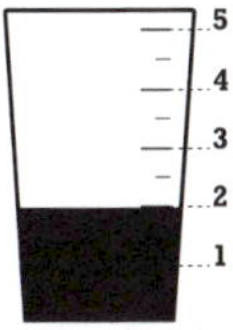

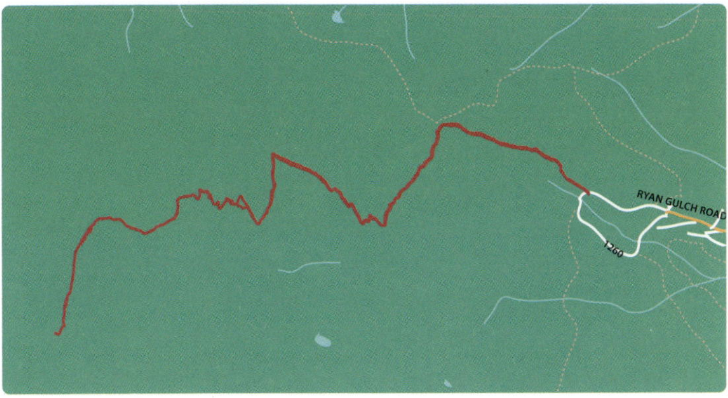

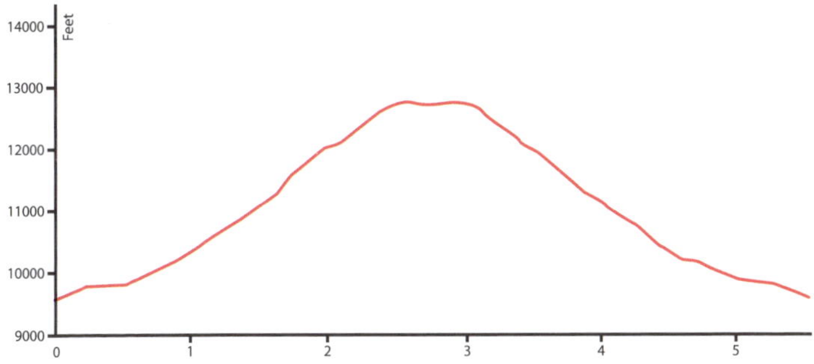

HIKE DESCRIPTION

Bag this classic peak with a combination of hard hiking and mild scrambling, then enjoy a German-style wheat beer named after the mountains.

Getting up Buffalo Mountain is no walk in the park, but if you're up for the challenge, you'll be handsomely rewarded. The route offers fun scrambling and route finding through the talus slopes, bird's-eye views of the Dillon Reservoir and nearby Grays and Torreys peaks, and a chance to see the herd of mountain goats that frequents the upper slopes of this mountain. Plus, after a hike like this one, the brown ale that awaits you at Brewers' Bakery will taste all the more magnificent.

The hike begins at a relatively mellow grade, passing old mining ruins and subalpine forest on the way into the Eagles Nest Wilderness. After the first mile, you'll begin encountering sizable talus slopes. Be mindful to follow the cairns to guide you through any areas in which the "trail" becomes difficult to find. Hundreds of cairns exist in these boulder fields, easing your way to the summit with an established climbers' route. Nonetheless, you're likely to need both hands at times to help you scramble over certain sections. This trail is not for the faint of heart.

As you climb, enjoy views of the Dillon Reservoir behind you. At just over two miles, you'll emerge from the largest talus slope at the saddle of a false summit. Next up is another, slightly smaller talus slope and more cairn-following before you emerge on the ridgeline. The true summit is here—so if you're ready, make yourself at home, layer up against the wind, and enjoy the panoramic views. Keep an eye out for mountain goats, which love to roam the alpine meadows here; you'll no doubt find clumps of their white hair clinging to rocks along the summit.

For the bravest of souls, there is an optional scramble with some moderate exposure to a secondary summit farther along the ridgeline.

Start this hike early in the day, check the forecast to avoid thunderstorms, and budget lots of time; picking your way through the rock gardens and talus means mandatorily slow going for much of the way. Also, even on a hot summer day, be sure to pack a jacket, warm cap, and gloves for the brisk winds you're likely to encounter at the summit.

TURN BY TURN DIRECTIONS:

1. At 0.57 miles, bear left at the four-way trail intersection.
2. At 1.15, start climbing steeply through the talus. Look for cairns to guide you and be mindful not to get off the main route.
3. At 2.2, emerge at the saddle of a false summit.
4. At 2.6, arrive at another talus slope. Follow cairns again.
5. At 2.8, emerge on the ridgeline and summit. An optional scramble (with some exposure) across the ridge takes you to a secondary summit at just over 3 miles.

FIND THE TRAILHEAD

Follow Wildernest Road south from Silverthorne, then west until it turns into Ryan Gulch Road. The well-signed trailhead sits at the top (west end) of this road.

ANGRY JAMES BREWERY

Back in 2014, husband-and-wife team AJ (Angry James) and Darcy ditched Denver to move west to the mountains and start working toward their vision of the Angry James Brewery, with the goal of creating not only world-class beer but also a community gathering place. With 16 taps, decadent Mountain Melt grilled cheese sammies, and a calendar packed with live music and trivia nights, Angry James is the perfect spot to refuel after a big day in the mountains.

CONTACT INFORMATION

U.S. Forest Service,
Dillon Ranger District,
680 Blue River Parkway
Silverthorne, CO 80498;
970-468-5400

BREWERY/RESTAURANT

Angry James Brewery
421 Adams Ave
Silverthorne, CO 80498
970-455-8800
Miles from trailhead: 3.4

STEAMBOAT SPRINGS

TWO MAGNIFICENT WATERFALLS FOR THE PRICE OF ONE

STARTING POINT	OBJECTIVE
FISH CREEK FALLS TRAILHEAD	UPPER FISH CREEK FALLS
BEER	HIKE TYPE
HOPPY HIKER IPA	MODERATE-STRENUOUS
FEES	SEASON
$5	JUNE TO OCTOBER
MAP REFERENCE	DOG FRIENDLY
TRAILS ILLUSTRATED 118: STEAMBOAT SPRINGS, RABBIT EARS PASS	YES (LEASH REQUIRED)
DURATION	LENGTH
3 HOURS	4.9 MILES
LOW POINT / HIGH POINT	ELEVATION GAIN
7,440 FEET / 8,780 FEET	1,470 FEET

ALCOHOL
6%
CONTENT

HOPPY HIKER IPA

BURNT GOLD

CITRUS,
PINE

DISTINCTLY HOPPY

BITTERNESS
IBU: 60

SWEETNESS

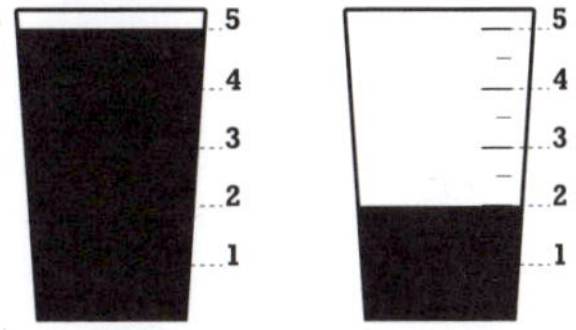

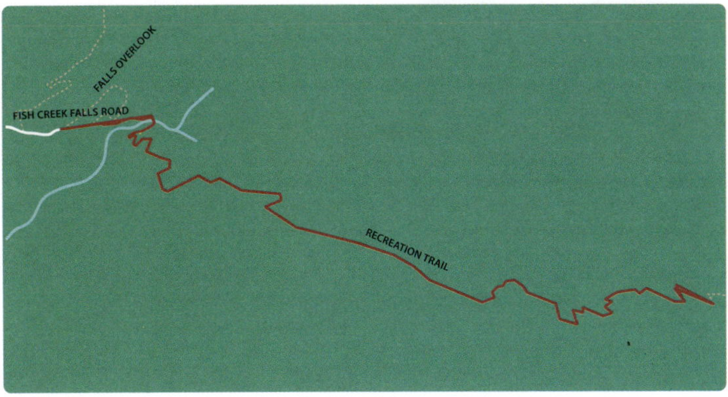

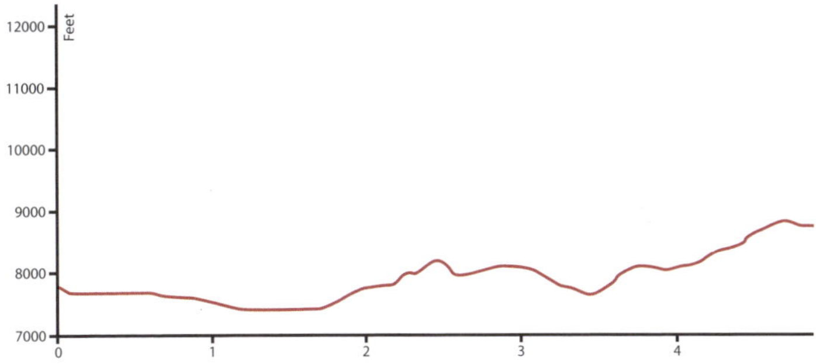

HIKE DESCRIPTION

Visit two magnificent waterfalls in a single hike before stopping in for a dry-hopped American IPA that bursts with citrus and piney aromatics reminiscent of the forests that surround Steamboat Springs.

Steamboat Springs is a town famous for its world-class skiing, extensive network of singletrack trails, abundance of geothermal hot springs and—yes—good beer. What's not to love? The town derives its name from the chugging sound that early explorers heard and assumed was a steamboat coming down the Yampa River—only to discover that the gurgling was, in fact, coming from the natural hot springs near the old train depot.

Fish Creek Falls is one of the most popular stops for visitors to Steamboat, especially in the late spring when the falls are roaring at their fullest and early-mid fall when the aspen leaves are changing. You can avoid the "strenuous" part of this hike altogether and head (nearly) straight for the taproom at Butcherknife by keeping your hiking adventure to the main Fish Creek Falls overlook, which makes for a scenic roundtrip hike of just half a mile—downhill on your way out, uphill on your way back. The bridge at the base of the 280-foot falls offers a lovely view from afar of the cascade, as well as the babbling creek into which they spill. Visit in mid-late spring to see the falls at peak runoff.

If you're game for a longer adventure and a way to escape the crowds, continue your hike beyond the bridge to a second waterfall higher up. Begin with switchbacks that climb up through the dense, shaded forest. You'll pass through some stands of aspen along the way, which turn to fiery hues come late September. After passing a second bridge across Fish Creek, the trail grows rockier and steeper yet. From the bridge, it's just over half a mile to reach the upper falls. Enjoy the views of the valley as they open up along this final stretch of the hike. The upper falls, though slightly smaller than the lower falls, are no less impressive. They're surrounded by rocks and boulders for scrambling up and relaxing on to eat a snack before heading back the way you came for noshing and a brewski back in town.

TURN BY TURN DIRECTIONS:

1. At 0.2 miles, reach the bridge overlooking the falls.
2. Continue hiking past the bridge, crossing another bridge at 1.5 miles.
3. Reach upper falls in just over 2 miles.

FIND THE TRAILHEAD

Head east out of downtown Steamboat Springs on Oak Street, which turns into Fish Creek Falls Road. In 2.4 miles, follow the road around in a sharp right to stay on Fish Creek Falls Road and arrive at trailhead in another 0.7 miles.

MOUNTAIN TAP BREWERY

Mountain Tap Brewery owner Rich Tucciarone began his brewing career after a somewhat random meeting with a fellow ski bum in Steamboat Springs that evolved into a friendship and eventually a job opportunity at a fledgling Denver brewery. In five years at Breckenridge Brewery in Denver, he worked his way up to head brewer and brewery operations manager. After that, he spent 12 years in charge of brewery operations for Kona Brewing Company on the Big Island of Hawaii. But Tucciarone never lost his love for the mountains, so in 2011, he packed up and moved back to Steamboat Springs to work as an industry consultant. In 2016, he and his wife, Wendy, opened Mountain Tap Brewery in the former Yampa Valley Electric Association building adjacent to the Yampa River.

CONTACT INFORMATION

U.S. Forest Service,
Hahns Peak/Bears Ears Ranger District,
925 Weiss Dr.,
Steamboat Springs, CO 80487;
970-870-2299

BREWERY/RESTAURANT

Mountain Tap Brewery
910 Yampa St #103
Steamboat Springs, CO 80487
mountaintapbrewery.com
970-879-6646
Miles from trailhead: 3.8

IDAHO SPRINGS

PAY A VISIT TO ONE OF COLORADO'S LAST REMAINING GLACIERS

STARTING POINT	OBJECTIVE
ST. MARY'S GLACIER TRAILHEAD	ST. MARY'S LAKE AND GLACIER
BEER	HIKE TYPE
BLOOD ORANGE IPA	MODERATE
FEES	SEASON
$20	JUNE TO OCTOBER (OR SNOWSHOE YEAR-ROUND)
MAP REFERENCE	DOG FRIENDLY
TRAILS ILLUSTRATED 103: WINTER PARK, CENTRAL CITY, ROLLINS PASS	YES (LEASH REQUIRED)
DURATION	LENGTH
1 HOUR	2 MILES
LOW POINT / HIGH POINT	ELEVATION GAIN
10,407 FEET / 11,207 FEET	735 FEET

ALCOHOL 6% CONTENT

IPA

CLEAR COPPER

BIG CITRUS

JUICY ORANGE, SLIGHT MALT

BITTERNESS
IBU: 55

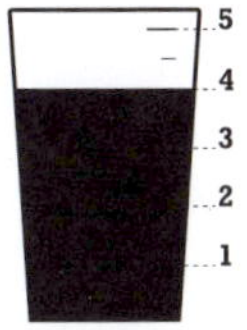

SWEETNESS

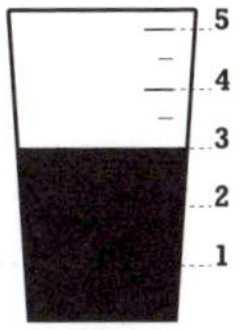

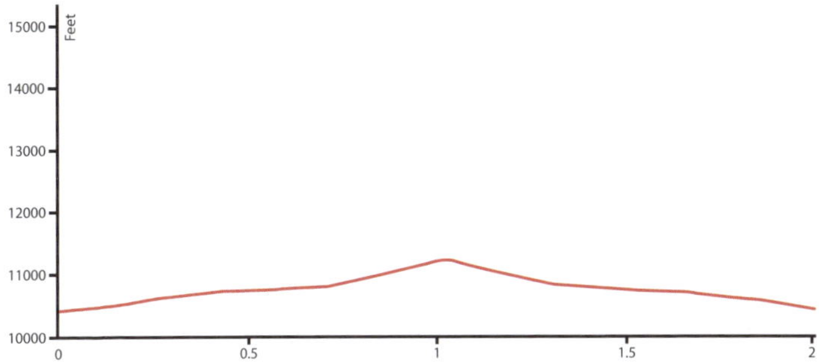

HIKE DESCRIPTION

Visit one of Colorado's few remaining glaciers on this rewarding hike that delivers you to the foot of a lake, waterfall, and small glacier in less than a mile.

To date, Colorado has just 14 officially named glaciers remaining, most of which lie within the boundaries of Rocky Mountain National Park, or in or near the Indian Peaks Wilderness. Tiny St. Mary's lies just above an eponymous lake on the cusp of private property, but a 0.75-mile trail is open to the public for those who wish to venture to its flanks. Rewarding you for your efforts on the rocky trail up are terrific views of the alpine lake, cascading glacier, and small waterfall between them, as well as the rocky slopes and cliffs towering over the lake.

In all months of the year, locals flock to St. Mary's for the chance to ski, snowboard, sled, or glissade, even if only for a minute or two on the short snowfield—hiking up to earn their turns even at the height of summer or fall. (Do beware that dangers exist year-round, ranging from precarious snow bridges in the summer to avalanche conditions in the winter; as signs as the trailhead will warn, there have been fatalities here in the past.)

Due to this hike's scenic destination, relative brevity, and its proximity to Denver, it gets busy by midday, especially on weekends. Plan to arrive early for a better shot at easy parking and a less crowded experience at the glacier. Hiking up above the lake and glacier also offers more solitude at any time of the day, as most hikers don't venture above the bottom of the glacier.

From the trailhead, follow the wide, rock- and boulder-strewn dirt road up. Several trails and road spurs splinter off in different directions, but the abundant private property signs tacked on to trees lining the trail should keep you on track. Within a half-mile, the lake, glacier, and waterfall will be within view, along with a beautiful grove of twisted old pines and the looming nearby Fox Mountain.

From here, it's largely a matter of choosing your own adventure on the various splintering trails around the lake and up near the glacier. Beyond what's visible from the bottom, there is a whole other section of glacier—not visible from the lake—if you venture up another quarter- or half-mile. Watch your footing on the loose earth if you opt to scramble up this way. A rough path snakes up along the northwest (looker's right) side of the glacier. Follow this up as high as you like, to the top of the glacier or even beyond to a higher pass with views toward the James Peak Wilderness Area.

When you're ready to call it a day, head back down the way you came up. A juicy blood orange IPA awaits you at Tommyknocker Brewery on the main drag in Idaho Springs.

TURN BY TURN DIRECTIONS:

1. At the first two wide junctions, stay left on the main road, continuing up.
2. At 0.3 miles, follow the trail to the right.
3. At 0.5, cross the bridge and arrive at St. Mary's Lake.
4. At 0.75, arrive at the foot of St. Mary's glacier. Turn around here, or continue up the trail along the northeast side of the glacier another quarter-mile or more for more glacier views.

FIND THE TRAILHEAD

Take exit 238 off I-70 and follow signs for the glacier, traveling north on Fall River Road for about 9 miles. Bring $5 (exact bills in cash) to park in either trailhead lot; both sit on private property. The well-marked trailhead sits between them.

TOMMYKNOCKER BREWERY

Tommyknocker Brewery has been brewing lagers and ales in the historic mining town of Idaho Springs since 1994. It's earned loads of Great American Beer Festival (GABF) medals over the years. Hearty, Rocky Mountain pub fare and a full array of not only beers but also house-made cream sodas, root beer, and even a non-alcoholic version of their flagship Blood Orange IPA let you fuel up for all your mountain adventures.

CONTACT INFORMATION

U.S. Forest Service,
Clear Creek Ranger District,
2060 Miner Street,
Idaho Springs, CO 80452;
303-567-4382

BREWERY/RESTAURANT

Tommyknocker Brewery
1401 Miner Street,
Idaho Springs, CO 80452
303-567-2688
Miles from trailhead: 11.3

NEDERLAND

STUNNING BACKCOUNTRY LAKES IN THE INDIAN PEAKS WILDERNESS AREA

STARTING POINT	OBJECTIVE
HESSIE TRAILHEAD 2WD PARKING	WOODLAND LAKE AND SKYSCRAPER RESERVOIR
BEER	HIKE TYPE
VERY NICE PALE ALE	MODERATE-STRENUOUS
FEES	SEASON
NONE	JULY TO SEPTEMBER
MAP REFERENCE	DOG FRIENDLY
TRAILS ILLUSTRATED 103: WINTER PARK, CENTRAL CITY, ROLLINS PASS	YES (LEASH REQUIRED)
DURATION	LENGTH
4-7 HOURS	10.6 MILES
LOW POINT / HIGH POINT	ELEVATION GAIN
9,012 FEET / 11,260 FEET	2,180 FEET

ALCOHOL 6% CONTENT

PALE ALE

BRIGHT STRAW

FLORAL; LEMON

HOPPY, TANGY

BITTERNESS
IBU: 33

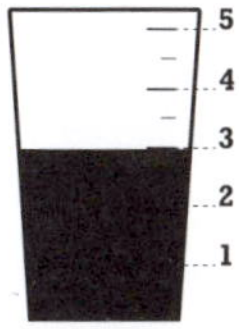

SWEETNESS

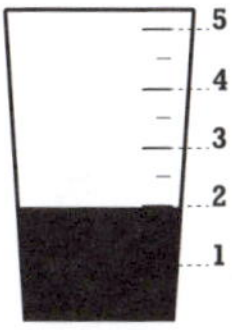

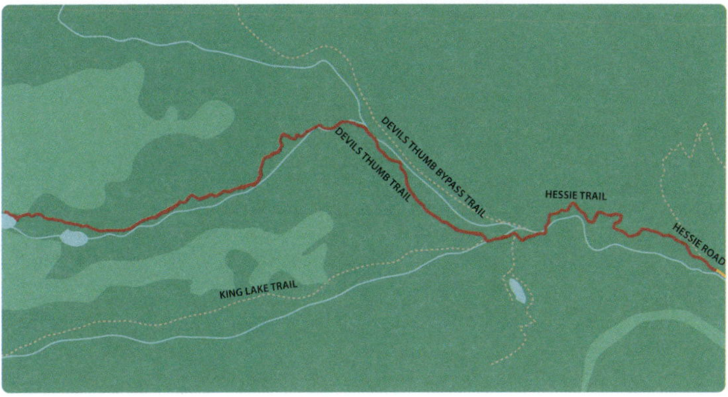

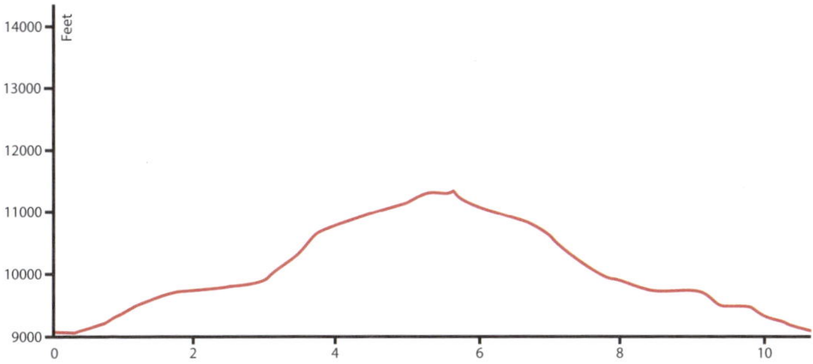

HIKE DESCRIPTION

The long hike in is worth it for a glimpse of these backcountry gems, let alone the refreshing pale ale that awaits you at Very Nice Brewing.

It's hard to beat the views at these scenic backcountry lakes, which are tucked into impressive, craggy cirques deep inside the Indian Peaks Wilderness Area. They're located at the foot of the Continental Divide. The entire area is pockmarked with dozens of picturesque bodies of water including Devil's Thumb, King, Bob, Betty, and Storm Lakes, not to mention Woodland Lake and Skyscraper Reservoir, your destinations on this particular trek.

Once upon a time, this region was a hotbed for mining, including the successful Fourth of July Mine. The ghost town of Hessie—which you'll pass early on your journey, and from which the trailhead gleans its name—served as a homesteading site for a number of silver miners in the 1890s and early 1900s. It drew its name from the wife of town founder Captain J.H. Davis, who set up a post office and became the town's first postmistress.

Today, the area is exceptionally popular for hikers and backpackers eager to soak up its breathtaking alpine views. That said, the majority of day hikers do not venture all the way to the lakes, most of which require several hours to reach. If you're game for a longer hike, it's possible to out-hike the crowds, especially if you take advantage of visiting on weekdays or in the fall off-season.

From the 2WD parking area along the sides of the road, your hike begins on a rocky jeep road for a half-mile before arriving at a bridge and the official Hessie trailhead. The hike in to Woodland Lake has a fairly mellow grade, with a few steep pitches here and there. The lake will be on your left, visible through the trees. If you opt to continue on up to Skyscraper Reservoir (absolutely worth doing if you have the time and energy for the bonus mile!), you'll enjoy even better views of Woodland Lake from above, where carpets of wildflowers also await.

Skyscraper Reservoir is appropriately named, as its glittering waters seem to kiss the blue sky beneath the Divide. Originally built in the 1940s for irrigation purposes for farmers and ranchers downstream, the reservoir is no longer maintained; however, it retains remnants of its original damming. Lots of beautiful driftwood graces its shores, with many rocks to scramble over on any further, off-trail meandering you want to do around the lake before hiking back down the same way you came up.

TURN BY TURN DIRECTIONS:

1. From 2WD parking area, follow the rocky, dirt road for 0.5 miles to reach the Hessie trailhead.
2. Cross the bridge, then stay on the main dirt road up.
3. Follow signs for Woodland Lake; trail junctions are well marked.
4. Around 5 miles, reach open view of Woodland Lake to your left.
5. Continue up trail for another quarter-mile to visit Skyscraper Reservoir before returning the way you came.

FIND THE TRAILHEAD

On summer weekends, take the free Hessie Trailhead shuttle from the RTD Park-n-Ride in Nederland. Otherwise, head out early for a good shot at the limited parking. From Nederland, drive southwest out of town on CO 119, then turn right on CO 130/Eldora Road. In 4.5 miles, arrive at Hessie 2WD Trailhead at the junction with Fourth of July Road. Park on the road in designated areas only.

VERY NICE BREWING COMPANY

This cozy, family-owned establishment sports a 3.5-barrel brewing system and a lineup of six flagship beers as well as a rotating menu of seasonals and premium beers. Locals are invited to bring in their own ingredients to contribute to small-batch experimental brews as well. With frequent live music and a family-friendly atmosphere, it's hard not to fall in love with this quaint little neighborhood watering hole.

CONTACT INFORMATION
U.S. Forest Service,
Boulder Ranger District,
2140 Yarmouth Ave
Boulder, CO 80301;
303-541-2500

BREWERY/RESTAURANT
Very Nice Brewing Company
20 Lakeview Drive, Suite 112,
Nederland, CO 80466
303-258-3770
Miles from trailhead: 5.3

NORTH BOULDER

A STEEP, SHORT TREK NORTHWEST OF TOWN

STARTING POINT	OBJECTIVE
2ND STREET AND DAKOTA BOULEVARD	HOGBACK RIDGE
BEER	**HIKE TYPE**
JAPANESE STYLE RICE LAGER	MODERATE-STRENUOUS
FEES	**SEASON**
NONE	YEAR-ROUND
MAP REFERENCE	**DOG FRIENDLY**
FOOTHILLS AREA TRAIL MAP AT BOULDERCOLORADO.GOV	NO
DURATION	**LENGTH**
1.5 HOURS	2.4 MILES
LOW POINT / HIGH POINT	**ELEVATION GAIN**
5,670 FEET / 6,417 FEET	700 FEET

ALCOHOL
4.9%
CONTENT

RICE LAGER

PALE STRAW

GREEN TEA, TOASTED RICE

CRISP, LIGHT-BODIED

BITTERNESS

IBU: 13

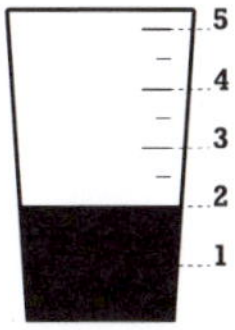

SWEETNESS

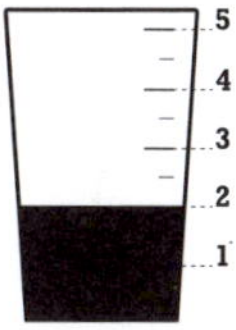

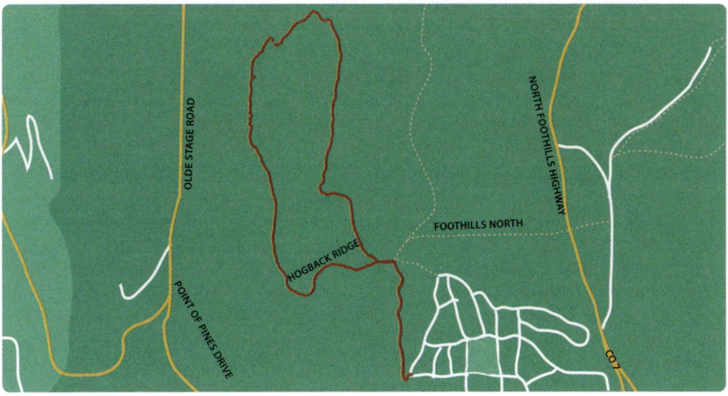

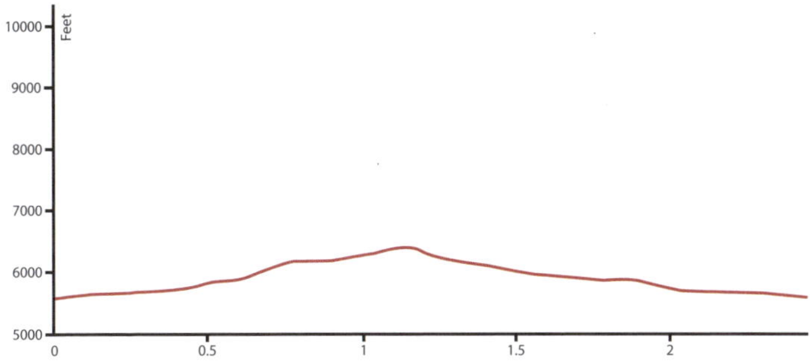

HIKE DESCRIPTION

Escape the Boulder trail crowds by venturing onto this steep, hiker-only loop northwest of town, then wash it down with a Japanese-style rice lager.

Boulder frequently appears on "Best Trail Town" lists—and for obvious reasons, with more than 200 miles of trails within easy range of downtown. Because Boulder's population has boomed in recent years, many of the most popular trails can get quite crowded, especially on summer weekends.

The solution? Venture to the lesser-known singletrack systems northwest of town on the outskirts of North Boulder, or "NoBo" as it's called colloquially. Because neither dogs nor mountain bikers are permitted on this loop, it's a great choice for hikers desiring a bit of solitude outside a city otherwise bustling with fellow outdoors enthusiasts.

"Hogback" is an actual geological term for a long, narrow ridge created over time by erosion. Colorado is chock-full of trails called "Hogback" that traverse such ridgelines, and this one is no different. It's a relatively steep climb up, but absolutely worth the short trek for expansive views of the eastern plains, sparkling reservoirs, neighboring foothills, the Boulder Flatirons, and Mount Sanitas.

Wear a hat and ample sunscreen, as there's hardly any shade on this trail other than the brief respite offered by some scrubby pines near the top of the hogback itself. Otherwise, the trail is mostly desert grasses and rock or log stairs. Admire the beautifully designed rock staircases you encounter along the way.

The Hogback Loop is a lollipop loop that begins with a section of the Foothills Trail. After a quarter mile on the Foothills Trail, veer left and head uphill to begin the Hogback loop. Stay to the left when the trail splits to continue on a clockwise circuit of the loop. The trail continues by descending the hogback and closes the loop just before rejoining Foothills Trail.

Do keep an eye out for rattlesnakes, as they enjoy sunning themselves on the rocks along this trail. Other wildlife sightings are common as well, including mule deer and coyotes. After soaking up the views at the top, descend on the north side to complete a clockwise lollipop loop before heading to Upslope Brewing's NoBo taproom less than a mile away on Lee Hill Drive.

TURN BY TURN DIRECTIONS:

1. From the trailhead, follow the clear uphill trail to your right.
2. At 0.3 miles, go left at the junction, then arrive at the well-signed Hogback Loop, which can be hiked in either direction.
3. If you go left (clockwise), reach the high point at 1.1 miles. Scramble up to your right to reach the very top before rejoining the trail.
4. Continue on the loop, descending north.
5. At 2.1, rejoin the original trail by going left at the first junction and right at the second junction.

FIND THE TRAILHEAD

Go west on Lee Hill Drive out of North Boulder. Make a right on 5th Street, then a left on Dakota Boulevard. The small trailhead is at the corner where Dakota meets 2nd Street. Park on the street.

UPSLOPE BREWING COMPANY - LEE HILL

Upslope is named for the meteorological pvhenomenon responsible for many a snowstorm in Colorado's Front Range. The name is an ode to Upslope's founders' love for snow, mountains, and adventure. When the team of three first opened Upslope in 2008, their mission was to "make a better beer rooted in the outdoor lifestyle." They have six core styles, with a number of popular seasonals ranging from a pumpkin ale to fruity sour ales to an IPA brewed with spruce tips.

CONTACT INFORMATION

Open Space and Mountain Parks (OSMP),
3198 N. Broadway,
Boulder, CO 80304; 303-441-3440

BREWERY/RESTAURANT

Upslope Brewing Company - Lee Hill
1501 Lee Hill Drive,
Boulder, CO 80304
303-449-2911
Miles from trailhead: 0.8

BOULDER

ASCEND A BELOVED LOCAL PEAK VIA THE FERN CANYON TRAIL

STARTING POINT	OBJECTIVE
NCAR TRAILHEAD	BEAR PEAK
BEER	**HIKE TYPE**
ANNAPURNA AMBER	VERY STRENUOUS
FEES	**SEASON**
NONE	MARCH TO NOVEMBER
MAP REFERENCE	**DOG FRIENDLY**
OSMP TRAIL MAP AT BOULDERCOLORADO.GOV	YES (LEASH REQUIRED)
DURATION	**LENGTH**
4-6 HOURS	7.5 MILES
LOW POINT / HIGH POINT	**ELEVATION GAIN**
6,109 FEET / 8,461 FEET	2,687 FEET

ALCOHOL **5.1%** CONTENT

AMBER

BROWN, REDDISH TINT

BISCUIT, CARAMEL

TOFFEE, BARLEY MALT

BITTERNESS IBU: UNLISTED

SWEETNESS

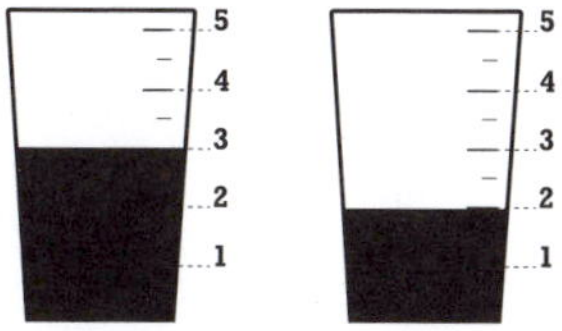

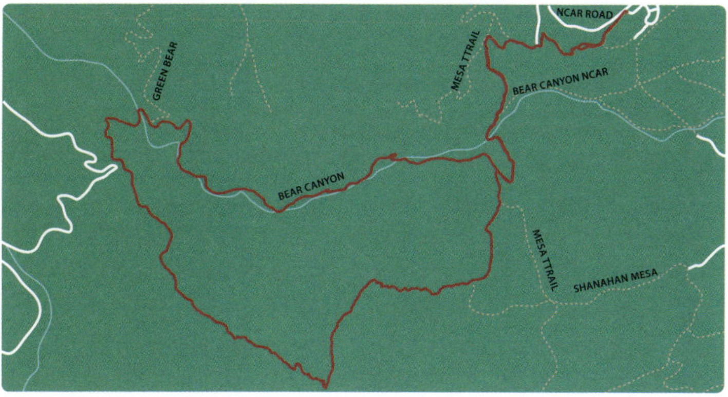

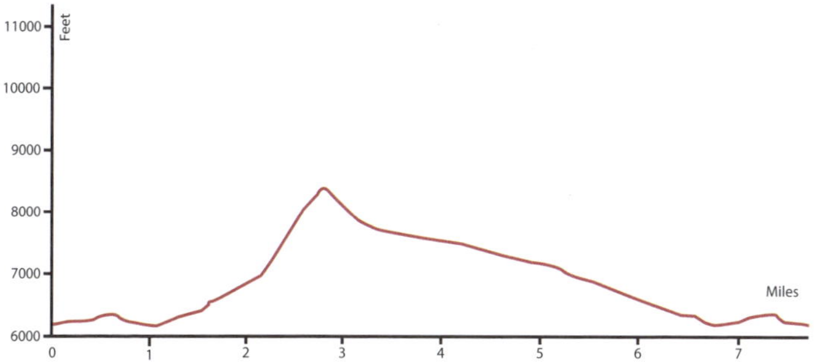

HIKE DESCRIPTION

Go for this "bear" of a climb and scramble up a famous local peak before visiting one of Boulder's original brewpubs.

The town of Boulder is framed on the west by a number of prominent mountains and ridgelines visible from most parts of downtown. These include the infamous Flatirons on the front flanks of Green Mountain, as well as Bear Peak and South Boulder Peak. With many trails weaving over their shoulders, all offer spectacular, challenging hiking and a bit of scrambling. From their summits, you'll enjoy spectacular views of Boulder to one side and the vast Indian Peaks Wilderness to the other.

If you're in the mood for a slightly shorter hike, you can do this summit of Bear Peak as an out-and-back in a little over five miles. However, the longer descent through Bear Canyon provides a lovely amble through the trees and over a number of creek crossings—and it's a more forgiving route on the knees and quads than coming back down the much steeper Fern Canyon Trail you'll ascend on your way up.

From the National Center for Atmospheric Research (NCAR) trailhead, the initial approach on the Mesa Trail passes through dry, dusty desert environs. It can get quite hot in the middle of the day during summer. But it won't be long before you get to duck into the trees and seek respite among the pines.

Once you turn onto the lush Fern Canyon Trail, be prepared for a staircase of a workout for about one mile until you reach the high, open saddle just beneath the 8,459-foot summit of Bear Peak, the second highest mountain in Boulder. From there, you can see the adjacent South Boulder Peak (8,549 feet) to the west, as well as the larger mountains along the Continental Divide on the horizon line. To the east, you get a bird's-eye view of Boulder and rolling plains that lead to Denver and beyond.

From here, you'll be able to see the Bear Peak West Ridge Trail snaking down the ridge to your right. A trail sign below the summit marks the turnoff for this route to Bear Canyon. When you're ready, and assuming you want to complete the full loop, continue in this direction for a descent that's initially steep but quickly mellows to a more flowing, roundabout hike through wildflower-studded meadows and mixed forest.

Before you go, check www.OSMP.org for current dog/leash regulations and trail conditions; portions of this route are subject to frequent closures. This route can generally be done year-round, though if you plan to hike it in the winter, traction devices (spikes) are highly recommended.

TURN BY TURN DIRECTIONS:

1. Stay left at the first two trail junctions at 0.6 miles and 0.7.
2. At 1.4 miles, make a left, followed by a right onto Fern Canyon at 1.5.
3. At 1.9, go right and up.
4. At 2.7, scramble up to reach the Bear Peak summit.
5. Follow signs for Bear Peak West Ridge (the trail winding down the ridge below to the northwest).
6. At 4.6, stay straight to stay on Bear Canyon Trail.
7. At 6.75, go left and up on the Mesa Trail, following signs for NCAR, then stay right at next three trail intersections.

FIND THE TRAILHEAD

From S. Broadway (Highway 93), drive west out of South Boulder on Table Mesa Drive. This turns into NCAR Road before arriving at the large, well-signed trailhead at the end of the road.

SOUTHERN SUN PUB & BREWERY

Southern Sun Pub & Brewery is one of three local branches of the Mountain Sun, a bohemian-themed neighborhood brewpub that first opened its doors back in 1993. Its south Boulder locale makes it a perfect stop after a day of hiking in nearby Chautauqua Park, home to Boulder's iconic Flatirons and many other beloved local hikes including this one. Grab a seat on the outdoor patio or a booth by the window for a great sunset view over the mountains.

CONTACT INFORMATION

Boulder Open Space and Mountain Parks,
66 S. Cherryvale Road,
Boulder, CO 80303;
303-441-3440

BREWERY/RESTAURANT

Southern Sun Pub & Brewery
627 S. Broadway,
Boulder, CO 80305
303-543-0886
Miles from trailhead: 2.6

ESTES PARK

A DAZZLING ALPINE LAKE IN ROCKY MOUNTAIN NATIONAL PARK

STARTING POINT	OBJECTIVE
LONGS PEAK TRAILHEAD	CHASM LAKE
BEER	HIKE TYPE
GALACTIC PORTAL HAZY IPA	STRENUOUS
FEES	SEASON
NONE	JUNE TO OCTOBER
MAP REFERENCE	DOG FRIENDLY
TRAILS ILLUSTRATED 200: ROCKY MOUNTAIN NATIONAL PARK	NO
DURATION	LENGTH
5-7 HOURS	8.4 MILES
LOW POINT / HIGH POINT	ELEVATION GAIN
9,426 FEET / 11,847 FEET	2,500 FEET

ALCOHOL
7.4%
CONTENT

HAZY IPA

CLOUDY YELLOW ORANGE

PINEY; TROPICAL FRUIT

PINEAPPLE, MELON

BITTERNESS
IBU: 48

SWEETNESS

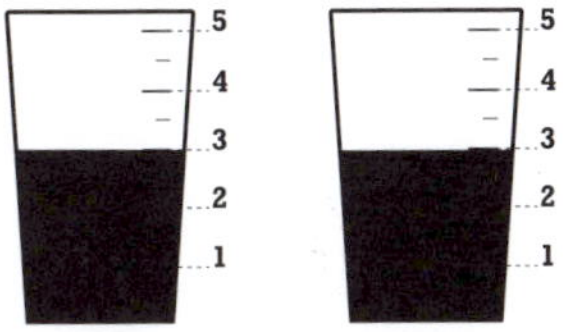

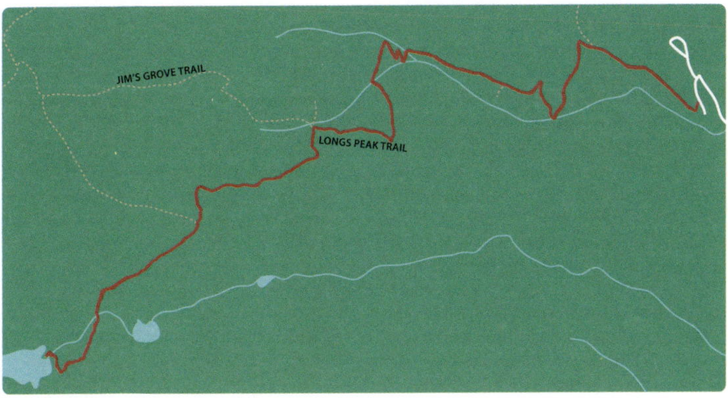

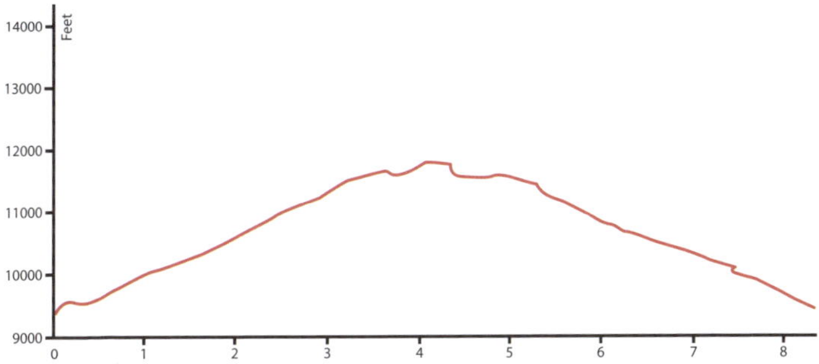

HIKE DESCRIPTION

This dazzling alpine lake sits at the foot of one of Colorado's most iconic, awe-inspiring mountain faces.

The crown jewel of Rocky Mountain National Park, Longs Peak is its tallest peak and only "fourteener," standing proud at 14,259 feet. It is featured on the Colorado state quarter, and its dramatic, sheer east face is known as "The Diamond" for reasons that will become obvious during this hike. Chasm Lake lies at the foot of the Diamond—a gorgeous alpine lake burrowed into the belly of a dramatic cirque, carved out long ago by glaciers. The one remaining sliver of a glacier on Longs Peak, Mills Glacier, sits just above the lake.

Find your trail behind the ranger station. You'll begin by hiking through subalpine lodgepole pine forest before emerging above tree line. Listen for the squeaks of pikas and chirps of marmots darting amidst the rocks and wildflower-pocked tundra. You'll pass the turnoff for the Boulder Field, where you'll part ways from hikers bound for the summit of Longs. Beyond there, admire the face of the Diamond as you traverse the alpine hillside toward it, passing Peacock Pool below to your left. Depending on the time of year you go, a waterfall often spills down between here and the rocky bluffs above.

There's a small scramble in the last tenth of a mile to reach Chasm Lake, as the "trail" snakes up and through a notch in the rock. Follow cairns to find your route. Enjoy the deep emerald hue of the lake with its beautiful reflection of the surrounding jagged peaks, snowfields, and rocky cliffs. Plenty of flat boulders around the lake's edge let you relax in the sun. If you've brought binoculars, it's possible to watch climbers ascending Longs Peak, which looms over the lake like a sentry.

Because this is also the trailhead for Longs Peak, the parking lot can fill up fast, especially on summer weekends. Plan to arrive early. Above tree line, high wind, harmful UV rays, and lightning can all be threats—so, wear sunscreen, bring layers, and be prepared to turn back early if thunderstorms begin to develop.

TURN BY TURN DIRECTIONS:

1. At 0.5 mile, go straight at the well-signed junction, following signs for Chasm Lake and Longs Peak.
2. At 2.5, go left at the well-signed junction.
3. At 3.2, stay straight/left at the junction with the Boulder Field.
4. At 4, scramble up the steep gully, following cairns.
5. In a tenth of a mile, reach the lake.

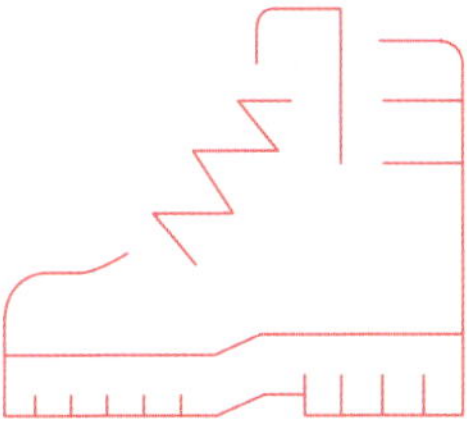

FIND THE TRAILHEAD

From Estes Park, head south on either Mary's Lake Road or South St. Vrain Avenue (Highway 7). About 5.5 miles farther south of where these two roads intersect, turn right onto Longs Peak Road. Arrive at the trail-head in 1 mile.

ROCK CUT BREWING COMPANY

Rock Cut Brewing Company offers a cozy, après-adventure spot to quench your thirst and rest your weary legs after hiking in nearby Rocky Mountain National Park. Located at the foot of Prospect Mountain with an outdoor patio overlooking Lumpy Ridge, this family-friendly tap-room pours everything from crisp IPAs to barrel-aged imperial stouts to a number of German-style brews.

CONTACT INFORMATION

National Park Service,
Rocky Mountain National Park,
1000 U.S. Highway 36,
Estes Park, CO 80517;
970-586-1206

BREWERY/RESTAURANT

Rock Cut Brewing Company
390 W. Riverside Drive,
Estes Park, CO 80517
970-586-7300
Miles from trailhead: 10.3

FORT COLLINS

TAKE THE HORSETOOTH ROCK TRAIL TO A FUN SUMMIT SCRAMBLE

STARTING POINT	OBJECTIVE
HORSETOOTH MOUNTAIN TRAILHEAD	HORSETOOTH FALLS AND HORSETOOTH ROCK
BEER	HIKE TYPE
ZWEI PILS BAVARIAN-STYLE PILSNER	STRENUOUS
FEES	SEASON
$9	MARCH TO NOVEMBER
MAP REFERENCE	DOG FRIENDLY
HORSETOOTH MOUNTAIN OPEN SPACE ON LARIMER.ORG	YES (LEASH REQUIRED)
DURATION	LENGTH
3-4 HOURS	6.1 MILES
LOW POINT / HIGH POINT	ELEVATION GAIN
5,745 FEET / 7,255 FEET	1,585 FEET

ALCOHOL 5.1% CONTENT

PILSNER

CLEAR, PALE STRAW

FLORAL, HONEY AND BISCUITS

CRISP, GRASSY, HERBAL HOPS

BITTERNESS

IBU: 36

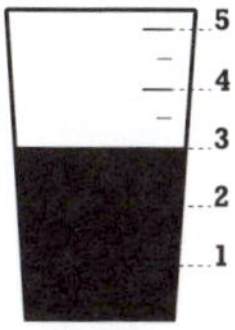

SWEETNESS

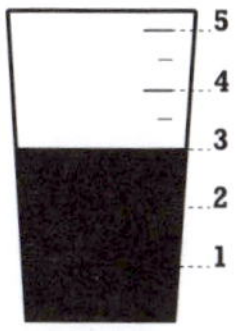

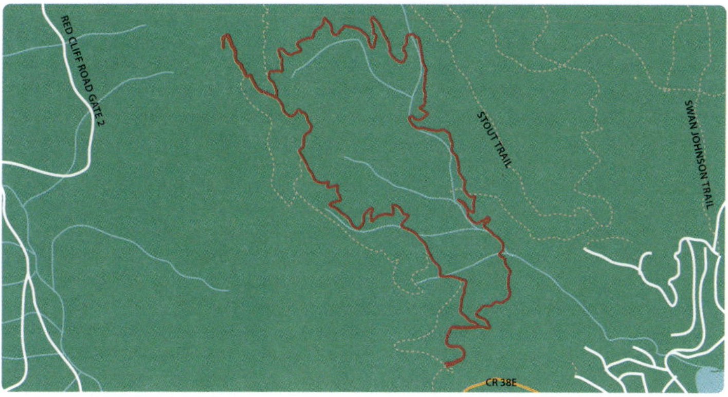

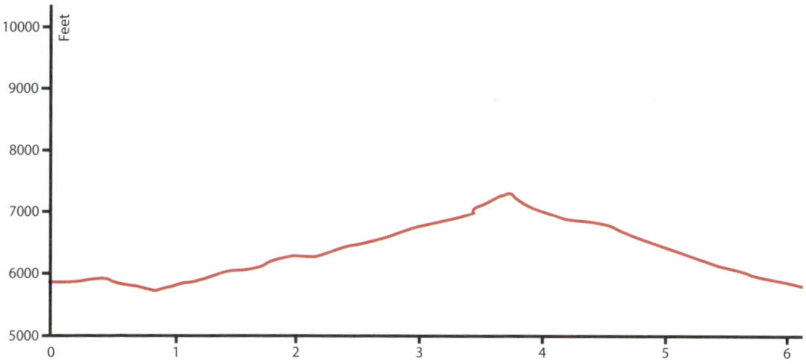

HIKE DESCRIPTION

No Fort Collins trip is complete without a trip to Horsetooth Mountain Open Space; this loop encompasses a waterfall, fun summit scramble, and an authentic German-style pilsner back in town.

Horsetooth Mountain—so named for its resemblance to giant, literal horse's teeth—is a landmark on the western horizon of Fort Collins. It's even a part of the official City of Fort Collins logo. According to Arapahoe legend, the rock is what remains of the heart of giant who once presided over the area before Chief Maunamoku killed him, cleaving the giant's chest into the rock formation we now see today.

Visible from many parts of town, it is an icon that beckons to be climbed.

Fortunately, nearly 30 miles of trails have been developed in the public open space that sits at the foot of the mountain. Often referred to as Horsetooth Rock by locals, Horsetooth Mountain is not only a doable (and justly popular) day hike, there are multiple route options for reaching its summit.

The most direct, and thus most crowded, hiking route up is the Horsetooth Rock Trail. This loop utilizes that trail on the way down, but on the way up, detours onto the Horsetooth Falls Trail—also a nice option for a shorter, easier hike if you don't want to venture all the way to the top. The falls are modest (and may be gone altogether during some times of the year such as autumn), but are a lovely spot nonetheless to enjoy a snack, tucked away in a quiet ravine in the woods. Reaching the summit via this trail permits a more forgiving grade on the climb up.

The dense ponderosa forest is home to mule deer, fox, black bear, and many species of birds, so wildlife enthusiasts will love this hike. As you near the top of Horsetooth Rock, the hike turns into a scramble, requiring a few Class 2 moves to make it to either the north or south summit rocks. From the top, the 360-degree views are breathtaking. Take your time up here, savoring glimpses of the nearby Mummy Range and much-adored 14er Longs Peak.

TURN BY TURN DIRECTIONS:

1. Start up Horsetooth Rock Trail to the right and continue following signs for Horsetooth Falls.
2. At 1 mile, go straight/left for a brief out-and-back to a viewpoint of the falls before continuing on up Spring Creek Trail.
3. At 2.1, go left onto Wathen.
4. At 3.3, go right onto Horsetooth Rock Trail and scramble to summit at 3.7 miles.
5. Head back down to junction with Wathen and go right this time.
6. Follow signs saying "Attention: Foot Travel Only" to stay on Horsetooth Rock Trail on your way down.
7. At 5.2, go right on Soderberg, then right again a half-mile later at the original junction with the Horsetooth Falls Trail.

FIND THE TRAILHEAD

South of downtown Fort Collins, take County Road 38E west to Red Cliff Road. The trailhead parking area for Horsetooth Mountain Open Space is to your right. Ample parking exists, but the lot can still fill up on busy days, so plan to arrive early to ensure a parking spot.

ZWEI BREWING

This German-inspired brewery in Fort Collins crafts authentic German, Belgian, and Czech lagers, as well as some small-batch American-style creations such as IPAs, red ales, and brown ales. Their flagship beers include this Bavarian-style pilsner, a Munich-style Helles, a Munich-style amber dunkel, a Bavarian hefeweizen, an Austrian-style lager, and an American IPA. A sunny outdoor patio with lawn games, a ping-pong table and rotating food trucks on site round out this lively tap-room experience.

CONTACT INFORMATION

Larimer County Open Space,
200 W Oak Street,
Fort Collins, CO 80521;
970-498-7000

BREWERY/RESTAURANT

Zwei Brewing
4612 S Mason Street, Suite 120,
Fort Collins, CO 80525
970-223-2482
Miles from trailhead: 8.9

GOLDEN

TOUR THE TOP OF A 60-MILLION-YEAR-OLD MESA FORMED BY LAVA

STARTING POINT	OBJECTIVE
NEW TERRAIN BREWING COMPANY	MESA TOP
BEER	HIKE TYPE
CRUISE RIDE AMERICAN CREAM ALE	MODERATE
FEES	SEASON
NONE	YEAR-ROUND
MAP REFERENCE	DOG FRIENDLY
NORTH TABLE MOUNTAIN PARK MAP AT JEFFCO.US	YES (LEASH REQUIRED)
DURATION	LENGTH
2–2.5 HOURS	4.2 MILES
LOW POINT / HIGH POINT	ELEVATION GAIN
5,656 FEET / 6,444 FEET	780 FEET

ALCOHOL 5.6% CONTENT

CREAM ALE

HAZY GOLDEN

BISCUITY; HONEY

TART LEMON; SMOOTH, CRISP

BITTERNESS
IBU: 13

SWEETNESS

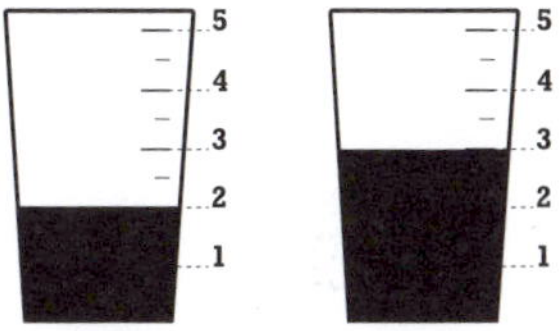

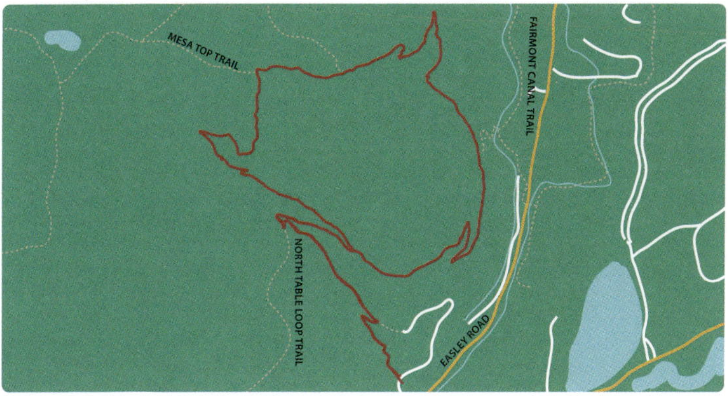

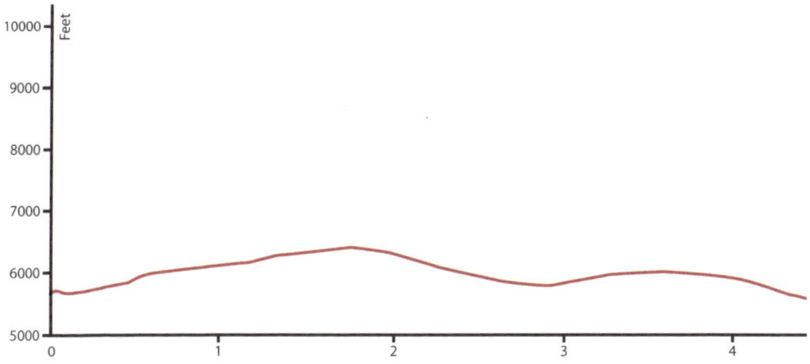

HIKE DESCRIPTION

Take a tour across the top of a 60-million-year-old mesa, formed by lava, that's now home to raptors, rattlesnakes, and panoramic views.

With bluffs and geologic formations beckoning to be explored, the 2,000-acre North Table Mountain Park looms over downtown Golden. Multiple trailheads lead to some 17 miles of trails set over the park's dry, desert-landscape mesa, so check out a map before you start. (And don't forget to lather on sunscreen!) This lollipop loop offers a good tour of the eastern side of the park, which tends to be a bit quieter than the western side.

The mesa that sits at the heart of the park was formed by lava flows thought to have occurred some 60 million years ago. To reach the expansive, flat top of the mesa, you'll climb up a dramatic drainage toward towering bluffs. The power lines over them are a bit of an eyesore amidst the otherwise pristine landscape, but the cliffs are still an impressive sight to behold. Soon you'll be atop them.

Keep an eye out overhead as you climb for raptors such as hawks, eagles, and falcons. At the same time, watch your step, for rattlesnakes are known to frequent the grasslands here. Indeed, the prairie serves as home to an impressive mix of flora and fauna in addition to the aforementioned, including deer, coyotes, cacti, cattail, and yarrow.

Many options exist for a longer excursion, including a loop on the Rim Rock Trail (closed February to July for raptor nesting) that tacks on about two miles atop the mesa. But if you choose to follow the turn-by-turn directions for this loop, you'll enjoy a brief tromp atop the mesa before dipping down singletrack on its east side. From here, enjoy the soaring views of the urban lakes and reservoirs below, and the Denver skyline farther off in the distance.

Watch for mountain bikers, as this park is popular for biking. In the summer, shadeless as they are, these trails can turn into a furnace in the middle of the day—so if you do go, get an early start to beat the heat. Otherwise, spring, fall, and even winter—depending on snow conditions—are all good seasons to take advantage of these trails.

TURN BY TURN DIRECTIONS:

1. From the west side of the brewery's parking lot, head north, then west, on the dirt path.
2. After a quarter-mile, go right to cross the bridge and road.
3. At 0.5 miles, go left on the trail. After several switchbacks, stay left to go clockwise on the North Table Loop.
4. At 1.5, stay right.
5. At 2.5, turn right onto the Mesa Top Trail.
6. At 3.1, turn right onto the North Table Loop.
7. At 3.5, reconnect with original junction. Go left to return the way you came.

FIND THE TRAILHEAD

This loop hike can be done from the parking lot of New Terrain Brewing Company, located on Table Mountain Parkway in Golden.

NEW TERRAIN BREWING COMPANY

With a motto like "For those who wander" and a location tucked away on the fringes of Golden's North Table Mountain Park, New Terrain Brewing Company is a no-brainer destination for all the hikers, trail runners, and mountain bikers who frequent the nearby trails. Opened by beer-industry professionals in 2016, the thirty-barrel brewhouse, taproom, and beer garden (complete with farm-to-fork food-truck cuisine) offer terrific views of the local foothills.

CONTACT INFORMATION

Jefferson County Open Space;
700 Jefferson County Parkway,
Golden, CO 80401;
303-271-5925

BREWERY/RESTAURANT

New Terrain Brewing Company
16401 Table Mountain Parkway,
Golden, CO 80403
720-697-7848
Miles from trailhead: 0

EVERGREEN

HIKE THE FOOTHILLS IN ALDERFER/THREE SISTERS PARK

STARTING POINT	OBJECTIVE
EAST TRAILHEAD, 30299 BUFFALO PARK ROAD	EVERGREEN MOUNTAIN
BEER	**HIKE TYPE**
ANGRY ELK AMBER ALE	MODERATE
FEES	**SEASON**
NONE	APRIL TO OCTOBER
MAP REFERENCE	**DOG FRIENDLY**
ALDERFER THREE SISTERS PARK ON JEFFCO.US	YES (LEASH REQUIRED)
DURATION	**LENGTH**
2.5–3.5 HOURS	6 MILES
LOW POINT / HIGH POINT	**ELEVATION GAIN**
7,513 FEET / 8,556 FEET	990 FEET

ALCOHOL 5.8% CONTENT

AMBER ALE

CLEAR AMBER

MALTY, SLIGHTLY HOPPY

CRISP, MEDIUM-BODIED

BITTERNESS

IBU: UNLISTED

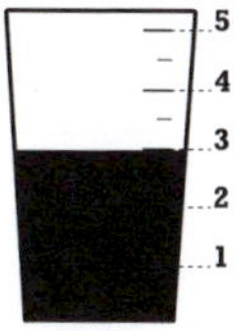

SWEETNESS

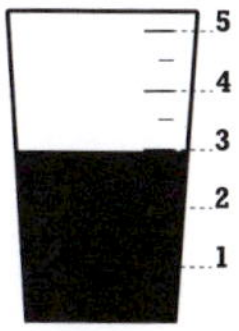

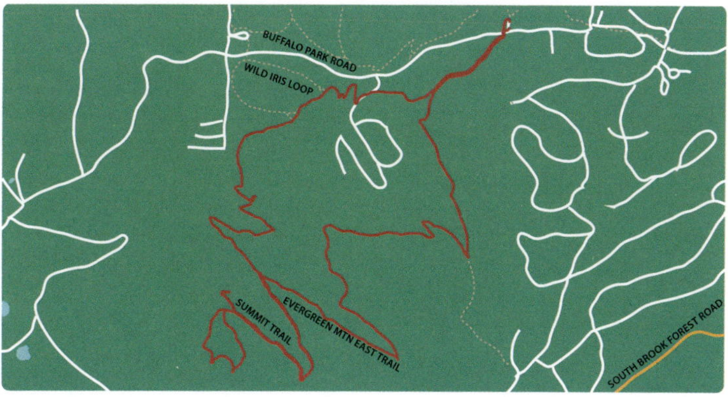

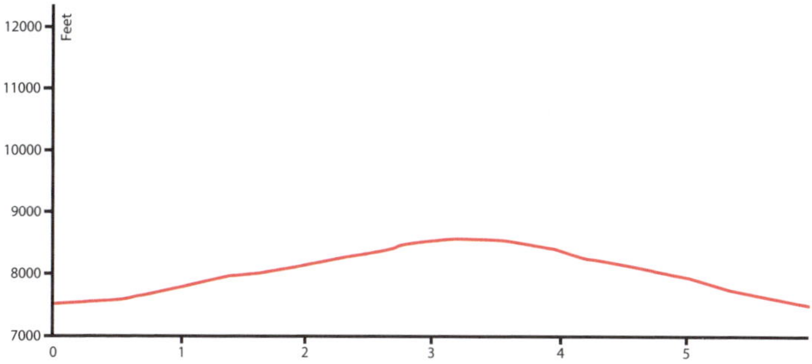

HIKE DESCRIPTION

Spend a day basking in Colorado sunshine on this terrific day hike in the Evergreen foothills, followed by an amber ale on a scenic outdoor deck.

Alderfer/Three Sisters Park was once a working cattle ranch. These days, however, it's a public open space with some 15 miles of trails for hikers, mountain bikers, and equestrians to enjoy. The wildlife, flora, rock formations ideal for bouldering, historical structures, and dense, diverse forest offer a bit of everything for every kind of outdoors enthusiast.

The rocky outcroppings of "The Three Sisters" (North, Middle, and South) and "The Brother" dominate the skyline of the north side of the park, while Evergreen Mountain is the park's most prominent point on the south side. From its modest summit, it's possible to glimpse the Continental Divide and nearby 14,264-foot Mount Evans.

Many loop options exist to take you around either side of the park. This particular loop is a nice sampler platter of the park's terrain, leading you through nicely shaded lodgepole and ponderosa pine forest and cresting out at its high point atop Evergreen Mountain. However, you can also view the park trail map online at www.jeffco.us, or pick up a paper map at the trailhead and design your own loop.

In the late spring and early summer, wildflowers blossom abundantly. These are also popular seasons for trail users of all kind in this park, especially mountain bikers. Though the area receives ample snow in the winter, the trails are popular enough that the snow remains fairly packed—so it is possible to hike in the winter as well, and doing so will likely afford a more solitary hiking experience than in other seasons. (Wear traction devices on your shoes or boots if you're worried about slipping.)

After a few hours in the park, there's no need to head indoors; the expansive, sun-drenched back decks and dog-friendly beer garden at nearby Lariat Lodge Brewing await you.

TURN BY TURN DIRECTIONS:

1. From the East Trailhead, cross the road to pick up the Evergreen Mountain East Trail.
2. At the fork at 0.3 miles, stay left to initiate a clockwise loop.
3. At 2.2, go left and up the Summit Trail.
4. At 2.8, check out the scenic 0.1-mile spur before continuing on up to the 0.5-mile lollipop summit loop, which you can do in either direction.
5. On your way back down, make a left at the well-signed junction with Evergreen Mountain Trail West to complete a loop back to the trailhead.
6. Stay right at the next two intersections until you see a sign pointing you onto Ranch View Trail. Take that until you rejoin the Evergreen Mountain East Trail. Go left to return to the trailhead in 0.3 miles.

FIND THE TRAILHEAD

This is a very popular trailhead, so plan to arrive early. From downtown Evergreen, head west on Highway 73. Make a slight right onto Buffalo Park Road. In just over a mile, the East Trail parking lot for Alderfer/Three Sisters Park will be on your right, located at 30299 Buffalo Park Road.

LARIAT LODGE BREWING

The highlights of this brewery are its massive outdoor decks and beer garden—half of which is dog friendly—with expansive views of the surrounding mountains and woods. The inside is cozy and rustic as well, though. With the brewery's constantly rotating taps of classic beer styles and seasonal experiments, as well as a delicious menu (the Brussels sprouts salad is phenomenal), you'd be hard pressed to find a better place to refuel after your hike.

CONTACT INFORMATION

Jeffco Open Space,
700 Jefferson County Parkway,
303-271-5925

BREWERY/RESTAURANT

Lariat Lodge Brewing
27618 Fireweed Drive,
Evergreen, CO 80439
303-674-1842
Miles from trailhead: 2.9

COLORADO SPRINGS

VISIT A 250-FOOT WATERFALL IN NORTH CHEYENNE CAÑON PARK

STARTING POINT	OBJECTIVE
GOLD CAMP ROAD	ST. MARY'S FALLS
BEER	HIKE TYPE
LAUGHING LAB SCOTTISH ALE	MODERATE-STRENUOUS
FEES	SEASON
NONE	YEAR-ROUND
MAP REFERENCE	DOG FRIENDLY
POCKET PALS TRAIL MAP #3: NORTH CHEYENNE CAÑON AREA	YES (LEASH REQUIRED)
DURATION	LENGTH
3-4 HOURS	6 MILES
LOW POINT / HIGH POINT	ELEVATION GAIN
7,533 FEET / 8,950 FEET	1,400 FEET

ALCOHOL
5.4%
CONTENT

SCOTTISH ALE

CLEAR AMBER

BREAD; NUTTY

MALTY, SMOOTH

BITTERNESS
IBU: 19

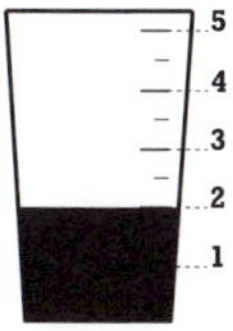

SWEETNESS

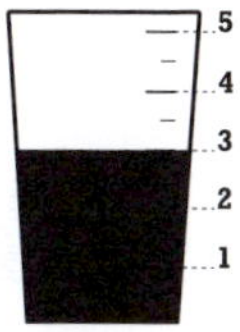

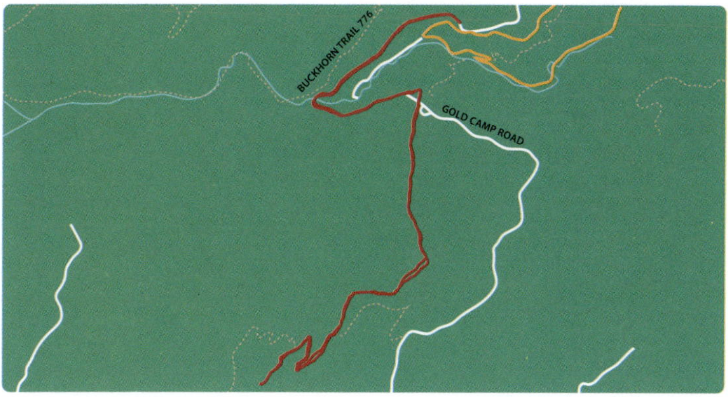

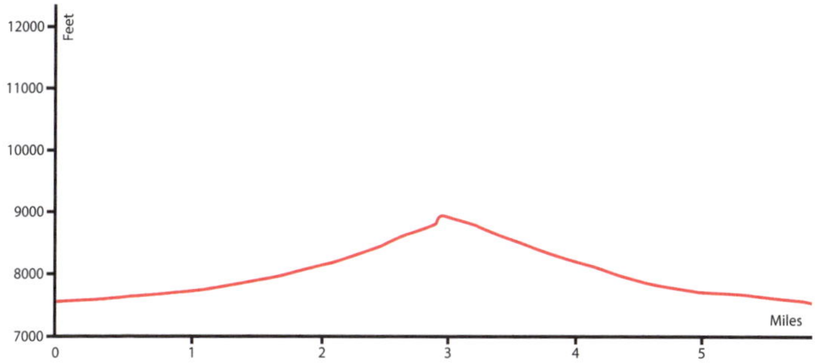

HIKE DESCRIPTION

There's no better way to celebrate completing this popular waterfall hike than with a crisp, sessionable Scottish Ale that's been a perennial award winner.

Once a popular site for Ute Indian tribes, North Cheyenne Cañon Park today is an enchanted labyrinth of trails, waterfalls, rock formations, historic stone bridges, and other remnants of Colorado's gold rush days.

The first part of the hike follows the decommissioned Upper Gold Camp Road, first traversing the north side of a gully before making a 180-degree turn to traverse the south side. The gravel path here is wide, relatively flat, non-technical, and exposed to the sun. In just over a mile, you'll come to the gated entrance of an old tunnel. It was originally constructed in the 1800s during the gold rush as part of a railway before being converted to a toll road for cars. In the late 1980s, the tunnel collapsed and was never repaired, thereby shutting down vehicular access to Upper Gold Camp Road—and creating infinite fodder for Springs locals' ghost stories and haunted tales of paranormal occurrences in the creepy, fenced-off tunnel.

After you bypass the tunnel, the trail narrows to singletrack into an area called Buffalo Canyon. Shortly, look to your right for a sign marking the way to St. Mary's Falls. From here, the route is a fairly gentle climb up through mixed pine and spruce forest and along the babbling Buffalo Canyon Creek. A few minor trail junctions exist along the way, though most routes quickly reconnect. (Just ignore the offshoot trails on your left that go all the way down to the creek.)

Only the final third of a mile offers significant steepness as you approach the falls on a series of switchbacks. Enjoy watching the lovely, 250-foot cascade tumbling down the imposing granite wall above you. Depending on what time of year you go, the falls may be roaring (spring), more of a trickle (fall), or frozen altogether (winter).

Though this hike is doable year-round, if you go between November and April, snowshoes or traction devices and trekking poles are advised, as areas can be snow-covered or slick with ice.

On your drive back toward the Springs for your post-hike beverage, pull off about a half-mile down N. Cheyenne Canyon Road to check out the magnificent Helen Hunt Falls just off the road.

TURN BY TURN DIRECTIONS:

1. Start hiking on the dirt road at the back (northwest corner) of the parking lot.
2. After passing the tunnel, go right at mile 1.2, following the sign for St. Mary's Falls.
3. At 2.6, make a sharp right in front of the St. Mary's Falls sign and follow the trail up.
4. At 2.8, stay left and reach the falls in another quarter of a mile.

FIND THE TRAILHEAD

Drive southwest out of Colorado Springs on Cheyenne Boulevard, then make a slight right onto N. Cheyenne Canyon Road. Drive 3 miles to the end of the road and park in the gravel parking lot at the intersection with High Drive and Gold Camp Road.

BRISTOL BREWING COMPANY

Bristol Brewing Company is located inside the old Ivywild School, an elementary school built in 1916 and converted in 2009 into a multi-use community space filled with art, food, music, and, of course, a brewery. An independent, family-owned brewery that aims to do the classics well, Bristol has been making great beer since 1994, with numerous Great American Beer Festival medals to their name.

CONTACT INFORMATION

U.S. Forest Service,
Pikes Peak Ranger District,
601 S. Weber Street,
Colorado Springs, CO 80903;
719-636-1602

BREWERY/RESTAURANT

Bristol Brewing Company
1604 S. Cascade Avenue,
Colorado Springs, CO 80905
719-633-2555
Miles from trailhead: 5.8

MANITOU SPRINGS

HIKE THROUGH DRAMATIC SANDSTONE FORMATIONS

STARTING POINT	OBJECTIVE
RIDGE ROAD TRAILHEAD	RED ROCK CANYON
BEER	HIKE TYPE
HIGH GROUND IPA	MODERATE
FEES	SEASON
NONE	YEAR-ROUND
MAP REFERENCE	DOG FRIENDLY
RED ROCK CANYON MAP AT COLORADOSPRINGS.GOV	YES (LEASH REQUIRED)
DURATION	LENGTH
2 HOURS	3.4 MILES
LOW POINT / HIGH POINT	ELEVATION GAIN
6,191 FEET / 6,627 FEET	430 FEET

ALCOHOL **6.9%** CONTENT

IPA

CLEAR, BRIGHT GOLDEN

GRASS, GRAPEFRUIT

PINE; ZESTY, HOP-CENTRIC

BITTERNESS
IBU: 125

SWEETNESS

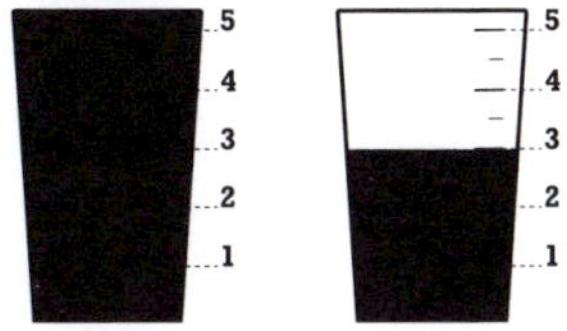

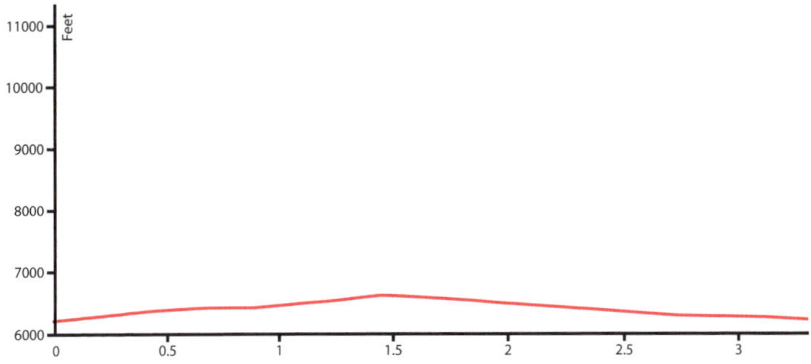

HIKE DESCRIPTION

Red Rock Canyon is a less touristy alternative to the nearby, infamous Garden of the Gods, yet features many of the same dramatic sandstone formations.

This loop hike offers a solid tour of some of Red Rock Canyon's spunkiest singletrack, scenic ridges, eye-popping geologic formations, and a lovely, quiet pond—watch for geese and herons—with which to wrap up your hike. A number of trails exist in this park, so the loop suggested here is merely that—a suggestion. Plenty of other routes exist, too; your best bet is to carry a map and explore to your heart's delight.

True to the park's name, the crushed-gravel trails wind through many a red-rock landscape. The rock here is primarily sandstone of the Fountain Foundation—formed some 300 million years ago by the erosion of the Ancestral Rocky Mountains. The same Fountain Foundation composes Boulder's iconic Flatirons, nearby Garden of the Gods, and Denver's famous Red Rocks Amphitheater. It gets its color from the copious pink feldspar grains embedded in it.

This hike takes you through a mix of Douglas fir and ponderosa pine forest in the shadier stretches of the canyon, as well as more desert-like environs replete with Gambel oak, pinyon and juniper trees, yucca, and prickly pear. Keep an eye out for the rustle of birds, deer, coyotes, or other smaller mammals in the bushes around you as you hike, as the area is filled with vibrant wildlife. And, of course, soak up all the impressive views along the way of the park's namesake red-rock formations.

If you bring Fido with you, you can also make use of the off-leash dog area (include a short loop trail in addition to those included in this hike) just west of the Mesa Trail, shortly after you begin hiking. Either way, when you're ready to venture out onto the loop, stay on the Mesa Trail and enjoy the views of Pikes Peak on the horizon to your right before getting on the Roundup Trail and returning on the Red Rock Canyon Trail. At times along this hike, you'll also be able to catch glimpses of the slanted red rocks of Garden of the Gods to the north.

Though nearly 100 technical climbing routes have been established in the park for permitted climbers to tackle, be aware that rock scrambling more than 10 feet off the ground (sans permits, ropes, and harnesses) is illegal in this area, and punishable by fines and/or jail time.

TURN BY TURN DIRECTIONS:

1. Start up Mesa Trail from end of the parking area.
2. At mile 0.55, make a right on Quarry Pass, following it until mile 0.8, when you'll wrap around red rocks onto the Roundup Trail.
3. At 1.2, follow a switchback around to the left, staying on Roundup Trail.
4. At mile 2, at the bottom of the hill, go left, then left again in a tenth of a mile onto Red Rock Canyon Trail.
5. At mile 3, make a slight left (and stay left) to return to your car.

FIND THE TRAILHEAD

Red Rock Canyon Open Space is located along Highway 24 at 3550 W. High Street. From Manitou Springs, drive east on Highway 24, then make a right on to Ridge Road and immediate left (via roundabout) onto High Street. Park in the first lot on your right.

MANITOU BREWING COMPANY

Manitou Brewing Company is located in a former burro stable, where hikers in the late 1800s who wanted to summit Pikes Peak could rent a donkey to aid with their journey. Today, it is a thriving spot for both craft beer and craft food, with beautiful repurposed wooden décor, a scrumptious menu, and a wide variety of house beers and guest taps alike. This High Ground IPA is dry hopped with more than five pounds of hops per barrel, and earned a World Beer Cup Silver Medal in 2016.

CONTACT INFORMATION

Colorado Springs Parks,
Trails & Open Spaces,
1401 Recreation Way,
Colorado Springs, CO 80905;
719-385-5940

BREWERY/RESTAURANT

Manitou Brewing Company
725 Manitou Avenue,
Manitou Springs, CO 80829
719-282-7709
Miles from trailhead: 2

ALAMOSA

GREAT SAND DUNES NATIONAL PARK'S OTHERWORLDY LANDSCAPE

STARTING POINT	OBJECTIVE
DUNES PARKING AREA	HIGH DUNE
BEER	HIKE TYPE
VALLE ESPECIAL MEXICAN LAGER	VERY STRENUOUS
FEES	SEASON
$15 (OR ANNUAL PASS)	YEAR-ROUND
MAP REFERENCE	DOG FRIENDLY
GREAT SAND DUNES NATIONAL PARK VISITOR GUIDE AT NPS.GOV	YES (LEASH REQUIRED)
DURATION	LENGTH
2 HOURS	2.6 MILES
LOW POINT / HIGH POINT	ELEVATION GAIN
8,071 FEET / 8,720 FEET	670 FEET

ALCOHOL 4.2% CONTENT

MEXICAN LAGER

GOLDEN

FAINT CITRUS, APPLES

LIGHT-BODIED, GRAINY

BITTERNESS
IBU: UNLISTED

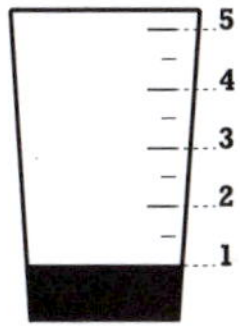

SWEETNESS

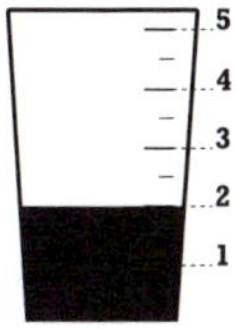

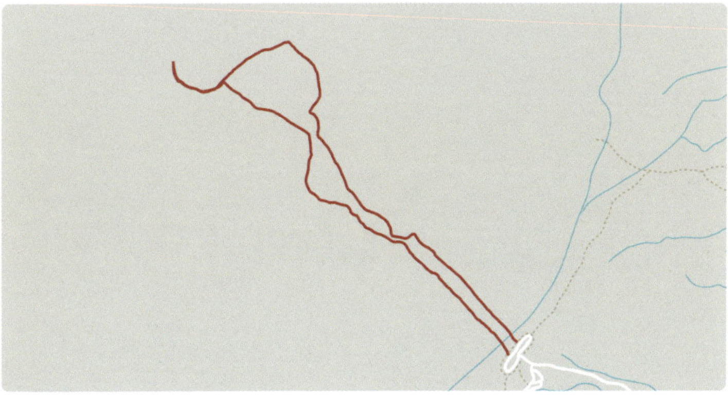

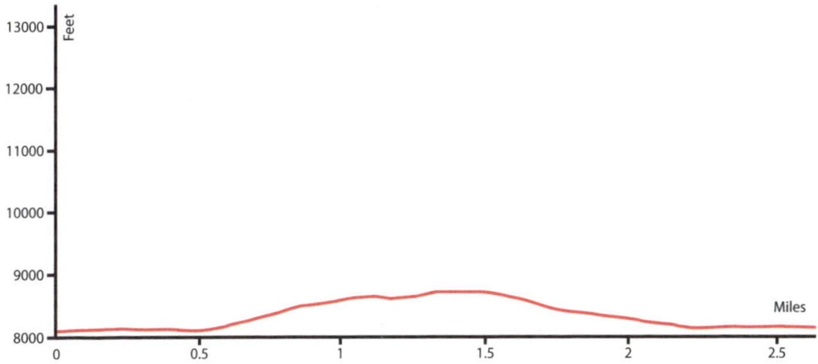

HIKE DESCRIPTION

Get a dose of desert dunes in this otherworldly landscape—trekking up North America's tallest sand dunes, nestled at the foot of the jagged Sangre de Cristo Mountains.

Great Sand Dunes National Park is home to the tallest sand dunes on the continent. The dunes in this one-of-a-kind park are estimated to be nearly half a million years old and have remained surprisingly unchanged for at least the last century—which is rather amazing, given that they're essentially just massive mounds of sand, originally deposited by volcanic activity and resculpted daily by the whims of the wind.

For reasons that become obvious when you see how quickly wind erases even the deepest footsteps in the sand, there are no formal trails through the dune field. However, many park visitors delight in climbing High Dune, the most prominent mound on the eastern ridge of the dune field. It rises nearly 700 feet above the San Luis Valley. Climbing to its summit on soft sand (more than 8,000 feet above sea level to boot) is no easy feat—but the payoff is huge.

It's a "choose your own adventure" route to the top of High Dune, with many options for wending your way among the sculpted dunes and dramatic, curved ridgelines along the way. For an extra dose of fun and adventure, rent a sand board or sand sled at Great Sand Dunes Oasis (near the park entrance) to allow for a fast, adrenaline-filled ride back down.

Do beware that sand surface temperatures by midday in the summer can reach a scorching 150 degrees Fahrenheit. Do not venture out into the dunes without proper shoes (not sandals) to protect your feet—and, if you're hiking with a dog, not without booties to protect your pup's paws as well. Your shoes will inevitably fill with sand as you hike; if the sand temperature permits, it can be more enjoyable to hike barefoot, but always carry proper footwear with you in case sand temperatures heat up while you're out. Also beware of developing thunderstorms, as it's very dangerous to be in the dunes when lightning is present.

Of all the hikes in this book, this one is located the farthest away from its accompanying brewery—but the drive is worth it to visit this wildly unique landscape. You will feel as though you've arrived on a different planet from the rest of Colorado, let alone the rest of the continent.

TURN BY TURN DIRECTIONS:

1. Set your sights on the highest dune on the ridgeline visible from the dunes parking area.
2. Choose your own route to the top and back.

FIND THE TRAILHEAD

From Alamosa, take US-160 east out of town for 14 miles. Turn left (north) onto CO-150 and drive another 19 miles. The Dunes Parking Area is just past the visitor center.

SAN LUIS VALLEY BREWING COMPANY

After a hot day in the dunes, the light-bodied brews at family-owned San Luis Brewing Company hit the spot. The Valle Especial Mexican-style lager is served with a slice of lime—or, if you're in the mood for a little more heat, order a Valle Caliente for a green-chili infused rendition. The brewpub, which opened in 2006, is located in a gorgeously restored building downtown on Main Street. Head brewers Scott and Angie Graber also roast their own coffee beans, available for purchase on site.

CONTACT INFORMATION

Great Sand Dunes National Park
and Preserve,
11999 Highway 150,
Mosca, CO 81146;
719-378-6300

BREWERY/RESTAURANT

San Luis Valley Brewing Company
631 Main Street
Alamosa, CO, 81101
719-587-2337
Miles from trailhead: 34

GO BEER HIKING!

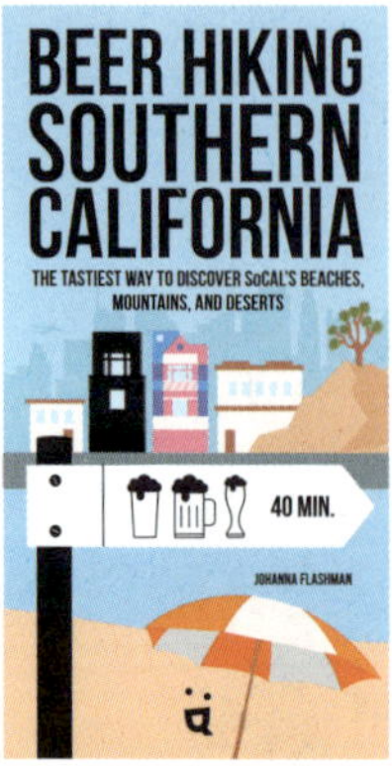

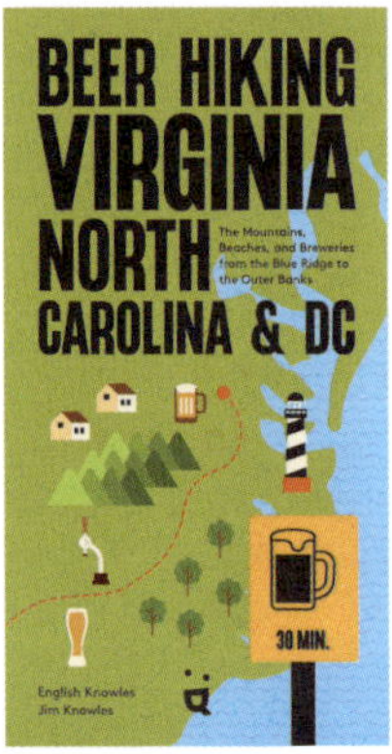

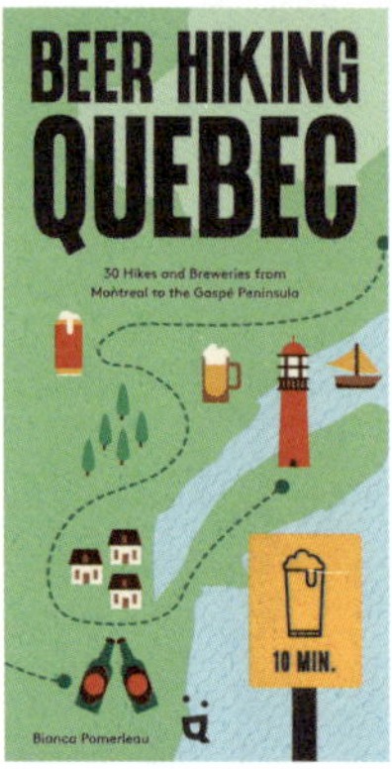

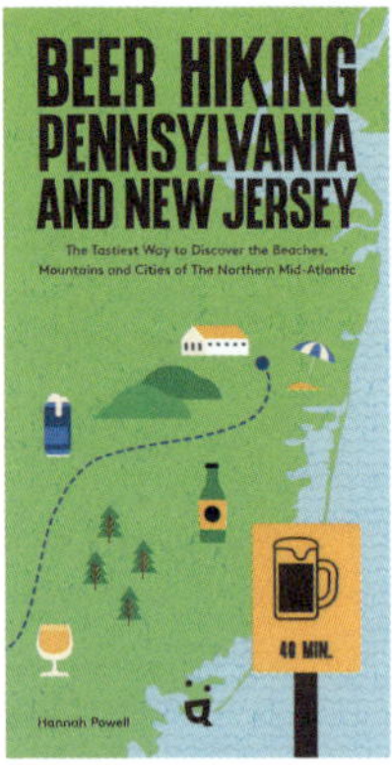